DRIVING

DARK

AFRICA

The Journey of an Accidental Adventurer

MICHAEL BANKS

This book is dedicated to Helen, my ever faithful and ever following companion, without whom I could never have travelled so far.

I would also like thank my daughter-in-law, Marie, who has helped me put pen to paper.

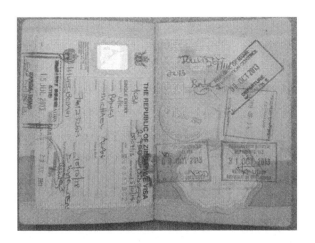

FOREWORD
Marie Banks, July 2015

I married into the Banks family. It was a full eighteen months after meeting Mick's son, Nick, before I met my prospective father-in-law. All I knew was that he had rented out the family home and was 'somewhere in Asia'. I eventually came to know and love a man with a huge appetite for travel and adventure, who always had a story to tell.

Mick's memory for detail was astonishing and he could recount with accuracy a host of exotic encounters from time spent backpacking in South America, cycling around the world or driving through Africa. He was one of life's characters. Whilst he often struggled with the foibles and bureaucracy encountered, he kept a sense of humour – even if it was somewhat dry.

This book describes an overland journey from Rochford in Essex, UK, to Cape Town in South Africa; a journey of 28,000 miles, crossing twenty-five countries in eleven months. This would not have been possible without the company and support of his wife, Helen, with whom he had shared many of his previous travels.

Sadly, this was the last adventure that Mick and Helen were able to have together. At least two further generations of adventurous Banks are already following in his footsteps; his eldest son, Matthew, and three grandchildren having emigrated to Australia, and Nick and I also relishing periods of wanderlust.

He lives on through our memories and his words, and it was a pleasure working with him to record this tale for others to enjoy.

As a family, we would like to raise awareness of oesophageal cancer. Recognising the early, and seemingly innocuous, symptoms - for example, persistent hiccups and acid reflux - and seeking advice and treatment can make all the difference. Find out more on the Cancer Research UK website: www.cancerresearchuk.org/about-cancer/type/oesophageal-cancer/

PREFACE

The accidental adventurer

I have always been an armchair traveller. I would watch programs featuring the likes of David Attenborough and Chris Bonnington - even the odd travel show - and I would wish that I could go to some of those exotic places. But, even whilst thinking that, I was aware that the only reason I was not exploring any of these far off lands was me. My biggest obstacle was myself.

But then, in 1999, Helen and I embarked on an epic international cycle ride. This was a complete accident; I had intended to tag along with some blokes who were planning a big adventure, and eventually none of these 'men' committed to it, but I was psyched up and eager to go. I am not a lone traveller though and, rather foolhardily, my new girlfriend, Helen, volunteered to accompany me instead. In those days the internet and e-mail were almost complete strangers to us; I tried to do some research but decided that my fifty-six-year-old brain would never remember it all. So we set off and made it up as we went along. We took eighteen months, crossed twenty countries and cycled 14,000 miles.

After a while back at home, we got itchy feet, so we set off to backpack around South America. We bought a plane ticket and sorted out our first night's accommodation after landing in Rio. This was followed by backpacking around Australasia, Asia and other *ad hoc* travels, all with the same amount - or lack of - planning and preparation.

An idea is born

The pre-cursor to our really big adventure happened in 2010 and little did we know at the time what it would lead to. On a flight of whimsy, Helen and I decided to go to South Africa, buy a 4x4 and travel around several of the countries in Southern Africa for nine months. We'd have a great time, then sell the car and come home. And that was more or less the end of the planning.

As soon we arrived in Johannesburg, everything seemed to fall apart. The hostel we were planning on staying in was supposed to pick us up at the airport, but that did not happen. We tried phoning them, but their phones were out of order. So late at night, in a strange land, we had to make our own way into what is called a 'dangerous city'. When the taxi dropped us off at the hostel we were confronted by eight foot high solid steel gates topped with razor wire. After a lot of banging, a small door was opened by the drunken owner of the hostel and we were in.

Security seemed to be an issue; all the properties had walls and fences of the same height, all topped with broken glass, electric wire or razor wire. We had never seen anything like it before. And most of them had a

4

placard outside warning that they were protected by an armed response security company. We may have been seeking adventure, but this was not the start we were looking for. This was a world we knew nothing about and were totally unprepared for. And, under the circumstances, we felt the need to buy a car quickly and leave town as soon as possible.

The following day, as we started to look for our new mode of transport, we were shocked at the price of cars; they were two or three times the price of the equivalent in the UK or Europe. I had done some research - if looking on the internet a couple of times at 'cars for sale in South Africa' can be considered research - but it appears that it was all wrong.

The first error was that I had not taken into account the size of South Africa; some of the cars for sale could be several days' travel away and we would need a car to go and see them. We would look in a paper at 'cars for sale' and they would be listed in some district or town, or even only a postcode area, and we would have absolutely no idea whereabouts in the country that may be. Also in my mind was that if anything serious should go wrong with the car, or if we cannot sell it at the end of our tour, then a very expensive purchase would be a lot of money to throw away. The whole idea was suddenly starting to lose its glamour. But we were there and we had to do something. The new plan was to buy the first car we could find that we could afford and we would only go only where the car - with whatever ability it has - could go.

We bought the most impractical car possible. It was a small Volvo, made in Holland, and very suitable for Dutch roads, but eventually we took the car to places that the designers and manufacturers had never intended for it to go - or possibly never even knew existed. Several times we took it beyond its physical limits, as proved by the amount of damage on the underside and the number of body bits and light fittings that kept falling off that I had to keep refitting. I managed to crack the sump, bend the exhaust in several places, and dent lots of things. This was totally unintended; the plan was to stay only on the roads that the car could cope with. But we had no idea what the roads would be like. In some places it was easier to drive on the dirt at the roadside than on the remnants of tarmac.

Somewhere along the way the 'man factor' crept in. There were a number of places where there were only gravel roads, and most of these were good, extremely good, but there seemed to be a natural gravitation towards the not quite so good ones. We coped OK with these, but from then on it was a downhill slope towards what in all practical intent and purposes were four-wheel-drive-only tracks. For the avoidance of doubt, those who usually only use a 4x4 to mount the kerb outside of a school would feel very inadequate; these roads could consist of rocks, deep sand, water or just a rough, unmaintained track where truly only a 4x4 would do. There were not too many of these and finding them was always accidental.

One day, heading for Opuwo on a fairly good gravel road, we came to a section that had been washed out

by the previous rains. Helen said, 'We must go back!' I
was not in favour of that, not only did it go against my
grain, but, according to our map, and guessing where
we may be on the road, it was 140 miles back to the
turning, so I walked the degraded bit of road to check it
out. It was only about 30 metres long and I worked out
a possible route through this disaster. In preparation for
driving this short stretch I chucked some rocks in a
couple of the big holes, and sent Helen on ahead to take
photos of my amazing driving. As I drove my chosen
route, Helen stood in front, waving her arms about,
shouting, 'No, stop! Go that way! Go this way! You're
going to crash!' Needless to say, I was as pleased as
punch when I cleared the obstacle but, unfortunately,
my arm-waving photographer took not one single
picture.

When we were booking into a camp in town, the
guards, looking at our car, asked us if we came by the
gravel or tar road. 'Gravel', we said. They were amazed
as big pick-up trucks have turned back to take the other
road. Unfortunately, we did some more of this until the
car became a bit of a wreck. It looked good on top, but
underneath, due to the very low ground clearance,
everything that could be bent got bent. Many fitments
kept falling off and had to be wired or glued back on and
in a manner that was better and more secure than the
makers had originally fitted them. I had the whole front
bumper off twice, so twice we both had to struggle to
get this weighty unit back on the car. It was one of
those big moulded sections that seemed to make up
half of the front of the car. It also had integral light
fittings, so when it came off, there was a danger of
dragging some of the wiring out. The first time it

happened I just put it back onto the maker's fixings. The second time I did it properly, my way. Everywhere we went I would look for bits of wire - there was nearly always some laying around where there was fencing - and as bits came adrift from the car I would wire it up. For some things I had to resort to Gripfix, or at least its African equivalent.

At some point, in rural Tanzania, the engine blew up and no amount of wire or Gripfix could sort the problem and we had to abandon the car. So, from this remote village miles from anywhere, we continued our journey through the rest of Tanzania by bus, crossed the River Rovuma in a rowing boat to get into Mozambique and then on into Swaziland through to South Africa and to the airport for home, travelling by bus, pick-up truck or whatever means was available.

At different places during this fantastic touring trip, we saw Land Rovers with English registrations and each time I just had to ask the owner if he had driven all the way from the UK. But in every case it turned out that the owners were German and they had bought their cars in England, because of the right-hand drive, had shipped them out to Namibia, and left them there for their annual holidays. They could just fly out to their car and they were ready to go. This inspired us to consider if we could do this thing properly, that is, buy a car in the UK and drive all the way from home to Cape Town.

Planning the return

I just had this vision of me driving our rugged and kitted out Land Rover across the deserts, jungles and the savannah of Africa. *I am British and I should have a British car to do what I consider to be a very British trip!* A load of rubbish my dreaming turned out to be. Time will show my imaginings to be a mirage of a time gone by.

I have a number of friends who know a lot less about driving in Africa than I do, and they eventually talked me into a Toyota. Land Rover does seem to have a bit of a reliability issue, and that had always lingered in the back of my mind, so possibly I did not take a lot of persuading. I was looking for a car big enough to sleep in if there was a need to; diesel engine, economic to run, easy to maintain - that is, no engine management, electronics or super but unnecessary gizmos. Above all, it had to have a high ground clearance and it needed to be rugged. And cheap. I thought that we would be going into the relative unknown; I wanted fitness and reliability, but if it all went tits up, it needed to be something that would not be too big a financial disaster to walk away from.

Much later, we were to learn that you never abandon a broken down car, as you will probably come back to a wreck. We will, in time, on our drive through Africa pass countless vehicle body shells on the roadside. We will also come to see adverts on TV for vehicle breakdown and recovery services, which claim a broken down car left alone can be completely stripped down by four men in an hour. They also claim to respond to any call in less than two hours. I think they may have their sums wrong somewhere. But that is Africa. Breaking down does seem to be a thing best to be avoided, for all sorts of reasons.

No car would ever cover all the criteria I wanted, but I ended up with a 1994 Toyota 4Runner, which probably covered the least number of them.

We bought a basic eighteen-year-old car and did a few modifications. In the first flush of excitement, I had the idea of a big luggage rack on the roof with a ladder on the side of the vehicle. After some thought, I realised that we had no idea how much this trip was going to cost, and the more we spent kitting it out, the less money we would have for the trip itself, and the more luggage we had, the more we would have to leave behind when we finished, as our plan was to sell the car at the end of our journey. Also, I had some concern as to whether the extra weight on the roof would alter the handling characteristics of the vehicle, and all the extra weight may also increase the fuel consumption. So, no roof rack meant no ladder. I did so want a ladder, a more realistic approach was needed.

Some of the gadgets we fitted we would possibly need, and some of them were 'boys' toys' thinking. I made and fitted a snorkel, not for four-wheel-drive swimming, but to keep the air intake as far from the dust and sand as possible. I searched the internet for a snorkel for our car and had no luck whatsoever, but I found someone who had bought some aluminium bends and made his own. So I went down that route; buying the bits, cutting them to suit and epoxying them together, cutting a hole through the wing and the inner wing into the engine bay, and diverting the air intake from the air filter to my snorkel.

I made a spare wheel carrier for an extra spare. In the event it proved unnecessary, we never used the second spare, but we did go to a lot of places that I would definitely not have liked to have gone with only one spare wheel. I also made a rack to carry a 20 litre jerry can, mainly because I thought it would look good. A long way down the road, somewhere in deepest Africa, I came to realise our car had much too small a fuel tank for the route we took, and especially for the places we wanted to go to but were unable to, even with the extra 20 litres on the back. The various other things I fitted were two 12 volt power points for charging our electronic gizmos - batteries, camera, laptop. I also fitted an inverter to provide 230 volts for the same reason. There were other bits and pieces, some used and some not. And I fitted a winch - not for using, but for the macho look. Everything I was doing was a complete guess, a total shot in the dark as to what we may or may not need.

When I said I made a spare wheel carrier, what I really mean is I bought the metal, cut it and shaped it, and the tricky and clever welding was expertly done by Steve at Transweld of Pagglesham. He lives just down the road from us, which was quite handy as I spent a lot of time running backwards and forwards, wanting bits and pieces done - the spare wheel carrier, and the carrier for the jerry can for spare diesel. Also, a 5 litre petrol can, fuel for our petrol driven cooking stove, and a seemingly endless list of odd bits, including new jacking points for our new high lift jack.

And a huge amount of assistance came from a good friend, Keith, a motor engineer and pre-war Riley Specialist, with a part-time interest in one particular post-war Toyota 4Runner. He helped sort out and repair a number of faults on our eighteen-year-old car, and made it ready, or at least as ready as we could make it, for its drive of a lifetime.

We were on holiday in France a while ago and I came across some wartime, and now ex-War Department, jerry cans in a car boot sale. I bought one date stamped 1943, and now this war veteran is going to Africa.

And the need for padlocks: the high lift jack mounted on the outside of the car had a padlock on it; the spare wheel had a padlock; the diesel jerry can, padlock; the fuel cans and the spare wheel on the back of the car were mounted on swing gates and when they were both closed they were padlocked together. The petrol can and the spade were also padlocked. The rule of thumb for Africa is: anything on the outside of the car must be padlocked. With all these locks around the vehicle, I simplified the key system by getting sets of padlocks that were keyed alike, that is, one key fits all. I had two different-sized padlocks, so it was actually two keys fit all. The padlocks, although they worked, required constant maintenance. They were supposed to be outdoor, waterproof, all weather locks and with a guarantee. However, they went rusty and stuck; keeping them oiled and greased led to sand and dust sticking to them, clogging the key hole. Being somewhere in Africa with a stuck padlock bought from a company in the UK, there was no chance of making any use of the guarantee. Security is supposed to be our watchword.

I also made a little cubby hole under the floor and carpet (with a lock, naturally) and made a secret place to put some spare money, in an old electrical box from the car breakers. I took all the bits out of it, and mounted it behind a panel in the foot well, alongside some other electrical boxes. It had some wires coming out, not going very far but out of sight. I also put tinting on most of the windows, in the hope of keeping some of the heat of the sun out, and in the hope of keeping prying eyes out.

Now the race is on; my driving licence will expire next year when I turn seventy, travel insurance will be difficult, and my body is probably getting towards its sell by date. I am not sure how fit one has to be to do something like this, but I am fairly sure that the younger one is, the better.

The plan, such as it was, was to drive from home in Essex, UK to Cape Town, South Africa. I am a bit of a 'buy the ticket and go, sort the rest out when we get there' type of person. For this trip, I obviously had to plan a bit more. *On the way, I want to see Sudan, go to the Masai Mara and see the Shoebill Stork, and of course the gorillas... the rest we will have to make up as we go along, as per normal. Helen wants to go... no, Helen will go wherever I take her!* Our plan in a nutshell was to drive from Rochford to Cape Town and take in the sights and experiences along the way.

As regards research, I looked at a map of Africa, found out which countries needed a visa in advance, and what countries the government's Foreign and Commonwealth Office advised against. I did try to look at the weather and the seasons along the route, but some countries have a winter and summer, some countries have one wet and one dry season, and some have two wet and two dry seasons, and, on top of that, we did not know when we would be able to get away, so we decided that we would go when we could and would have to take the seasons as they come.

In preparation, we acquired a carnet de passage for the car, arranged travel insurance for ourselves, basic camping equipment, a couple of old guidebooks and a bird book. Nothing was high tech. At the end of our journey, we hoped to sell the car and most the rest of the stuff could be sacrificed; we would come back with only what we could carry.

After a long, unplanned wait, we secured a tenant to rent the house and as long as he keeps paying the rent we can afford to be on the road.

This is the story of *our* trip to Africa.

Preparations at home
Practicing with the new heavy-duty jack

Driving Dark Africa

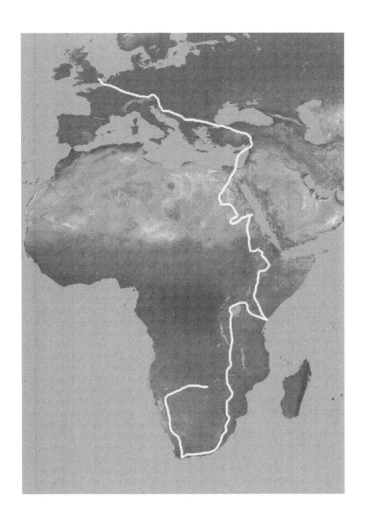

DRIVING DARK AFRICA

EUROPE
1 December 2012

Delays, hiccups, cock-ups, war and pestilence, plus my son and his fiancée needing my presence at their wedding, all contributed to our late departure on this trip. I am not sure where the pestilence comes into it, but I am certain it had a part to play somewhere.

According to the HM Government's Foreign & Commonwealth Office, all the main routes down the east or west coast of Africa include a number of countries that are too dangerous to travel through. The risk stems either from armed civil unrest, bandits or outright civil war. I am a big fan of the FCO's travel advice pages. I do tend to think that they err on the side of safety, but they do give practical and realistic advice. Also, if we go to an area that the FCO advises not to, our travel insurance will be voided, so it is best to heed the advice. I have looked at travel advice from American and Australian government websites, and they are awful, providing a much-reduced level of detail, so, despite being run by the British Government, I am grateful for the sound service of the FCO.

Unfortunately, most of the government advice precludes us doing the west route. Much later, we would speak to more than one person who had driven down the west route without any worries, so Who knows? But we still need to find a route to Africa. One of the three options in the past would have been a ferry from Spain to Morocco for the western route. The ferry is still there, but the FCO is not too keen on some of the route. Parts of some countries - Algeria, Nigeria, Chad, and Niger - are patrolled by bandits and/or revolutionaries. For the eastern route there is, or rather was, a choice of a ferry from Italy to Tunisia then drive to Libya and then Egypt, but since the fall of Gadhafi, Libya is considered unsafe. The other option is to drive around the Mediterranean, which would require driving through Syria but, with a war currently waging, this country is also considered unsafe in the extreme.

I keep searching the internet, and eventually I find a new ferry has started running from Iskudendrun, a port in Turkey, to Port Said in Egypt. It is late in the year, but at least now we have a route.

We set off on a sunny but crisp and frosty December morning to get our ferry at Dover and our all-important international driving permit. There are two versions of this document - a 1949 and a 1921 - but for the countries we are going to we should only need the 1949 convention. Amazingly, it looks like it is still made of cheap paper left over from 1949. I have spent a fair bit of time sorting out which particular convention we need, or whether we need both, and at the ferry terminal enough time is taken getting these valuable documents to ensure we have to take a later, and more expensive, ferry. And ultimately, in the twenty-five countries that we drove through, anybody that asked to see our license was happy with our British one, so, for all this grief, the international driving permit never saw the light of day.

Damp, dismal France and Belgium. Our first night on the road and we arrive in Lille in the rain, via the motorway. As we approach the city we turn onto what seems to be another motorway. We are hoping to see something like a Formula 1 hotel to stop the night in, but instead all we appear to be doing is turning onto another high-speed road to God knows where. But we do eventually find a hotel, book a room and venture out to look for something to eat. Across the road is a Buffalo Grill. I have seen these a lot in France but have never been in one. *Now is my chance!* The cowboy surroundings and mediocre food do nothing to excite us. We will only try one again in future if we get desperate.

Next morning, we decide to settle for a McBreakfast. Unfortunately, they do not open until 10.30, presumably because all the locals have their breakfast brandies in the local cafés. So, back to the hotel to make ourselves a coffee. *Luckily we came prepared with a supply of cereal bars!*

Now the saga of trying to find our way out of town, but, in the daylight and without as many people on the road in a desperate rush to get home, it is a bit easier, and at least, for the moment, it has stopped raining.

Germany, and now we have snow. We stop for the night in Saarbrucken and find a Christmas market on the go. We wander around for a short while but, as nice as it is, we don't really have the clothes for a cold, snowy December night. So for us the plan is to find a restaurant, eat, and get back to the hotel, and as quick as possible.

Somewhere short of Munich we stop again for the night so we can face the city ring road with a fresh mind. In the morning, we find the road is well sign posted and easy to drive; in no time at all Munich disappears from the rear view mirror.

As we approach Austria, I decide to get off the dreary motorways and cut across country. The smaller road is much more pleasant to drive on and going up into the Austrian Tirol is spectacular; the snow covered mountains and trees are beautiful. As we trundle up one high pass, a lorry in front of us is having great difficulties. I execute my passing manoeuvre and the car gets into a bit of a wiggle on the ice. I engage four-wheel-drive, *super!* I am quite excited, as this is the first time I have done this in earnest, and it certainly makes the car more stable.

On the way down, for some reason known only to mechanical science, I lose the use of my clutch. Here I am, mid gear change, with no clutch and no gears. *Great! I am on a virtual ski slope, I have all my wheels engaged but none of them are connected to the engine!* My Sat Nag who sits next to me and usually says something like 'You want the next left, err no, sorry, the other way' is not quite so cool; she is screwing up the map and saying, 'Wa'sappened? Wotawegunnerdo? W-w-w-w-what?'

We make it down the mountain and to a town. I have spent most of my life driving old, worn-out cars, so the lack of a clutch is no big deal, well, at least temporarily. We are lucky to see a café with an easily-accessed car park, and there is no traffic on the road, so no stopping and straight across the road and in. We stop for a coffee and give the car, and Helen's nerves, a bit of a rest. When we return to the car, all is well; some mystical magic must have overheated the clutch fluid on the snow covered mountain. *So, we have no real problem. Yet!*

We decide to stay the night here, and then, if we have problems in the morning, at least there is a garage in town. We find a typically old Austrian hotel down the road. It is fantastic and, although not real cheap, it is not as dear as I would have expected. It has tradition and character, good food, beer and promises a good night.

At 4.30am, we are woken by snow ploughs driving up and down outside the bedroom window. This is not an encouraging start for the new day's journey. To my mind, the sound of snow ploughs is a sign that there is more snow.

After breakfast and having no problems with the car - apart from scraping the ice and snow off it - we continue through the spectacular winter wonderland. Descending out of the high mountains, I ponder, *If my clutch fluid can overheat in the ice and snow, what is it going to be like in Africa?* It seems illogical to me, but it must have been something to do with the cold.

We had been warned that we would need a vignette to drive on the motorways of Austria, so we had bought one as soon as we saw somewhere selling them. They are quite cheap and there is a hefty fine if you are caught without one, so it made sense. We had no such advance warning, however, that we also need one in Slovenia, so in total ignorance we enter and then drive across Slovenia unvignetted, with no obviously dire consequences that we are aware of yet.

We stop for the night in the town of Postponja. The hotel is vast and quite expensive, so we eat out in a restaurant down the road. In the morning, upon coming downstairs for breakfast, we are astounded; the buffet table is some 30 feet long, laden with every type of food imaginable. Different types of meats, varieties of cheeses, eggs cooked four different ways, breads and almost every type of fruit possible. The amount of food is astounding, and pasted on the wall along the length of the table are signs stating: 'No bags'. Obviously, with the amount of food on offer, people are loading up with stocks to last them for God knows how long. We sneak a little bit to have for lunch later, *naughty, naughty!* The dining room itself is vast, with seating for well over a hundred people, but no-one else comes in while we are having our breakfast; we are the only two people in this huge expanse of tables and chairs, with mountains of food.

The highlands of Slovenia are beautiful and from here we drop down into Croatia and to the Mediterranean

Sea. Once out of the mountains and meandering down the Adriatic coast, the sun is shining and everything in the world is lovely. We had thought of holidaying here at some time in the future, and it looks really nice. There are a lot of caravan and campsites along the way. The road is empty now, but, in my imagination, I see these small roads full of campervans and caravans. This puts us off wanting to come back in the high season.

Crossing into Croatia is a piece of cake, and the nice man at the frontier gives my navigator a map, and off we go. After a while, I query Helen's directions, and she assures me all is well, she has the map. After a bit more time, I just have to stop and look for myself. The map she was given has only got motorways on it, and we are going the wrong way because that is all she has on her map. If only she had stuck to using our map, the map with all the roads on it, but some little charmer at the border gives her a smile and a free map, and she is all over the place. Eventually we are able to turn around at an intersection, pay another toll and we double back along the motorway, get down on to the coast road, and, by now, the steam has finished evaporating from my ears, so all is well again.

After a long day's drive, we for stop for the night on the outskirts of Zagrad. Unfortunately, there is something in the back of the car that Helen desperately needs, so, even though I am tired after a long and unnecessary drive, I have to empty everything out. And all to no avail; after loading it all back in again having not found it, Helen finds the object of her desire was on the back seat all the time. The steam is starting to rise again.

The next day, we drive along the coast all day and arrive

at Dubrovnik in the early evening. It is starting to rain. We find a rather grand hotel, or at least it seems grand to us. It is built on a hillside - or more like a cliff side - overlooking the harbour area. The entrance at road level is actually on about the eighth floor, and on the other side there are spectacular views across the town and harbour. Even with the odd shower, we still enjoy a beautiful sunset. And we are warm and comfortable.

As we set off again on not the best of roads, it is pouring with rain and awful driving conditions. I am sure that in some places the water on the road is deeper than the sea on our right, and by the looks of the road, where it is visible, and some of the surrounding ground, these sorts of conditions are not ever so unusual events. There are eroded channels down the hillside and eroded tarmac to match in a number of places. Even though it may possibly be a normal winter event, it would seem to be a first-time experience for an awful lot of people, judging by the driving skills of most of the locals. I have to admit that this is probably my first experience on roads like this in conditions like this. But hopefully I am not driving as badly as some of the other fools on the road. I cannot believe their terrible driving practices in such adverse conditions.

Escaping Croatia into Montenegro, the roads and the rain get even worse. I think they must have used water soluble bitumen on the roads, as there seems to be no tar but an awful lot of mac. And in a lot of places it is difficult to see where the road is, as the water is so deep. Having left Dubrovnik at 8.30am, we don't reach Shkoder in Albania until 4.30pm - a total of 142 miles of driving and eight hours of possibly the worst conditions

I have ever driven in. The Sat Nag has a bit of a problem as well; there are no road numbers, also no town names, and very few direction signs. Even if there is a sign to somewhere, we have no idea if we have reached said town, or in fact already gone past it.

I am a bit surprised to find that all the fuel pump prices in Albania are in Euros and not the local currency, the Albanian Lek. We pay for everything else - hotel, food, drinks - in Lek, but the petrol and diesel are priced in Euros. I pull into a service station and a scruffy little man comes running out. He stands by the pump and says, 'Euro'. So I reply, 'Yes'. He says it again and this time louder (probably because I am a foreigner) and also with his hand out, 'EURO!'

Aah, I think, *he wants paying first*. Not knowing how much fuel I want, I just give him two 20 Euro notes. He takes the notes, counts them, and then appears to do a lot of mental calculations and types into the gadget on the pump: 56 Euros. Again, he says something in fluent Albanian to me, or at least I assume it is fluent Albanian. I am a bit bemused as to what he means, so I just shrug my shoulders. He shouts across to a colleague standing in a doorway - I assume for confirmation of his mental calculations - and gets some sort of a grunt as a reply to his query. And so he puts 56 Euros worth of fuel in the tank, and then says something more in fluent Albanian.

I stand, totally puzzled, as I am expecting him to have his hand out to ask for more money and I have my hand in my pocket ready, but all I get is a lot of hand gestures and more Albanian. I am completely lost as to what is going on. He speaks louder and increases his hand waving, and I begin to think that he is indicating something to the effect of, 'Bugger off, I am a busy man, have a nice day'. So I slowly get into the car and he watches us drive off.

As we drive down the road, Helen gets the calculator out to do some cross checking - cost of fuel per litre, number of litres poured and 56 Euros - but the 40 Euros I paid does not fit into the equation anywhere. I am still not sure if he was missing something or whether I was.

Passing through the shambles that is the capital Tirana, the road leads us to the mountains again, and more snow, deep snow. We travel over two high passes and both sides are strewn with stuck lorries and cars. Signs everywhere indicate that snow chains must be fitted. We don't have any with us as they will have limited use in Africa, but luckily we do have a 4x4 and new, or nearly new, overland tread tyres, so I weave in and out of everybody else on the way up and down. Getting a bit excited, I declare to Helen, 'I am going to get one of these when we get back!' Then I remember that I have one of these already and I am driving it. And I do not really want one when we get back.

This time, no matter how deep or cold the snow, I manage not to boil my clutch fluid. I am not sure if it is me getting better, or whether the conditions are a bit different now.

At the border with Macedonia we have to get car insurance. Our car insurance at home included thirty days' green card for Europe, but when I applied for it I was told that these countries are not in Europe and, therefore, not eligible for their green card. I thought of giving the girl on the other end of the phone a lecture on geography, but I knew I would be wasting my breath, so I just thought we would carry on and worry about it as the time came. And now the time has come. The border control says we need insurance. We ask where we need to go, and, with a flick of his head, he says, 'There'. So off we go, but we still do not know where 'there' is. We ask someone else where the insurance office is and he points to a small brick building about 200 metres away. We are soon trudging through deep snow. It is cold and we now have wet feet, but as we open the door to the shed, we are hit by an avalanche of super tropical heat. And smoke. The woman we meet must have all the heat there is turned full up, and supplement it by continuously lighting up cigarettes. I am sure all of this gets added to our bill as we have to pay a whopping 50 Euros for fifteen days' cover.

We get back to the car and turn the heater full blast onto our feet to warm up and dry out after our two-way trek through the snow field. Unfortunately, I also need all the heat on the windscreen so I can see where we are going. Driving in these kinds of conditions, and at this time of year, was not part of the plan at all.

In one town, morning checks of the car reveal that it has frozen; the wipers are frozen to the windscreen, the door locks are frozen and the doors are frozen to the car. The staff, noticing our plight, come out with kettles of hot water, and slowly we get everything working. *We are packed for Africa, not the Arctic!*
Now we are entering Greece and driving down to the Mediterranean coast where it is sunny and warm and

everything in our world is well again. At least, until nightfall. We turn off the motorway into the town of Xanthi and find a place to stay. We dump our bags; our priorities are to find an ATM and some food. We set off down the road with directions and, after walking about a mile and a half in the dark, we find an ATM, but food doesn't seem to be so easy; there are no cafés or restaurants anywhere. This is obviously no holiday destination, in fact, I cannot see it as any sort of destination. After a long search we find cheese, ham and Russian salad in a supermarket, but we have to eat in our hotel room. *Such is our journey of a lifetime!*

Continuing along the coast, we enter Turkey. We stop briefly in Istanbul with the idea of going to the Sudanese Consulate to try and get our visas for Sudan there to save us going into Cairo, which is having a bit of civil unrest and we thought Istanbul would be a better place to stop. We have been to Istanbul before and enjoyed it, but last time we were without a car. This time with the car is a nightmare; every road is jam-packed with traffic, and after missing a turning it is impossible to turn around. I hate it. When we finally reach the consulate, we find that they do not issue visas to people on holiday. I am afraid that goes straight over my head, as we need a visa to go there on holiday. And apparently the same is true at the Sudanese Embassy in Ankara. So we are going to have to wait until Egypt for the visas. But we come across a copying shop and we know that in a lot of countries you need a photo for almost everything, so we take the opportunity to prepare and stock up on copies of our passports and photos, so that we will be ready for the bureaucracy and visa issuing later.

This is another country where you need a prepaid card to use the motorways, luckily we found this piece of information on the internet. We find an office selling these permits, but after queuing for a while we are told we are at the wrong counter, so off we go to join another queue the other side of the room. Eventually we get our permit, which comes in two parts; one part goes in the glove box, to never be seen again, and the other part is a strip with a barcode on it, which has to go in an exact place on the interior mirror facing the windscreen. It comes with a complete set of instructions and measurements for three different categories, we assume for different classes of vehicles, and one needs to go through the right channel for that particular format - like a toll booth but with traffic lights instead of toll collectors.

Off we go, spending a moment to pick the right channel. We get to the camera, but for us the traffic light does not go green. We wait. Nothing. I think we must be in the wrong lane. Luckily there is no-one behind us, so I reverse out and move to the next lane, but exactly the same thing: no green light. I have no idea whether my barcode has been read or not, so we proceed anyway, and we drive right across Turkey without a green light at any of the toll booths. Luckily there were only traffic lights to stop us and not barriers. We still do not know if it was because our barcode on the mirror was in the wrong place, or upside down. There is even the possibility that, as we are right-hand drive, the interior mirror was pointing the wrong way. Who knows? We later came across someone in Africa who did not know about the motorway prepayment scheme and he had driven along in ignorance until the police caught up with him and escorted him off the motorway and told him never to come back again.

In Cappadocia, we realise we have some spare time in an area we have previously visited. A few years ago we were staying with some friends on their boat and we left them to make an awful journey across Turkey to see this region, a torture we had to endure, as we may never pass this way again. Now it is right on our route. The ferry to Egypt runs twice a week. The next one due to go will arrive at Port Said in time for the weekend when all the staff are off, and a two-day wait in the port before starting the two-day formalities for getting out does not sound like much fun. So we opt to stay here for a few days and will catch the next boat. *It's a funny old world.*

In the town of Goreme, we look around some of the houses and churches carved into the rock faces, and look at the weird and wonderful fairy chimneys. Last time we were here it was summer and it was fantastic, but now, in mid-December, it is cold, and snow is coming, so we leave and head down to the Mediterranean. We will wait for the ferry that will whisk us over to Africa in the port town of Eskenderun.

Amazingly, we have crossed thirteen countries to get here. Even though we have been on the road for about three weeks, we are only now getting to the real start of our journey.

Road to Africa
Not the weather we were prepared for

FERRY TO AFRICA
22 December

We find the name of a ticket agent for this boat on the internet. Apparently, this route was started up to move freight between Egypt and Turkey, but had been interrupted by the war in Syria and we have been told it has been unreliable ever since it started. Driving around the streets of Eskenderun, asking several people the way, we eventually find the ticket shop. Then we have to drive around some more looking for somewhere to park.

Several hours pass in the ticket agent's office - form filling, photocopying passports, car documents and tickets, money changing hands - and we eventually get our hands on our ferry tickets. We are instructed to be down at the gates by 8.30 tomorrow morning, gate number one.

Now we can get excited; although some of the drive through Europe was pleasant enough, most of it was just a slog, something that had to be done to get here. But now our spirits are up as tomorrow morning we will board the boat and at 12 noon we will be away.

Nineteen hours later, Port Said. *Africa! Africa, the real start of our journey!*

By 10am, after we have been sitting outside the dock gates for a long time, we are told there is no ferry. Maybe nine at night, maybe midnight, maybe tomorrow. We are gobsmacked. We have paid £450 for this ticket, you would think the least the ferry could do is turn up.

We head back to the agency with all speed, where we are told the ferry is delayed but, 'Maybe tonight, maybe tomorrow'. They advise us to go back to our hotel. *But, if we are leaving tonight we won't need a room at the hotel!* It is later confirmed the ferry will definitely go in the morning for sure, and we must be at the terminal by 8am tomorrow. So we trudge back to the hotel and book in again. It seems that the stories I have read about this ferry are probably true after all. Sometime later we were told by another driver that he was informed of this delay when he bought his ticket two days earlier, but, as we were already on the boat by then, it was a bit late to go back to the ticket office and scream at somebody.

A rest overnight has done us good and some of the frustrations of yesterday have evaporated. Arriving at the gates at 7.45am, full of anticipation for our journey to begin, we are told to wait. No further explanation. This isn't looking too good but, after a few hours, the guards usher us all forward. The drivers all surge at the small opening and, forming a perfect wedge, totally block the gateway, so none of them can get through until at last one of them backs up a bit. The good old

British sport of queuing would make things run so much quicker here. The officials at the gate have no idea of organisation and I can only assume that this doesn't bode well for the rest of the day's proceedings.

After a time, we get our turn to be shouted at. 'Here! Lift the bonnet. Move over there', from one officious man. 'Stay here!' from someone else, competing for authority. 'Documents!' All in fluent Turkish, or maybe Arabic, but we can just about work out the meaning. One of the other drivers comes over to interpret for us and, with his help, we at least know for certain what is being asked of us, but the organisation of the whole operation still doesn't make much sense. We are eventually told to move over to somewhere else and wait. When our queue has enough vehicles, an escort car comes and we are led down to the dock area. I ask where our vehicle documents are, but get told, 'Later'.

Whilst settling in for what we realise could be a long wait, some scruffily dressed men with big cardboard boxes come round to collect everyone's passports. We are used to Customs and Immigration officials wearing some sort of uniform, but these bods look like they have just had a rough night sleeping on the street. They and our passports then disappear. Having to surrender your passport to a tatty cardboard box managed by an un-uniformed man is not normal, at least in my experience, but I have been told by someone who travelled this route that this is the normal routine, so we try not to worry unnecessarily. There is no waiting room, cafeteria or seats, so we just hang around for hours on the dockside, without our passports and without our car documents, and without a clue as to what is really going on. There is a lot of muttering in four or five languages amongst most of us waiting. 'What the heck is going on now?' Some of the others waiting may know the answer, being from the region themselves and used to the organisation. But confusion is certainly the sentiment amongst the Europeans in the contingency.

There are many Syrians waiting for the ferry, escaping the slaughter in their homeland. We cycled through Syria some twelve or thirteen years ago. It was a fantastic country and the people were extremely friendly and very helpful. It is devastating to see reports on the news of places that we had visited now destroyed, and the thought that some of the people that helped us may now be homeless or murdered. Standing on the dockside amongst these people fleeing their country is very saddening.

Eventually, the passports come back. We find that Helen's has been stamped but mine has not, and the car documents have been returned but have not been stamped. There are a number of other people with similar problems, so a small group of us wander from shed to shed to try and get these things sorted out. In each office we are told there is no problem, or we are just sent to the office next door. Eventually I get mine stamped. One Italian traveller is not so lucky and his passport has been altogether mislaid. He starts searching through all the piles, with officials telling him, 'It not there'. Eventually he does find it himself, but the immigration officers are then reluctant to stamp it, probably because he has just shown their system up as being a mess. After a lot of arguing, he too gets his stamp. After my passport is stamped, we have to go to two more tin sheds to get the carnet sorted out. The whole thing has been a right royal shambles, but on the bright side, it has used up an hour or two of the boring waiting time. There appears to be a similar mess going on with the vehicles leaving the ship, as there is a queue of vehicles and a lot of disgruntled drivers.

During the morning it becomes very obvious that the ship is not going to leave at mid-day. In fact, as far as I can see, there is even a possibility that it will not leave today at all. A long and tedious day unfolds, with nothing to eat or drink apart from the drop of water and the sweets that we have in the car. But, at 6pm - six painful hours after our supposed departure time - the ship starts loading.

We park the car and make it up to the passenger lounge, where the passport saga continues as they collect them all up again for the duration of the voyage. It is a long voyage and there are cabins available but at 300 US Dollars, we decide not to take up that option. So we try and make ourselves comfortable somewhere amongst the mass of refugees fleeing the carnage in Syria. They seem to have about four million screaming kids with them, so sleep does not come easy. I think any other time this would make me irritable, but I can only feel sympathy for their tragic circumstances.

The boat is a mess. After only a very short time one set of toilets are awash, the other set are locked, presumably to keep them clean. At around midnight local time, Christmas Eve no less, one day and twelve hours late, we set sail. *We are leaving Europe at last.*

Our ticket includes two meals. As meal time comes around, the lorry drivers get the first sitting. Luckily the stewards are benevolent towards us and usher us in with the lorry drivers too. This is something like sitting in an average cross channel ferry cafeteria with only twenty-five or so people in it. So we have our meal in relative peace. When we are all finished, the doors are opened and all hell breaks loose as the stampede of Syrians enter the dining room.

We dock in Port Said twenty-four hours later. Some Immigration officials had boarded the ship with the local pilot some time ago, but it is only after we have docked that they start their stamping duties. Three hours later, they start handing out our passports; one man standing behind a counter picks up a passport and calls out a name to the masses of people. *This is going to take quite a while.* We car drivers have to go and get the cars off and park them on the dockside, then we have to get back on the boat and continue to wait for our passports; the slow handing still goes on. A long time later we successfully retrieve our passports, then we have to wait for God knows what at the gangplank before we can get off the boat. As the crowd of passengers is waiting and moaning, a contingent of Syrian gypsies bursts through the line of sailors and Customs Officers, with all their goods and chattels on their shoulders, marching down the gangplank. The picket line breaks to chase the gypsies and provides an opportunity for us to follow. We gain no great advantage though as, once on the quay, we still have to wait a bit more for some lorries to move, as all our vehicles have been blocked in. By and by, we get the cars out and have a police escort to the Customs Office. Here we have to wait yet some more.

During this long wait, one of the Italians realised it was past midnight and it is, therefore, Christmas Day. He breaks out a bottle of Martini and five of us stand on the dockside and drink ourselves into... a small martini. *Happy Christmas!*

After the contents of the cars are cleared by Customs, we have to take our vehicles to a compound where they are parked up and locked in. Now we can leave the port and try and find a hotel. It's 2am.

Early the next morning, without time for breakfast, we arrive back at the port to start the procedures to get the car out. First we have to get vehicle chassis and engine numbers verified, which involves someone climbing into the engine bay and under the car to take rubbings of the actual numbers on the engine and the chassis. Reading the vin plate, or reading the engine and chassis numbers, and then writing them down is apparently not good enough. The rubbings are then cut out and stapled to the appropriate form.

The next step involves going round several offices - some of them more than once - and shelling out a fortune. We seem to be clearing the Egyptian national debt and topping up a few retirement pots.

These offices are from a world gone by. Some of them look like derelict buildings from the outside, all of them on the inside look like something from the 1940s. Apart from the computers, they only look like they are twenty years old. The shambles, the mess and the chaos is unbelievable. And the noise. A host of Arabs all trying to get the attention of somebody behind a desk. I am not sure how the filing system works; there are stacks of paper piled high, filling up all the ancient shelving and piled up on any available patch of floor space.

Every office has someone behind a desk surrounded by a crowd shouting at him. With every new folder put in front of him, he interrupts what he is doing to look at it, often whilst talking on the phone as well, and the paperwork created is incredible. Unsurprisingly, we uncover a number of errors made in all this chaos, so that means, after moving on to the next shouting match, we need to go back to the previous office to get the error rectified each time. One fellow has the biggest rubber stamp I have ever seen, the full width of an A4 sheet, and an ink pad about a quarter of the size of the stamp, so he spends a lot of time dabbing around the ink pad. He puts the stamp on the paper and thumps all around the edges with his fist, the end result of which is about half of the intended imprint and it is smudged and illegible, although that may be only to us as it is all in Arabic.

We have a scrap of paper that allows us to leave and re-enter the port. When we leave to buy a cup of tea, the paper is diligently examined and again on our way back in. The tea vendor is right next to the dock gates; the guard actually watched us buy the tea but then still scrutinises our passes on the way back in. We do also have to venture further afield; it seems regular visits to an ATM are necessary to get enough money to pay for everything. Eventually Day One of the port clearance saga draws to a close and we return to the hotel to recharge.

Today, hopefully, we get the car out! We begin another round of frustrating paperwork. We have a fixer to do the work. Prior to this trip, I had never even heard of a fixer, but Antonio the Italian has obviously done more research than me and gave us the phone number for one. I think we were very lucky to bump into Antonio as it would be impossible to do this without a fixer; the offices are in the town, in the docks, down alleys, anywhere. Few of them actually look like offices, all of them look like they should be demolished before they crumble of their own accord. Even though our fixer is doing the biz and dealing with the frustrations of officialdom, we have to be with him. It gives us a chance to interact with the locals; there is always someone who can speak a little English.

> 'Where you from?'
> 'England.'
> 'Aahhh, Manchester United.'
> 'No, London.'
> 'Manchester United?'
> 'Yes.' It seems easier to concede.
> 'Goood.'

Saints be praised! By 3.30pm we are out. We have our carnet stamped. We have our new Egyptian driving licence - a sheet of cheap paper covered in Arabic, but we are told it is a driving licence. And we have our new Egyptian number plates. New to us, that is, the plates themselves look like they have been through a few wars. We tie them on with string.

Although everything is done, cleared and stamped to satisfaction, we still have to get the engine and chassis numbers checked again at the exit gates. Is this to ensure that we have not sneakily changed the engine or chassis while the car has been locked in the Customs compound? All is well, we are out, and we are on the road south. I'm sure one day I might look back and think this whole procedure comical.

From turning up for the non-existent ferry in Turkey to getting on the road in Egypt has taken five days. And it would seem we have been lucky; I have since heard tales of people having more trouble than us. We spoke to people who had spent four days getting clear of the docks. And for one unlucky group, due to uprisings in Egypt, the ferry anchored offshore for five days before docking, and only then could they start the two days of clearing the cars. It would seem we have had it relatively easy, but if anyone ever complains to me about the immigration queues at Heathrow, or their train being ten minutes late, I shall screeeeam!

EGYPT
26 December

We have been to Egypt before, so we think we will give the tourist attractions a miss and head straight for Sudan. I then spot a detour that will take us well into the Sahara, so that will be our route, but it means we will have to go through Cairo. We had planned to give Cairo a big miss as there is some political turmoil at the moment; the TV news has shown pictures of barricades and armed rioters. We also expect driving in the city will be a nightmare, having walked there and experienced the roads in taxis. But as we now need to go through the city, I guess it may be to our advantage to get our Ethiopian visas sorted whilst there.

Also, on our previous holiday in Egypt, we came across road convoys. There were some areas where traffic was only allowed to go in convoy and with military or police escort. A couple of times we were on a bus that had to wait for a convoy before it could go. I believe there were areas where unescorted tourists were not allowed to go at all, with or without a convoy. This time, we are on our own and I have no idea if such restrictions are still in force. We will find out, I suppose.

Unfortunately, we are running out of daylight and realise it is now too late in the day to make it to Cairo. We should have stayed in Port Said for the night and left tomorrow morning, but I was just in a rush to leave. We turn off to spend the night in Ismalia and as we drive around this strange town darkness falls quickly. We have already fallen foul of our number one rule: No driving at night. We are now driving around a town with no street lights, and donkeys, carts and cyclists all over the place. We have no idea where we are or where we are going. We ask several people, 'Where can we find a hotel?' After some time, as feelings of panic rise, the lights of a big and expensive hotel suddenly appear before us and, regardless of the cost, this ends our search and our desperate driving for the night.

Hopefully our ploy of going to Cairo to get our Ethiopian visas first will help us get our visas for Sudan cheaper and quicker in Aswan. I heard about somebody getting visas in Aswan and, although I cannot find anything on the internet about a Sudanese consulate in the town, I am hoping that the traveller's tale is true.

We arrive on a Thursday afternoon, too late to go to the Ethiopian Embassy; tomorrow they are closed for the weekend, so we have three days to enjoy the locale around our hotel. Cairo, the city of filth, noise and pollution, with a population of twenty million. I think everyone must have a car and be on the road twenty-four hours a day. The only code of driving seems to be: Use your horn as much as possible. The noise is deafening and disorientating as they whiz past in all directions, seemingly out of control. Abysmal driving techniques, but boy can they make a noise!

We had met an Egyptian called Sary on the ferry. He had been living in London but was returning to Cairo and we manage to get in touch with him here. He and his brother kindly offer to pick us up from the hotel and drive us at breakneck speed into the centre of Cairo. We have a beer over a catch up on his efforts to clear his belongings through Customs. His van is still locked in the compound, but he has managed to get his piano out! It is a great chance to see a bit of the nightlife in the inner city with a local for a guide and we enjoy the view of the cruise boats lit up like Christmas trees lining the Nile.

Monday morning and, bright and early, we set off again for the Ethiopian Embassy. We ask the man at the hotel to write the address in Arabic for us to show the taxi driver where we want to go. After asking a few people on the way, we reach the right street. Then we drive up and down asking more people where the actual address we want is. Twice I point to the building with the Ethiopian flag flying, but to no avail. Our taxi driver finds it in the end though. He tells me he did not know we wanted the embassy, as on the piece of paper it only had the building number, and he had been asking people in the street where number twenty-one was.

After several hours, the formalities are finished and have our visa. We find a taxi and present the card from our hotel; this appears to be a lot easier to find as the return journey is a lot quicker.

Visa'd up and filling the car with diesel for £5 - a little bit different from the £70 or so that it costs in England - something to cheer us up after the misery of escaping the port. We are finally on a roll. As we come to the edge of Cairo, we can just see the outline of the Sphinx in the distance through the smog. Somewhere to the west, we find our way to the Western Desert road. We have to ask a couple of people, even a policeman on point duty, who has to ask the driver of a passing car, and that driver then leads us to the turning we need.

We turn south into the desert through miles of flat, unchanging scenery for miles all around us and eventually come to Bahariyya oasis where we stop for the night. It is called Eden Lodge and we have a small, round, thatched hut. The camp is complete with a thermal pool – this bit must be the Eden for Helen. Here in the arid desert is an oasis that provides drinking water and a spring that provides naturally heated bathing water. It is New Year's Eve and we are invited to join our hosts in a large Bedouin tent for a bit of a bash. We enjoy a meal around the fire in the centre of the tent and then a live band - an electric synthesiser, three men on drums and a man playing a local flute - entertains us with traditional Bedouin music into the night. There is an endless supply of traditional Bedouin tea to keep us going. What a do! It is great to mix with the locals in their celebrations, although I am afraid all the music sounds the same to our western ears.

In the morning, our host helps us find some diesel on the black market. We are now having to pay double the price. On our way here, we passed miles and miles of oil wells, but the pumps at the service stations only serve petrol. I think there is something amiss, I was told that since the new (Islamic) government has been in power there have been a lot of problems with fuel, in turn there have been shortages of gas, petrol, oil and diesel. Buying diesel on the black market is the norm for most of the rest of our stay in Egypt. Setting off each day is a little bit nerve racking, wondering if we are going to get enough fuel to get us to the next place that has no diesel. This stop serves us well, as we are not sure if we would have had enough to get us back to Cairo if we couldn't buy any here.

We make one black market diesel stop from two men, one holding a funnel and the other tipping the fuel from a 25 litre can. They manage to cover half of the car in diesel and splash it up to only just short of roof level. With the second can they make the same mess but they don't stop pouring until the diesel is overflowing the tank and running freely down the side of the car. They then ask me if it is full. 'YES, FULL', I reply enthusiastically, 'it is overflowing!' They indicate there is a little drop more in the can (a mere litre or so) so they try topping up the already overflowing tank. And now with more diesel running down the side of the car and round their feet, they are happy. I can't help thinking there could be lot more of this to come.

We travel from oasis town to oasis town along this road into the Western Desert. In Farafa, we stop at a hotel next to the main road, where we camp in the grounds but are able to use the ablutions and wifi in the main building. Putting the tent up for the first time is not straight forward, it is cold during the night and the airbed deflates, but apart from that we have at last spent our first night under canvas and cooked our own food. We pack up and leave the next morning with a small sense of achievement.

48

We pass a number of small, Spartan, adobe-built oasis towns, like Mut, El Qsar and so on. We still haven't come across the traditional ideal of an oasis - the palm tree-lined pool of water - but all the towns and villages here are sited on a water supply, an oasis of some sort. There are some stunning desertscapes, with intricate shapes carved in the semi-solid sand by wind and weather. One area is called the White Desert because of its pale sand, and another is called the Black Desert. This I cannot understand, as it does not even look particularly dark. We stop at the Black Desert café for a chai tea. There appears to be nothing for miles in any direction, except for this shed proclaiming itself the Black Desert Café. Unfortunately our Arabic is not up to asking about the name for the area, in fact, our Arabic is barely up to finding out how much the tea costs.

We have encountered road checks all over Egypt, but the ones on this road are the most fun. Either side of the road is miles of nothing but sand. Coming to a check point, which consists of a few rusty drums, some bits of fencing and even pieces of junk, we spot amidst all this rubbish the shiny cat's claw, waiting. Waiting for what, I do not know. Every time we stop, we have to wait for someone to get off his backside and come out with his grubby exercise book and ask his questions.

'Where you come from?'

'Farafa.'

'Where you go?'

'El Qsar.'

'Passport.' He takes the passport, writes down all the details, and then asks, 'Italiano?'

'No, English.'

'Aah, welcome!'

49

A further 30 miles down the road, when faced with the next 'Where you come from?' there is an inner voice desperate to say, *The last effing check point and I am going to the next effing check point - there is nowhere else to go to, or come from!* But I am not brave enough, especially when they are armed.

'Germany?'

NO! Look at the bloody passport! (if only) 'No, English.'

'Welcome.'

'Thank you.'

I am completely baffled as to how they can make a big deal of copying all the details of the passport down, and still not know the nationality of the passport or its bearer. Maybe the car's temporary Egyptian plates has them fooled.

Some Austrians had told us about a desert road to Aswan, from El Kharga, where the turn off is. As we approach El Kharga, a police car stops us. We are still some six miles out of town and he *was* going the other way, but did a quick turnaround to chase us. My pulse quickens and I glance warily across at Helen as he approaches the car. He checks our passports, asks where we were going and then escorts us to town. *What have we done wrong?*

In town, we are led to a couple of buildings with no-one in. This man is now starting to be a pain; we have no idea why we were stopped or where he is taking us. I am really fed up. I see a hotel across the road, so I point to it and say, 'We are going there'. We get into our car and drive over to the hotel. He gets into his car and also drives over to the hotel.

Later on, we go out to see some of the local historical ruins and our new-found police escort follows us and escorts us back to the hotel afterwards. We take a walk to find the tourist office and they continue to follow us. I demand - well sort of demand - to know what is going on. He replies that he is concerned for our safety. We just want to find out where this desert road is; the tourist office was non-existent, despite two signs advertising it. The local police and army tell us there is no such road, and we are advised to go to Qena and Luxor; they even phone someone to explain to me in English that there is no short-cut across the desert.

However, I have more faith in the Austrians than I do in the local militia, so we decide to leave town and manage to give our ever-following escort the slip. We find a road going south, so we head that way. At the edge of town we see another police car and, at the risk of drawing attention to our safety again, we ask them where our desert road is. They kindly lead the way and we follow until we come to the turning of a superb road (by Egyptian standards). We thank our latest police escorts, these ones being welcoming, helpful and friendly, and we set off on our short-cut road. This road obviously is on the radar of the police and army, as there are check points along the way, two of which were only three miles apart. This route is 250 miles shorter than the way the locals wanted us to go. *How did their colleagues in town have no knowledge of it?*

We meet a Dutch couple who brought their car over to Africa ten years ago. They holiday, park the car somewhere, go home, come back next holiday and repeat the process. Over that ten years, they have been here fifteen times, and they have visited forty-two of the forty-eight countries of mainland Africa in their 2CV. I kid you not! Around Africa in a Citroen 2CV! And here I am thinking we are ill-prepared. It just goes to show...

Obviously their journey was not totally without car problems. At times on their return visits they had to bring out odd bits, like a new engine, new suspension arms, and new wheels. But I think almost any parts for a 2CV can fit into your luggage with no problem. At some point they needed some welding done on the underside of the car. The welder and his mate just tipped the car on its side, and he was able to stand alongside it and do his job. *More power to them,* I say, *it would seem the spirit of adventure is not yet dead*.

Now we are on the road properly, Helen - not much of a Domestic Goddess at home - is getting us into our travelling domestic routine. We do our laundry as we shower. I think this is so that I do my own and she does not have to lay her hands on my underwear. From here on in, all the laundry - well, the smalls and shirts - are done by hand, and the big things have to wait until if, or when, we come across a launderette. Or until Helen gets really desperate.

After finding our desert road, and a few hours' drive through the Sahara, we cross the River Nile and come to Aswan, effectively the end of the road for us in Egypt. So now it is a boat on the lake for us. Well, two boats really. A couple of days later we will get the ferry and the car will get the barge.

Egyptian numberplates

The Dutch Citroën 2CV

LAKE NASSAR CROSSING
7 January

Leaving Egypt, we have to go through the reverse of the routine for bringing the car into the country. This time we have a fixer, named Kamal, recommended to us. He helps us with driving from one run-down office to another, filling in forms, greasing a few palms - including a well-spent 50 Egyptian Pounds to avoid having to empty the car and put the contents through an x-ray machine - and handing back our Egyptian number plates and Helen's Egyptian driving licence. The car is in Helen's name, so Helen gets the licence, but I have to do all the driving. Luckily I have not been caught out yet, even with all those security checks. But the most important thing here is getting our carnet stamped. The process seems a lot easier and a lot quicker than the entry formalities in Port Said. I am very sad to see our Egyptian number plates go, they would make nice souvenirs.

Kamal then shows us a garage where we can fill up with diesel. He guides us there, but stays down the road, telling us to go to the driveway, ignore the man on guard at the front stopping everyone; drive past him, and go round the back. Aha! Round the back there are two pumps. Elated, I jump out of the car and almost fall over, the floor is like a skating rink, awash with diesel. Luckily, I manage to hang on to the door, which saves me from lying flat on my back, or my front, in all the sludge. *Why, when there is such a fuel shortage in the country, do they tip so much of it on the floor?*

With all these things done, I load the car onto a barge. Trying to manoeuvre the car through all the goods haphazardly stacked on the quayside and up two ramps, parking the 5 metre long car on a 6 metre wide hatch cover with six or seven Arabs all shouting something in the way of directions is a touch nerve-racking to say the least. But, after a while, I get the car on, with the handbrake hard on, and I leave it in gear. There it is, all ready and waiting. I have a celebratory cup of chai with the skipper in his galley-cum-cabin-cum-engine-room, and wish him and our car 'bon voyage'.

Sometime later, the barge sets sail, leaving us with our fingers crossed and hoping we will see it again - and all in one piece - as it goes out on to Lake Nasser for its voyage south to Wadi Halfa in Sudan.

With all this going on, we also have to get our Sudan visas. Our fixer takes us to a run-down, high-rise council estate. I wonder what on earth we are doing, but it appears that the Sudanese Consulate operates from some rooms in one of these Russian-designed and -built concrete towers - definitely not the usual embassy or consulate setting. We are used to embassies of one country having different rules in different places, but Sudan has just taken the proverbial biscuit. Sudan's embassy in London wants at least six weeks to grant a visa and it charges £100. Their embassy and consulate in Turkey does not give visas to foreign tourists, I am still a little confused with that one. The Sudan embassy in Cairo wants a letter of introduction from the UK Embassy (£45) and 90 US Dollars plus one week for a visa. But in Aswan we get our visa the same day, and at a cut-price rate of 50 US Dollars and NO requirement for a letter from Her Most Britannic Majesty's Government. But then I suppose if they are working from a run-down council tenement, they can afford to sell off their visas cheap.

Our fixer also suggests that we change some money into Sudanese Pounds. This is probably a good idea, as we are unlikely to come across an ATM in Sudan for at least a few days. He provides us with a great wad of dosh - 5,000 Sudanese Pounds, about £500 - a bit more than I was expecting, but no matter, a couple of trips to the ATM to pay for it and we are all sorted.

Off we go to the port again next morning to get ourselves onto the ferry. We are told there are only second class seats left, and, with the grim stories we have heard about this boat, we are not looking forward to it. We see a huge mass of Arabs and their luggage, scrambling and fighting for tickets. *Can it be any worse than we have already imagined?* But our fixer comes to the rescue and gets us into a back door of the ticket office, and I am asked if I want a cabin. It means spending an extra £30, but as Helen is a bit under the weather, I go for it.

Once on board, I have to admit that it is a cabin, but I have probably stayed in better sheds. It is scruffy, but then the whole ship is scruffy: paint worn right off a lot of the steelwork, the constant rub of bodies and luggage keeping it shiny; the toilets are broken, awash and disgusting; the dining room, if it can be called a dining room, beggars belief. Obviously Health and Safety Officers have never visited here.

We take our food back to our cabin - although grubby it is in slightly better condition than the dining room - so we sit on the bunk, eating our meal, trying not to think of the state of the kitchen where the food came from. At least in our own cabin we can lay our heads down overnight and, for the duration, it is our own personal bit of scruff - we do not have to share it with the rest of the passengers.

When the locals travel, they seem to take two or three camel loads of luggage with them. There are bodies, sacks and boxes all around the ship. There probably was a time when I would have been looking for a bit of spare dirty steel plate amongst this chaos to get my head down, but that was some time ago. Now I think, *no matter how grubby or how small, I am really glad we have a cabin*. I must be getting old. Later, we found out that lots of Sudanese get the ferry to Egypt to stock up on goods to take back to Sudan and sell. That goes some way to explaining the amount of junk they all have.

Sometime during the night, our ferry overtakes the barge with our car on it. The barges are slower and do not have GPS so they only sail during daylight hours.

Our ferry will take twenty hours, and the barges take a lot, lot longer - two days longer for our car's particular barge to complete the same journey as the ferry.

When we dock, the chaos of the Arabs with all their goods and chattels all trying to get off the boat at the same time creates a spectacle. The passageways are blocked solid. People are trying to lower their goods over the side of the boat. The crew are trying to get some organisation going; there is a lot of Arabic being shouted from various directions, but it is not terribly effective at organising the crowd. They even shut the outer doors, presumably in the hopes that it will instil a sense of quietude and order in the rabble. *Some hopes,* I think.

Somehow, we end up getting dragged into the chaos. Using sign language, one man asks me if he can lower his stuff out of our cabin window. With hindsight, I now know I made a mistake agreeing to this. Our cabin has enough floor space to allow six to eight people to stand in very close proximity, and in no time at all it is full with ourselves and six to eight Arabs, with all their chattels, arguing as to whose turn it is next. I reach the limit of my patience; I can't physically throw them out - the baggage they are toting is heavier than I could shift - so all I can do is shut the door and, as each one leaves, not let them back in, gradually regaining control of the situation. Eventually the packed crowds thin out a bit and we make our own attempt to disembark. In a short while, we are on dry land. We only have Customs and Immigration to face before we can enter a new country.

I have since read on the internet that there is a new road being built through desert, linking Aswan with Wadi Halfa. Although I can't find much evidence of it, some hard-bitten overlanders are regretting this progress as it will take some of the spirit out of the journey. In the same vein, I am glad we came this way. But if the road does happen one day and it puts that awful ferry out of business, *good job,* is all I can say.

Hanging around Wadi Halfa is dreary; it is definitely a one-horse-town, or at least it would be if the horse in question had not died of boredom some years ago. There are a number of scattered and run-down adobe buildings surrounded by a lot of sand. Wadi Halfa is effectively the end of the road in Sudan but, unlike Aswan, it is a small place. It is possibly more like the end of the world rather than the end of Sudan. I learn that the original Wadi Halfa is about 25 miles north of here, and, under the flooded Nile valley that is now Lake Nasser, so the present day town is relatively new. It doesn't look like it from where I am standing.

We have to spend two nights here whilst we wait for the car to turn up. We pick a rather crummy hotel, which I was told is the best hotel in town. Our choices of entertainment while we wait for the car are: sit on the bed in our dismal room and read our books, or wander around the dismal adobe town and have a coffee at one of the many little stalls. Very nice coffee, I admit, and this was to be the start of our love affair with Sudanese coffee, but you can only drink so much.

But we do have the fortune of catching up with some Spanish motorcyclists staying in the same hotel as us.

We first met them when we were loading our car, and them their bikes, onto the barge. And again, at the chaos of the ticket office, but we did not see them in the mass of humanity on the ferry. Here we have a chance to talk about our plans, and compare the mistakes we have all made so far. *And there is ample time to make plenty more.*

The great day arrives; our Sudanese fixer comes to the hotel to inform us that the barge is in. I am told I can go down and drive our car off and take it to the Customs area. Walking down the pier I realise I can't see the barge with my car on it. There is only one pier and only two barges, *It cannot be that hard to find.* But I am looking for my car standing proud, on top of a hatch cover, for all to see and, when I finally do find it, I am gobsmacked. In Egypt I drove the car onto the top of a hatch cover and then, after I left, they filled the holds up, covered the hatches and did not stop loading until they had also completely covered the car. The Spanish motorcyclists had loaded their three bikes onto the same barge as us in Aswan and now only a part of one wheel of one bike is visible. So much cargo has to travel on this one route that they are experts at stacking, even around, on top of, and integrated with our vehicles.

It takes a bit of haranguing before I can get enough cargo shifted to get to the car, and it takes a bit more time and cajoling to find the ramps under some cargo elsewhere. All this is done by hand, piece by piece taken off the barge and into waiting trucks. Putting the ramps under the car would be so much more sensible and a lot easier but they don't seem to have that mindset.

As we wait, we watch some of the unloading. Heavy boxes get dropped, light boxes get thrown, and a number of boxes get broken, along with their contents. Sometimes odd pieces come adrift from the main component; these bits are thrown onto a truck and, hopefully, will be reunited with their bigger parts at some later date.

Another two or three hours of paperwork and we are in. Having squared up with the hotel and the fixer, we are on the road. Certainly a lot easier than Egypt, and hopefully crossing borders to the rest of the countries we visit will be easier still, but for now I'm adamant, *No more ferries... EVER!*

I have seen this ferry a couple of times on television programmes; I can't remember exactly what occurred, but I know it was *this* ferry on *this* lake. I do remember that the participants of the filming, the crew, plus anybody else who may have been involved, seemed to have plenty of room to wander around and watch the world go by. I do not know if we were just unlucky with the crowds, or whether film companies pay for special arrangements. I have to admit that I have grown rather cynical about what is presented to us as real life on the square box. Travelling can do that to you. But I know this is the richer, and more real, experience.

This is the last time that we will need a fixer. When we were on the ferry from Turkey, we met a couple of Italians who had obviously done a lot more research than I had; they had a phone number of a fixer to help get the car into Egypt. We simply got him to sort ours as well, and from then on we were in a network, as he gave us the number of a fixer in Aswan, and he gave us the number of a fixer in Wadi Halfa. I am not sure of the detail of what they actually did, but I do believe we could never have got our car in and out of Egypt without them. From here onwards, sorting out the carnet should be relatively simple, even if frustratingly slow, and we can do it ourselves.

The Spanish bikers did not want to pay 20 US Dollars for help to get their bikes through Customs, in fact, they went as far as calling the fixer and Customs Officers 'the Mafia' - that probably did not help their cause too much. After a lot more hassle than we had, they manage to get away the following day.

Lake Nasser barge – driving the planks

Lake Nasser barge – spot the car

SUDAN
8 January

Heading south from Wadi Halfa, we continue through the Sahara on the lookout for pre-Egyptian temples. The view here meets my long-held vision of the Nile: only about ten metres wide, and lined with palm trees both sides. That was my vision before I ever went to Egypt anyway. The Nile is the longest river in the world. It starts in Burundi and/or Rwanda, passes through Uganda and then South Sudan, through Sudan and then through Egypt to the Mediterranean, and the only part of this long river that matches the image that I have had in my mind for many years is this stretch of it in Sudan.

Despite the fact that we know there are a lot of temples on the banks of the Nile, we only manage to find one. Named Wawa, it is signposted, but we are in a village on one side of the river, and the temple is on the opposite bank. After wandering around the village for a while, we find a boatman willing to take us across the river, and, after a short walk, we come to a few standing columns. As we stand looking at them, we are told it costs 500 Sudanese Pounds each to go in. That is not a lot of money, admittedly, but there doesn't appear to be much temple, so we decline. Our boatman takes us back again, gives us tea, and then we pay him and continue our journey.

We don't have much of a map for this part of the journey; there are a few place names on it, but none of them seem to really exist, and along the road there are quite a few place names, none of which appear on our map. Very few of them seem to exist on the ground either; there might be a place name sign for either end of an area but, as far as we can tell, there is only desert in between.

Further down the road we look for a quiet spot somewhere off the road to pitch our tent for the night. This is a liberating opportunity, just pulling over somewhere out the way and being able to pitch the tent within our own stretch of desert. It feels like there is no-one else for miles. There must be someone about though, as most of the bushes have litter snagged on them. This is a real shame; a beautiful area, but with scattered rubbish.

Camping at a totally deserted spot, we struggle to connect one of the pegs fixed to the edge of the tent into the end of the tent pole, and, as we are fighting with this problem, a group of Arabs walk by. They stand watching for a while. We can't pull the tent fabric past the end of the pole enough to get the peg to go in. Then one of them steps forward to help and he pops it together in just a second or two. We thank him profusely and after this brief encounter, he and his mates just wander off into the desert.

Two days later, we come in from the sandy tranquillity of the desert to the frantic bustle of Khartoum. There are more cars trying to get through one crossroad than we have seen in the last 600 miles. We stop at a place called the National Camp; it seems to be some sort of army place. It is OK, but too far from the centre for the things we need and want, and it is a bit dingy and run-down. It had been recommended by another overlander on their blog site. We come to the conclusion, after this and other 'advice', that they write a load of tosh on their blog. So we decide to move on.

In our preparations for leaving, we wander over to the office to pay. The two bods there are not too interested in us and indicate that we should come back later and see someone else. So, a little later, Helen goes back to the office and two different men this time just wave her away. When we are all packed and loaded, we drive over to the office for our third visit, and, this time, we can find no-one anywhere. *Isn't this some sort of military establishment, and so shouldn't it be run with some sort of order?* After waiting a while, we just leave.

The rather grand sounding Blue Nile Sailing Club also turns out to be rather dingy and doesn't really live up to the grandness that its name suggests. The toilets are not up to much, but the locals are friendlier and the actual pitch is better, and the view is better. It looks to me more like a place where old dinghies go to die; there are loads of them laying around covered in grot and not looking like they have not seen water for a long time.

But there is some history in the area - just down river is the site of Gordon's Last Stand. General Gordon had a successful career in many conflicts in many parts of the world, but possibly he is most famously known as 'Gordon of Khartoum' and his demise occurred not 500 metres from our tent, as local legend has it. He was killed in 1885 in what is now the presidential palace. And amongst the dead and dying dinghies where we camped is the Melik, Lord Kitchener's gunboat. Now high and dry, and being used as an office for the sailing club-cum-camp ground.

A bit further down the river is the confluence of the Blue and White Niles. We go and take a photo of this geographical feature, even though it is not all that picturesque. There is a guard on the bridge and I ask him if it is OK by holding the camera up and pointing. He nods.

In Khartoum, as in most of Sudan, on street corners or any piece of waste ground, you will find ladies operating coffee stalls. They sit on very low stools with an upturned box in front of them and a couple of kettles on the go beside them simmering over some hot charcoal. On the box, they have a row of jars, containing coffee, tea and a selection of herbs and spices. They ask you in fluent Arabic what you would like in your tea or coffee. Our Arabic is not up to knowing what they are saying, but we understand roughly what they were on about, so we have a sniff of the line of jars and make our choice - from ginger, cinnamon, cardamom, etc. There is also a box of fresh mint leaves and a box of grubby sugar and, as they make our drink, it is like watching some alchemist mixing an elixir of life. Watching the making is as much a pleasure as the drinking of the final product.

We wander around Khartoum from one ministry office to another, being passed from one person that does not know what we are talking about to someone else who has no idea. We need a permit to travel and a permit to use a camera, but nobody in these government offices knows what government edict we are required to conform to, or which government department issues the aforementioned permits. Two days later, after visiting about six government departments, we get it all sorted with the help of a Greek hotelier. It is a very smart hotel and, although we are not even customers, they offer their services for free, and get our permits in an hour or two. It is not what you know but who you know.

Now we are all certificated up and free to travel, but only to the places designated on our permit. And we are free to photograph, as long as we don't take pictures of things on the long list of forbidden subject matters. I normally feel that no photo collection is complete without a snap of a government office building, petrol station or some public utility, but on this occasion I have to give these and various other photogenic sights a miss in order to stay on the right side of the law.

Our next minor problem is that we changed some Egyptian money into Sudanese as we changed countries, and now in Khartoum we find that the ATMs only accept some local Islamic card and not our Western ones. So no withdrawals for us. This means we have to adjust our spending policies. This may not be as easy as you might think; we are already living in a tent when we can, which is free - we just pull up in the desert and become Bedouin - and are acquiring food and fuel as cheaply as we can. But, most telling of all, Sudan is 'dry' in more ways than one, so we have wasted, if that is the right word, not one penny on alcohol. I am now very glad that we did not spend the money to look at the temple columns; our Sudanese cash is going to become very precious to us indeed. I now realise why our fixer in Aswan suggested that we got some Sudanese cash before we entered the country.

We are in the district of Obdurman where, some thirteen years after Gordon's death and the end of British rule in Sudan, the then General Kitchener and his Anglo Egyptian forces fought against the Mahdist (Dervish) forces in the so-called battle of Obdurman, which eventually led once more to British rule here. So, on our last night in Khartoum, we visit a mosque on the banks of the Nile to see some whirling dervishes for ourselves. There is a lot of singing (or possibly just chanting) and stomping, but not a lot of whirling. Everyone forms a huge circle, the local men making an inner circle and everyone else stands behind them. Then the chanting and drumming starts and some men, whose dress makes me think they may be priests, walk around the outside of the circle, encouraging the chanting, whilst another man waves a pot of burning incense. Every now and then one of the men in the middle twists round and round on the spot. We watch for an hour and a half, waiting for the manic whirling which we had anticipated from such an event, but there are only ever two or three men spinning at any one time and it is all quite controlled.   But it is great entertainment.

The next morning, we set off again out into the desert.

'Going out into the desert' is a bit of a funny thing to say as, wherever you are in Sudan, the desert comes in to see you. But we are off with a specific aim to see the pyramids of Meroe. These pyramids are not as big as the ones in Egypt but are more than a thousand years older, and quite fascinating. The pyramids here are not the only pyramids in Sudan, but they are the most famous. Architecturally, they have a bit more style than the ones in Egypt. They have a front doorway, rather than some secret entrance, and these doorways are adorned with columns and carvings. They are also much steeper on the sides than their later counterparts further north. But, to me, a little bit of an anti-climax. I had read a bit about them and I must have built them up in my mind to expect something more impressive than this. Maybe size does matter after all. None the more for that, there are some fifteen or more of them in the group, and we really enjoy the trip into the desert, and walking around these tombs of a long-forgotten civilisation.

The following morning, after leaving the pyramids, we drive into a sandstorm. I have to admit that this is not a sandstorm of Biblical proportions, but as far as I am concerned it is a sandstorm. There is a covering of sand on the road swaying like a moving pattern and a haze in the air. Sometimes this haze turns into quite a yellow fog, and I have to stop for five minutes as there is no visibility whatsoever. While we wait, I desperately hope that everyone else has also stopped. It is logical to stop if there is no visibility, but I have already seen that logic does not always play a big part in local driving decisions and I am dreading being run up the backside by some Arab truck driver.

I decide that we won't be able to put our tent up in these conditions, so we will drive on to the next big town on the map and stay in a budget hotel. As luck would have it, the big town in question consists of a couple of mosques, two petrol stations, a lot of wooden shacks, tin sheds and about five hundred Bedouin tents. Not only is there no room at the inn, there is no inn. We have to drive down the road until we find an area off the road with quite a few bushes around. We get as sheltered as we can, make a brew and eat a cold supper, and then sleep in the car. This will at least help us to save our precious few Sudanese Pounds.

There have not been many police checks on the road up to this point, but about three miles outside of Port Sudan - and Port Sudan is to all intents and purposes the end of the road - we are stopped and asked, 'Where are you going?' As always, there is the temptation to make a sarcastic remark, *Where else is there to go? That city you can see down the road, there is nowhere else to go!* And he wants two copies of each of our travel and photo permits. 'For security purpose', he says. I am not sure he makes me feel any more secure.

Every town and city that we have visited in Sudan is a shambles, even the capital, Khartoum, and they are covered in sand. Sometimes it is difficult to see the tarmac through the covering of fine particles on the streets and footpaths. I know the desert is a difficult thing to control - if nature wants to move sand, the sand will be moved - but in Port Sudan it is a different world, almost European: proper streets and pavements; clean, tidy, maintained, and without sand. Unfortunately, this cleanliness comes at a price, and I think a price that is

71

going to put too much strain on our remaining Sudanese pounds. But we find twenty-five Euros in the coffers and, after a bit of a search, manage to find a bank that will change these for some local currency. Every little helps.

Despite the clean streets, there are beggars in Port Sudan. It is a surprise as we haven't seen any in the rest of the country, in fact, we have been to a number of Islamic countries and have not really seen any at all, but here the number of them is unbelievable. They are all women, fairly aggressive and very persistent, and very, very annoying.

When we were in Aswan, Egypt, I had bought a jalabiya (a smock-like thing that Arabs wear) for my brother. We had failed to post it from there, as we were busy trying to get ourselves and our car out of the country, and the post office was never open when we passed it. In Khartoum we had more time, so we took our Egyptian smock to the post office there. Unfortunately, we were rather taken aback with the £20 postal charge - the thing only cost £15 to buy - so we abandoned that project. Now here in Port Sudan Helen wants to have another try so, against my better judgement, we go to the local PO, where we have a long, friendly chat with the man behind the counter and successfully send the Arab apparel off for a mere two pounds. Helen is right again. Sometime later, we receive an e-mail to say that it arrived safe and sound.

Other than that, the town is of less interest than we had hoped, so we don't stay long. At least we have had an opportunity to get ourselves and our clothes clean. So now it is back to the desert to look for a way out of the country.

On the way out of Port Sudan, the man at the checkpoint on the other side of the road to our previously security-conscious idiot just smiles and waves us through; he probably knows where we have come from. We stop to look at the ancient town of Suakin just down the road. Our guidebook covers the whole of Africa, so is rather short on detailed information for each country, and it is twelve years old, so maybe a bit out of date. Suakin is an ancient port and, according to the book, it costs 4 US Dollars to look around the historic buildings. Allowing for twelve years of inflation, that is too much in our present circumstances, but we continue on to have a look at what we can. The place seems to have fallen into serious decay since the authors of our book were here, so there is now no charge to see the piles of rubble. The adjacent wooden shanty town is also in a sorry state. Suakin is easily the most dilapidated town we have seen in Sudan and, considering everywhere is in a sorry state, that is saying something. But it probably is one of the most interesting.

Our final stop is Kassala, a stunning setting turned into a shambles by the local inhabitants. Yet again, rubbish everywhere. The roads and what pavements they have are covered in litter that has been walked and trampled over, forming a sort of carpet over the ground. Also, urine smells abound, and the general dilapidation of this bustling, thriving community is something to be seen, but probably best avoided, if I'm honest. But this is the land of the Fuzzy Wuzzy, who made their presence felt against Gordon of Khartoum and who were made famous by Rudyard Kipling's poem 'The Fuzzy Wuzzy'. Most of the men carry a stick for some reason, and a number of them carry a big sword across their back. I am not sure why, but they are possibly living on past glories. We find a grim place to stay, a good place for breakfast, and a good place for fruit juice. The eating at anywhere else is awful, and the litter is unbelievable; even for this country of rubbish, Kassala is a new low.

We have now run right out of money, so we spend our last one and a half days in Sudan with not a bean between us. On the last road heading to the border there is a toll stop, that is, a few tyres piled up either side of the road, a traffic cone in the middle, and a policeman. We tell him we have no money. He is a bit amazed and amused. As he looks at our passports, he realises we are from England, 'Manchester United?' and 'Do you know David Beckham and Michael Owen?' To these questions we give a sort of silly grin and a bit of a nod, and, with that, he lets us go for free. It is good when you have connections. Further down the road, another policeman wants to check our toll receipt, he is not interested in football, so we show him one that we had got a week earlier on a different road and he is happy. And so are we.

Now, on our last night in Sudan, preparing to leave for Ethiopia, we realise that not only will we leave Sudan, but we will leave the Sahara, *We will be leaving the sand, yippee!* We camp at the roadside, an hour or so drive from the frontier, so that we can do the border crossing in the morning, as we don't know how much time might be wasted with formalities. We were to find out that border crossings take about two hours on average. This one though is our first unassisted African border crossing. As we are packing up in the morning, a police car pulls up, and the occupants come over to talk to us. They sit on our seats chatting away; there is no mention of football, but they do ask us about our journey. After about half an hour they get up to go, but they do not go far - only back to their car and then set up a road block. Luckily, when we drive out from our camping place we are a good two or three metres past the road block. We give them a wave and then we are off.

Doing our border crossing in the morning may not have been such a good idea after all. There are a load of shanties by the side of the road and one of these is the Customs Office. Here we find out that we have overshot the Immigration Office, or should I say shed, by some way. All these offices that control the flow of traffic and immigrants are set way back off the road, and need to be hunted out by the unaware e.g. us. We have to drive back to try and seek it out. Job done and back to Customs, where we have the usual run around, one office to another, but this time all the offices we want have staggered breakfast breaks. Breakfast is an important meal in Sudan, and not to be interrupted. The first one is on his break when we arrive, so we have to wait. He comes back and, once we have finished with him, we get to the next office just in time to see them leave for their break. And the same thing again with the last one. Unfortunately, the last man wants 25 Sudanese Pounds. I briefly think about trying the 'we have no money' ploy. I even wonder about playing the 'I know David Beckham' card but, realistically, we have to dip into our secret supply of US Dollars. We give him five of those. We get a receipt. It is stamped. We then have to go back to one of the other post-breakfast groups and get it stamped again, and, after a few hours of this, we are done. Most of the time we have just been waiting for people to finish eating. Hopefully Ethiopia has no such eating rituals.

All in all, Sudan has been a disappointment. Although we enjoyed it, it in no way came up to expectations. Not that I knew what I was really expecting. I had been looking forward to visiting the country, but the amount of rubbish was really off-putting; there was litter everywhere, even in the desert. Every thorny bush had plastic bags or other rubbish snagged on it. At one point we saw a rubbish truck - we were truly amazed that any of this litter was collected - but, unsurprisingly, they just tipped it onto a vast pile in the desert and the wind scattered it in all directions. The desert is full of rubbish and the towns are full of sand.

It has always been a bit of a wonder to me how the poorest countries always seem to need the biggest armies and have the most bureaucracy. Sudan has a ministry for everything; they even have a ministry of ministries and they generally appear to have the least money to support them.

The tent is starting to get used though. It was only used twice in Egypt, and we were hoping to have camped more than that, but in Sudan we have spent ten nights in our tent, two nights in the back of the car, and the rest in grubby hotels.

But on to Gondar, Ethiopia. It is looking good already - they have beer, wine and, best of all, ATMs. So now we can upgrade our living standards to cheap.

The Whirling Dervishes

ETHIOPIA
27 January

Entering Ethiopia is easier than leaving Sudan; we wander around three wooden shacks, dealing with a few vagabonds to get our paperwork stamped. A scruff inspects the car - once again, the local officials are dressed in tatty and dirty clothes - and I really mean tatty and dirty - and, after all is done, a very rickety gate is opened and we are let in.

The change in countries is dramatic, from the nothingness in Sudan to busy, busy in Ethiopia. There are a lot of agricultural communities along the road, which itself is quite busy with cows, goats, asses and kids.

Here the jerry can comes into use for the first time. It was filled up in Egypt, and two or three times we came close to needing the extra fuel, but now in Ethiopia it becomes a necessity, and not because of the distance between filling stations, but because of the distance between ATMs. We have no money until we can get to the city of Gondar. The extra fuel gets us safely there and we find the only machine in town which seems to be on a real 'go slow'. Foolish of me, I know, but I wonder if its battery is going flat, or whether it is clockwork; it takes slow to a new definition. It only dispenses £70 at a time, so it takes several attempts to successfully top up the kitty.

We then have problems getting a sim card. We go to the main post office several times: we needed a photo and a passport; the man with the sim cards was not there; the lady with the receipt book was not there. In the end we get one - but then to get it working is another story.

Ethiopia is the first of the countries that we visit that uses the Julian calendar - the dates are about eight days adrift of us, and the day starts at six in the morning and not at midnight e.g. 7am for us is 1am for them, and 12 noon for us is 6am for them - so we have to watch the times and dates we are given. One time, on a previous trip to Tanzania, we were due to catch a bus at 2 o'clock in the morning, and I had very carefully confirmed the 2 o'clock timing. We were up early and left our hotel and sat outside in the dark for an hour. With no bus, fed up, we decided to abandon this idea and go back to the hotel; luckily the doors had not locked behind us. After a few more hours in bed, we were up having a cup of tea at 7.30 when the bus ticket agent came round to see if we were ready. This was when we found out that 2am to them is 8am to us. Now, forewarned is forearmed, and we are very careful to avoid such unnecessary early starts.

After searching for somewhere to stay, we find a cheapish but really clean and smart hotel - after coming out of the squalor of Sudan, it is luxury - but Helen decides that this is a good place to have a go at the sickness and exploding bottom routine. Luckily it only lasts one day. Amazing! After all the grubby places that we have stayed and eaten in, she has to go and get a dose of the D&V here in this spotless place. I may have to stop taking her to clean hotels.

Gondar is one of the old capitals of Abyssinia and is also dubbed Ethiopia's Camelot, so there are a number of historic royal ruins to see. Most of the palaces are in one enclosure, and there is a royal swimming pool elsewhere. The tour of the palaces and the history is all interesting, even the fact that the British bombed some of it during the war; the Italians were using one of the buildings as a headquarters. Our ticket entitles us to go to the swimming pool on the same day but as Helen has still not recovered fully from her bout of you know what, we give the pool a miss. All in all, I am not sure if it warrants being called Camelot.

The main diet of Ethiopia is 'Injera', which is a sort of very large pancake thing, with the look, feel and elasticity of rubber underlay - actually, it has more elasticity than underlay - with a sort of meat or vegetable stew on it. After reading the blurb and following the advice of a couple of locals, we try one for lunch, and decide that it is probably edible, but we will not bother having it again. We later learn from our guidebook that it is famous for making 'earth shattering' bottom wind (the book's author was rather more explicit about the wind). We wait some while, but have no problems. We are still not sure if this story is fact or fiction, but as we don't particularly like it anyway, we decide to stay away from it thereafter.

After a few days in Gondar getting our feet on the ground, we take a trip down to Lake Tana where the outfall is the start of the Blue Nile's 1,450km journey to Khartoum, where it meets up with the White Nile. We camp in the grounds of a hotel on the lake shore in the town of Bahar Dar, a couple of hours' drive south of Gondar. The location is beautiful with a huge number of colourful birds flitting around in the bushes by our tent.

We take a trip to see the Blue Nile falls, just 30km from our camp spot. Our plan was to drive out on our own, but the locals keep telling us we would be better off joining a tour. I don't believe them, but there are two other tourists going in a local car with a guide, so we join them. The cost for our half is hardly any more than we would have paid for diesel in our car, and I am not sure that we could have found the way on our own. The falls are quite spectacular, but water levels are low. Some photos we saw of the cataract from years gone by showed the water almost twice as wide as this. There is, apparently, now a hydro-electric power station on the river before the falls, and that appears to regulate the water flow somewhat.

On our way back to Gondar, we spend a couple of nights at the other end of Lake Tana, just outside the village of Gogora in a very nice campsite owned by a Dutch couple. Tim and Kim settled here a couple of years ago and are building up a nice campsite. They are a very likeable pair and, chatting over a beer, we mention our possible plan to leave Ethiopia via Lake Turkana and the potential problems with the lack of fuel supply, and he kindly gives us two plastic 20 litre diesel cans.

Back at Gondar, we decide to head to the Simien Mountain National Park, but we need fuel before we leave town, and so start the driving around in circles to try and find a petrol station with any fuel. On the fourth attempt we succeed, and are able to fill up both the tank and the jerry can. That might not seem much but we tend to find things like this some sort of victory. Hopefully the fuel situation is just a local situation and not a sign of things to come.

Although we are heading to the Simien mountains, we are not expecting to be able to do much there as Helen has a problem with altitude sickness, and most of the park is above her height limit. But, after being told the costs when we arrive at the park office, I do not think it is worth paying the entrance fee for both of us and the car, the fee to camp, plus the compulsory hire of an armed scout and a guide, plus tax, so we don't go in.

Debark, where we are, has four very upmarket hotels, and they are all out of our price bracket. The rest of the town is very bottom market - it is very dirty and unsavoury and the upmarket hotels seem very out of place - and so we decide to move on to the next town, where I have read there are some cheaper hotels. The next town, however, is not where I expected; it was much further away, and on our arrival we find it to be even slummier than Debark, and the best of the hotels is very unsavoury.

We need a plan B, so we will drive the 80 miles to Aksum. The start of this road is unexpectedly amazing as it winds its way through the Simien mountains, and, as we continue, it gets better, i.e. more exciting. This is, so I have been told, one of the roads featured in the BBC series 'The World's Most Dangerous Roads'. It is a fantastic drive. Helen, who is suffering from a touch of acute mountain sickness from the altitude, and a touch of vertigo from the sheer drops off the side, as well as a slight headache from the jolting on the poor road surface and a touch of nerves from my driving, is not the happiest navigator in the world.

There are a lot of hairpin bends and we descend some 5-6,000 feet. At times, I experience some brake fade and, when approaching yet another hairpin bend, I touch the brakes, and the pedal goes to the floor, but *Shite!* I suddenly need to burst into very quick pedal pumping mode, and rapidly change down the gears in order to get round the bend safely. This happens a few more times. I try only touching the brakes when really necessary, giving as long as possible between breaking to let them cool as much as I can. I try going down in a lowish gear, but we still go too fast, even in second; the engine breaking only works in first gear, but that is far too slow. Helen appears to be fully concentrating on holding herself together, so I think it best not to burden her with the problems I am having. I try slipping the clutch a bit, and, with the juggling of gears and brakes, we get down out of the big mountains. As far as I know, I think there are two ways of approaching this problem: one is to let the car freewheel, thereby letting air rush past the overheated parts, which would hopefully cool them down; and the other option is to stop and wait for them to cool down in their own time. I am not really one for stopping and waiting, and there was no café to wait in anyway. With hindsight, I think I had my foot hovering (or more likely it was a bit more enthusiastic than just hovering) over the pedals, causing the break fade.

We dropped a few thousand feet and now, in the lower mountains, there are no more big drop-offs to worry us, but 'Roads Ethiopia' are at work. Gone is the defined track; bulldozers and diggers are shifting earth and rocks all over the place. It's difficult to tell the temporary road from the surrounding countryside. With dirt and sand blowing about, it's sometimes impossible to see anything anyway. We are wondering if we are ever going to get to Aksum; it seems an awfully long 130km. As night falls, it's getting really tricky to follow the route - several times we have already had to back-track in the dark to find where we had lost the road. And several times, when the going was so bad I thought we had lost the road and I wondered if we should turn back and look for the right route, we would suddenly see a marker to show that these rough bits were actually on the right route. To be honest, by now even I am getting a little concerned, and Helen is getting into a real state of worry. We thought about pulling up somewhere and sleeping in the car, but at the moment we don't know if we are in the middle of being lost or the middle of the road.

At one small town, we got a bit lost. We asked for directions and have had the right way pointed out. However, as we trundle down the very rough and rocky road, we're unsure if we are still on the right track, so we stop and ask someone else. Once again we are pointed in the right direction - it would seem that we only ever get the first part of the route given, so we have to ask at every junction. We are getting very fed up with all this fumbling about in the dark, so Helen asks a group of girls who speak some English if there is anywhere to stay. It would appear that there are no hotels in town. Helen then mentions that we will just pull over somewhere and sleep in the car, but the girls all chorus, 'No, no, no! Do not stop anywhere, you must drive through to Shire' - not that we know what or where Shire is. It would seem that there are allegedly bandits about, which inspired the girls' concern, so no stopping until we are out of bandit country.

So, off we go, back into the dark. After a long time of this wilderness, we hit some tarmac and, because of this, I thought we were nearly there, so I gave it some welly for the final leg. My headlights are not the brightest in the world and currently they are covered in dust and dirt, so it came as a bit of a shock to suddenly see camel trains looming out of the dark as I am tearing down the road. I can see other cars, as they have lights, but all of the camel trains are unlit. We came across three columns of fully loaded camels so, even on the tarmac, there is no relaxing.

I am now getting desperate to get somewhere - anywhere - so I am going as fast as I can, but I still have to maintain concentration all the time, with the possibility of camels on either side of the road and maybe even lurking bandits. It hadn't occurred to us to worry about bandits but, now we have been told about them, we have to admit to being a little concerned.

Eventually, and unexpectedly, we arrive in a town, its brightly-lit presence rapidly looming out of the darkness. It is Shire, aka Inda Salasie, and it has a hotel with a bed and beer. We had no idea that this place existed, but we are bloody grateful it is here. Now we have stopped for the night we've discovered that our inadequate map is many miles adrift - Aksum was not 80 miles but nearly 160 miles away. So we still have a way to go. But, for what we did today, what a drive; *Boy, what a fantastic drive!* That said, we broke two rules on this stretch of road. One, as you know, was no driving at night - here we not only drove at night, we drove at night through what was possibly bandit country. Our second rule for African driving is that we should only do about 185 miles a day on good roads and 125 on gravel roads. Today we have done over 300 miles and mostly on bad, bad roads. As exciting as it may have been, I desperately hope we never do that again.

The next day we set off fresh and keen, and the way is all tarmac. As we pass Aksum airfield, we think we must be nearly there, but unbeknown to us there is a new bypass road and no signpost for the turning, so we overshoot the town. Luckily, we realise we have missed it before carrying on too far and, armed with fresh directions, we go back and find the town. It was a good job we spent the night in Shire and came to Aksum in daylight, because God knows where we would have finished up if we'd tried to find it in the dark.

We found out that Aksum was an ancient capital of Ethiopia and we decide to make use of a *tuk tuk* to do some sightseeing. I ask the driver how much it would be to go to the Lion's head, some well-noted stone carving, and also to some remains that are supposedly remnants of the Queen of Sheba's palaces.

'By argument', he replies. I do not like this idea very

much, so I ask another driver how much and he says, 'One thousand Birr'. Keen to strike a deal, 'Nine hundred Birr', shouts the first driver. I ask if he knows where it is, to which he replies in the affirmative. As we get out into the countryside, he has to ask someone in the fields a couple of times where we need to go. Not a good sign, but normal. On arrival to the proximity of the site, our driver points in a vague direction up the mountain, and says, 'It's up there'. So we set off and he goes to sit in the shade. Soon we are surrounded by a group of kids that offer to show us the way. We would never have found it without them, but it is a rather disappointing small carving on a huge rock, and probably not worth the hassle to find it. The palace remains do not fare much better. Although interesting, I cannot see these as the remnants of the home of the richest woman in the known world. We leave feeling a little disappointed, but the hassle is not over yet. When we reach the town, I give our driver his nine hundred Birr, and he moans that it is not enough, as it was a long time. I, of course, go through all the logical things: 'You quoted that', and, 'You said you knew where it was', but he carries on moaning, so I say, 'You wanted paying by argument and that is my argument'. I think we should have gone with the other man, but, then again, we may still have still finished up with a row.

This is the Tigray region, the home of legends about King Solomon and the Queen of Sheba. Sheba, I believe, is an ancient area that took in part of Sudan and this region of Ethiopia. On a tour of some ancient tombs and palaces, we are shown a rather large rockpool called the Queen of Sheba's swimming pool. I imagine some of the sites would have been grand in their day, but I have some doubts about these stories. It is a shame, because I love legends.

All the information we have comes from guidebooks and tourist brochures, but nowhere can I find facts to back up this story, so it seems that even the legendary King Soloman's mines in the east of Ethiopia are a myth as well. Although there is documentation to say that Soloman and Balkis, the Queen of Sheba, had met, I cannot find anything to say that Soloman had actually been to what is now Ethiopia. I am not sure if this is due to my limited skills in research, or that the facts do not agree with the legends. As we wander around more of the ruins of the supposed abode of Balkis, I still cannot imagine that they would ever have been fit enough for the wealthy Queen.

The church in Aksum has in its safe keeping the original Ark of the Covenant, a supposed present to the queen from the aforementioned king. The story, as far as we could make out, is that no-one but the high priest can cast his eyes upon the Ark of the Covenant and, as far as I know, no-one has looked into the box for many lifetimes. The ark is covered with a tapestry, so anyone paying to see this historic biblical artefact will only see a piece of cloth that is hiding a box of some sort. I am not sure how true any of it is, but it is all a good story.

There is certainly a lot of history here. In an area that contains some once-grand tombs of several kings, we met some archaeologists who were working on a tomb that was discovered only days before. A tour car had brought a group up to see some very ancient tombs and, during some manoeuvring, a wheel fell through the ground. This led to the present team of archaeologists exposing a previously undiscovered tomb. The leader of the team gave us an expert-led tour; it was very interesting and no bullshit.

We also visited a small but good museum and the grounds housed a collection of obelisks - one of them is supposedly the largest in the world, although what they are for, I do not know. And we took another *tuk tuk* ride out to see some 'stele' fields, the remains of inscribed stone tablets or monuments, much like Western gravestones but more elaborate; however, once again, in my opinion, our guidebook has extolled over virtuously on very little. For us, it was a lot of work for very little reward.

On the edge of town there is a small monastery on the top of a huge rock on the top of a mountain, albeit a small mountain. After a long walk up, we go through a gate to find there is a ticket office. We pay the required 80 Birr each to the honest and Godly monk, and only then Helen is told that women are not allowed in the monastery, and there is no refund. *That's religion and Ethiopia for you.* So I have a guided tour, which doesn't take long as it consists of only one room with some very faded painting on the walls. We are both allowed to see some historic artefacts, which consist of some books in an ancient script, and a couple of metal crosses. But the view from the top of the hill is good. There are some different mountaintop churches around Hawzen, which is our next destination, and yet some more of a different sort in a place called Lallebela.

We find there is a strange attitude to tourists (foreigners) in Ethiopia. The economy is growing and, as far as I can see, this is mainly through tourism, yet walk into a café or any room and the odds are someone will look and say, 'Faranji' (foreigner). In the street we often hear 'the call of gimme', as we have termed it: 'Gimme money', 'Gimme pen', or even in one case, 'Gimme trouser'. And there is even the odd bit of stone throwing. I find it strange, but it is a land-locked country, and the people are insular; the countries that border it are arid wildernesses and the only access for export or import is through one of the former Abyssinian Empire countries, with which they are not on the best of terms. It does not really affect us; I just find it odd that they treat the best income opportunities the country has in such a peculiar way. I am not saying that we in particular are their best hope, just tourism in general.

Our next stop is Hawzen, but first we have to find the town; our map is not the best of maps, and it does not seem to tally up with the actual roads too well. Our first plan for Ethiopia was to drive down to Addis Ababa, and then down to Kenya. Had we stuck to that, our map would have been OK. But now we are doing a tour of the country and exposing a number of shortcomings in the map department. This is one of the failings of not having a plan, or not sticking to it.

We need to turn off at the town of Adwa, but that does not agree with our map so I carry on until we find out that both I and the map were wrong. We have to go back to Adwa and ask several people the way and carry on what, for us, is an unknown route. Once again the journey is a lot longer than we expected, and it takes us through some spectacular mountain ranges. Luckily the road is tar all the way, so the driving is nice and easy.

We stop for lunch at a place called Adigrat and try to get our bearings. The lunch is very good, but our bearings still leave something to be desired; we can't get any information, so we decide to follow our noses, and what looks like the main road, until we are back where we started. From here, we take a scruffy looking road - the tar is in poor condition, the road strewn with debris and it is lined with a load of slum houses - it is a bit of a worry as to where we are heading, but it turns out to be the main road out of town. As we approach Hawzen, we miss the turning, and in a small town we stop for a drink and to get redirected. It would seem that our destination is in the sticks, down 60km of unmarked gravel roads, and not on this main road as our map indicates, so we will end up doing a little detour off the road to Hawzen. There were several places where we had asked the way and, as happens almost everywhere, the locals either do not understand us, or do not know, or do not want to talk to us, but now we find ourselves on the right road.

We come to a bridge. This is the dry season, so there is not a lot of water in the river below us, but it is a long way down. There are a few planks missing but, luckily, in front of us, there is a builder's truck with a few skimpy boards on it. We both stop to have a look at the situation and, after inspecting the problem, we lay four of his boards out, in the most needed places. It does not look too good, but we have to give it a go. He goes first, shattering one more of the original boards, and I follow, a little nervously. Helen, who is not even in the car, having walked even more nervously ahead, is now having kittens. It is a bit nerve-racking, not that the whole car could drop through, as the bridge is of steel frame construction, but even one wheel dropping through would be a bit of a disaster. But I make it across with no worries. I have to wonder what other people do; we are lucky enough to be following a man going to a job nailing four pieces of wood to something. I do not know how he or we are going to get back from Hawzen to the main road, but that is a problem for later. Someone coming from the other direction also takes advantage of the skimpy planks whilst we have them out and I don't know what he will do later either.

The area is very mountainous, and we are told there are one hundred and eleven churches or monasteries hewn out of solid rock on the top of most of these peaks. Visiting some of them is quite a feat, due to their difficult locations - the way up is to climb a sheer rock face, get hauled up by rope, or climb up pulling on a plaited goatskin rope. Helen is not really into rock climbing, and I am, but I am not sure how good I would be now; I have not done any for quite a while and the passing years have not added anything to my physical ability. We find ourselves a guide to show us around for a day, and we opt for one that is a long, steep, stiff walk rather than a sheer climb. Unlike the monastery in Aksum, Helen is allowed in, so we visit two which is enough to give us an idea of what they are like. These mountaintop spots are spectacular and quite amazing, but you have got to have religion bad to want to climb a rope every day with a hammer and chisel for the years it must take to carve out these great buildings. And the walls are covered with murals. We were told that these churches were built in these inaccessible locations to escape persecution. I would imagine that they escaped a lot of the congregation as well.

On our way back to the main road to return to Hawzen, a load of pack mules come out of nowhere onto the track. I swerve to the right to miss the train of animals and we fall down a secret hole. It is not secret any more, I know exactly where it is now. I'm feeling a bit stupid for thinking I could own the road. But, never mind, a quick flip into four-wheel-drive and I try to reverse out. Unfortunately, not enough of my four wheels are actually touching the ground to be effective - the front offside wheel is dangling down the hole, and the rear nearside wheel is up in the air, and, as I am trying to drive out of the hole, these two wheels just spin round on their own and the car stays where it is. Luckily I have this great big hi-lift jack and, with a number of willing helpers who appear as if by magic out of nowhere, we jack the front of the car up and shift what seems like half a ton of rock to fill enough of the hole to get us back on the road again.

I ask our guide about giving our new-found friends some money, and he said I should, so out comes my wad of notes. Our guide takes all the small denominations, counts them out and says it is not enough. I give him another 100 Birr - about £2.50 - he adds this to the wad and hands it over. The reception is not good, as they look at about three quid between five blokes, but it turns out it is not the pittance that they are grumpy about, it is the 100 Birr note - they have no way of splitting it.

The following day, on our way back to the main road and tarmac, we have to face the dodgy bridge again, and this time we do not have the benefit of the guy with the spare wood in his truck. Whilst in Hawzen, we had got some more information about the broken bridge, so we are a bit more clued up on this now, because the water levels are low at the moment, it is possible if you have a four-wheel-drive vehicle with good ground clearance to go off the track across a field, down the bank across river and up the other side, and … *Ta dah!* That is exactly what we do. *Who needs bridges?*

As we get back onto the road, a big, big army truck comes along. They ask what we were doing in the field, so I tell them about the bridge. They send a couple of men to inspect the dodgy crossing point and then decide to take the reverse of the route we have just taken. I did think that, with the size of their truck's wheels, there was no way they would fall through any of the gaps in the bridge, but the weight would have broken a lot more planks. Anyway, the route that we took may have been a bit daring for us, but it would have been bread and butter to them and their whopping great vehicle.

A few more hours' drive along the gravel track and we get back onto the main road. *Mekele, here we come!* We have heard of a place called Lalebella where a group of eleven churches are carved into bedrock. It looks, from the pictures I have seen, that they have not only hollowed out the rock for the church interior, but also channelled around the outside of the church as well, creating what appears to be a complete building within a cave, as if carving out the church alone was not enough. We have decided not to go there, as interesting as it may be. One week ago, the entrance price went up from 7 US Dollars each to 50 US Dollars each. Knowing that the price has only just gone up an enormous amount has put me off. In the 12th Century, King Lalebella had a vision, in which he was instructed to build a new Jerusalem, and this group of churches appears to be his interpretation of Jerusalem. I can only imagine that, even after all this time, the mortgage is still not paid off, hence the recent and hefty price rise.

From Mekele, there is a chance to go out to the Danakil Depression. This area is a vast desert of some 40,000 square miles consisting of sand, salt flats and volcanic areas. Despite the arid and fierce conditions, people live out there, which is amazing considering the daily temperature often exceeds 50 degrees centigrade. This famous desert is, I think, the start or finish of the Great Rift Valley, depending on which way you are facing, that runs a long way through Africa. Prior to leaving England, I had not thought at all about visiting the Danakil. Although some years ago I saw a program on television about this area and thought it was awesome, it never occurred to me that it would be a place that I could or would ever go to, and have since forgotten about it. But we are now on the doorstep of this wondrous place. The memory of that program has come back to my mind, so I have been asking around to find out if we could go there.

We were hoping to do this in our own car, but were told this is not possible. I did not fully believe them but with language problems and bureaucratic red tape, even just trying to find the right places to get the various permits, it is easier - though more expensive - to go with the flow. Helen and I have a lot of discussion about this, as it is not cheap. I really want to go and consider that it is a once in a lifetime chance. Helen is not as keen, as she is unaware of what I am talking about (no change there then). After a lot of mainly one-sided debate, we decide to go, and so we join a cowboy tour operator and his small group, on a four day trip into the unknown. *We are really going! I can hardly believe it.*

An early start is required, so we check out of our room. Our cowboy had said he would organise somewhere safe to leave our car. That hasn't happened, so we arrange to leave it in the hotel yard. After breakfast we set off, although not as early as we were supposed to leave, as our tour operator turned up late, but now, eventually, we are away, embarking on a hard drive which will supposedly take some seven hours. Along the way we stop at a village. Whilst we gather in a tin shed for a glass of tea, our guide-cum-leader negotiates for a local guide and an armed guard, which it seems is a requirement.

It's a rough dirt road all the way, and we drop from 2,000 metres above sea level in Mekele to 95 metres below sea level where we reach our first camp. It is a bit of a shanty; there are a number of very rickety shed-like structures for the tourist groups to use, and there is a small tin shack around a hole the ground for people to do the necessary. I look around at the other groups' smart new 4x4s and then at our group's beat up old Landcruiser and I hope that we paid a lot less money. After supper, we make camp on a charpoy and sleep outside under an open and spectacular sky.

The next morning begins an even harder drive. It's a good job we are in someone else's car. The long desert drive over some very harsh country is tough on tyres and the car and, although two cars are driving in convoy, we have already lost sight of the other two or three times. There seems to be no definite route to where we are going, it is just 'over there'. I am not sure if our driver knows the way as each time we lose contact with the other car, he seems to be a bit *not quite so cool.* The cars do make a lot of dust so sometimes there is a bit of a clue as to where the other vehicle is, as long as it's not another different car, or just wind-blown dust fooling us.

Along the way, we stop to pick up the local guide that had been booked and an armed scout from each of two tribes as we pass through their area. We also seem to have acquired an armed policeman from somewhere along the way; it seems that wherever you go in this country you need an armed escort. We notice that even the road making gangs have armed guards, all shabbily dressed and with holes in their shoes but carrying automatic weapons. I have never seen so many gun-toting ragamuffins in my life; half of the time we find it hard to be sure whether they are security or bandits.

There are five of us and between us we have two cars, two drivers and a cook. Then for each area we go to, it seems we need at least five other people: local guides, scouts, and, of course, gunmen. I do not think they are all necessary, I think it is just a way of creating employment for some of the locals, but I do know that they would not all fit in our car. After some time, we arrive at a sort of base camp. I think it may be an army

97

outpost. There are a few empty stone-built huts, and a few soldiers about, and here we are not ever so far from the border with Eritrea.

After dinner, and one hour before nightfall, we set off for a two-hour, dangerous trek up a mountain. This is not life-threatening dangerous, only ankle-twisting dangerous. After the best part of two hours, it becomes obvious that the time quoted from an Ethiopian, a country famous for long-distance runners, is not the same for someone from Europe, which is famous for old age pensioners. After three and a half hours, mainly in the dark, including a very short rest break, we make it. Food, drink and bedding had been loaded on to camels and sent up before us. *I think I should have smuggled myself onto one of those camels.*

This is where we will spend the night. But for now it is a rest stop, most of the clients have gone straight to sleep, that is, everybody bar me. I just can't get enough of the area. It is all black lava and, in the dark, there is not much to see, but the glow from the volcano has magnetised me. I am awestruck. Much to my satisfaction, there is to be more adventure tonight after all. Everyone is woken up from their rest snooze and we embark on the final leg to see the rim of the volcano. We start off on a narrow path going down a cliff face, only about ten or fifteen metres down but almost too much for some of the group. Once down, we start heading for the glow in the distance. Stumbling across a black lava field at night is not too easy. Over millennia, lava has spewed out of the volcano several times, which has solidified into sheets, one on top of the other, which have then broken up into platelets. Some of these are stable and some rock underfoot. Here we are walking over this vast area of black instability in the dark with only the aid of pathetic head torches. I suddenly realise that Helen is not with me, or even with the group; there are five of us clients and we have four guides, and Helen is lost. I back-track a bit and spot a glimmer of light in the distance. I want to run over there, but it is far too dangerous to do that, so the best I can do is stumble as fast as I can, all of the time calling for her to come towards me. It turned out that a shift in the wind had brought some acid laden air from the volcano in our direction. It had choked me a bit, but it had stopped Helen in her tracks and, unbeknown to me or our chaperones, she had got left behind. After safely gathering her up, we carry on to the cauldron and now, climbing up to the edge with the wind behind us, looking down at the boiling magma, it is breath-taking, astounding, amazing. I do not have enough words to explain the feeling, it is just incredible.

All this time, our leader and his three helpers have been totally unaware that two of their party are missing; the fact that the four of them now only have three people to look after, instead of five, seems to have gone right over their collective heads. But we made it, and standing on the rim of an active volcano makes it all worthwhile. Wow! It is such an unbelievable experience, apart from the occasional whiff of acid-laden steam as the wind gusted round, which totally takes your breath away. It seems to paralyse the throat. But now we can understand the point of arriving in the dark. It is an awesome sight; the enormous power of the volcano as it boils and splutters its bright red magma against the night-time back drop. I have been on volcanoes before, but standing on the rim of this one and watching molten lava being shot up in the air is definitely a once in a lifetime experience.

We retreat the several hundred metres back to our night camp spot to get away from the noxious gases of the volcano. By now we are ready for the bedding and food that had been carried up by the camels. A simple but delicious supper – so far we have been surprised at the quality of the food. Supper done, we prepare to sleep under the stars. The bed is just a thin mattress on the ground, and off to one side we have the red glow of the volcano - a bit like a giant night light - and above us, a starlit sky.

Our sleeping area is actually slightly higher than the 'top' of the volcano; the active part being a vast hole in the ground on top of a small rise. This was not the traditional or stylised vision of a volcano, illustrated by a tall peak with smoke pouring out of it.

Fairly early the next morning, we pack up and prepare to set off down the mountain. I must take one final look across to the volcano but, compared to last night, there seems nothing to see, just a few wisps of smoke coming out of the ground. Going down in the daylight takes us two and a half hours, to a very welcome breakfast, then back to our army base camp. Along the way, we dispense with our tribal escorts with little ceremony. The uniformed policeman left us at some point as well. On the way out we had gone into the villages and apparently negotiated for these men, but on the way back, it appears to be alright to just drop them off in the desert somewhere, pay them and let them walk home.

I never saw where the policeman went, but he had started off with us from base camp, and is not with us now.

By this, day four of our adventure, we are deeper into the depression and for this we require the assistance of another guide and four armed soldiers. I am still at a bit of a loss as to the need for all this protection; we are in a vast, harsh, barren wilderness, *Who is going to trek all the way out here in the middle of nowhere to try and start a war on some camera-toting pensioners?*

This area is considered the hottest place on earth, and we have dropped to 118 metres below sea level. I am not sure what temperature it is actually reading but it is awfully hot. The area is from another world; a vast lake with a crust on top, incorporating amazing formations and vivid yellows, browns and whites. It is a bit like a frozen lake, only the top is not entirely flat; there are crystalline layers built up in places, and nodules everywhere. The stunning colouring is like some vast and haphazard cake decoration. Under the colourful crust is thermally heated sulphuric acid bubbling away, so perhaps not a cake to enjoy with your tea. The crust, so I was told, is phosphorous (no smoking here then) and a guide takes me for a walk around. It is quite an eerie feeling, walking on this layer of hard phosphorous with even more dangerous stuff underneath. The lingering feel of acid on our skin and the taste of acid tingling on our lips leaves us with the desire for a hot shower, but we are on a trip that does not include showers - or any water to wash in, come to that - so we will just have to wait for these effects to wear off. *What a weird place!*

The outside edge of this acid bath is surrounded by unbelievable rock formations. Some are like slices of petrified tree trunk, only made out of marble. Others are like big, flat-topped mushrooms, again created out of some marble-like substance. There are vast areas of these natural phenomena and it is like nowhere else on earth. Or at least nowhere we have been to before. These are all natural formations and so unbelievably strange; some of them, with their flat, highly polished surfaces look like they were created by masons or sculptors, instead of some natural action.

After enjoying these wonders of nature's handiwork, we move on to see some rock salt. We could have been forgiven for thinking this would be more mundane but, unexpectedly, it is far from it. Great castle-like structures of salt, huge columns and even mountains - all rock salt. Here I go again: *Unbelievable! Amazing!* It is easy to spend an hour wandering amongst and admiring nature's architecture. I have no idea how or why there is so much salt here, but although this is the end of the rift in Africa I am informed that it continues up the Red Sea through Jordan, and to the Dead Sea, which is also salt-laden and below sea level. Whether that is significant or not I do not know.

Further down the road or track, whatever, we reach some salt pans. Here, men work day after day in the hot sun digging up salt. This trade is centuries old. The top layer of salt forms a crust some 1.5 inches thick, which is prised up and cut into oblongs. These are loaded onto camels, where camel drivers then walk with them for up to two weeks up to the edge of the Danakil to sell their wares. Knowing the average price of a block of the salt and the average load that each camel carries, I guestimate for this one-month-long round trip, each camel train would earn about twenty pounds, to be split between the camel drivers, the salt workers and maybe others. That also is amazing.

The track that we are about to go back up is in the process of being made into a proper tar road. Several people have told us this will make the camel drivers' lives better. I am not sure: it may only be me being cynical, but I believe the new road is to get the paying tourists in and out of the Rift Valley easier and quicker. I can also foresee this new road being the end of the road for hundreds of camels and dozens of camel drivers. And it will be a sad end to hundreds of years of tradition.

Now we travel back up the awful track from our present 100 metres below sea level to 2,000 metres above. It is still as bumpy and still as dusty, but the return journey does not take as long, mainly, I think, because we do not have to stop and negotiate for guards and guides. And, as far as I can see, the ones we picked up on our way down have had to make their own way back, even though they were taken a lot further from home than the previous ones we had collected and dropped off in the desert. I find it funny that we need guards on the way out but not on the way back, but then, as I think it is only 'jobs for the boys', it should be no real surprise.

As we get nearer to the top, the driver asks me if I want to close my window, as we are getting higher. I have heard of this peculiarity before so I know what it is was about, but this is the first time I have come across it myself. Rather like in days of old in England, when there was a belief that you would die if you travelled over 20 miles per hour (or some such speed), here in Ethiopia, people believe that travelling fast at altitude will cause you to come to some similar sort of physical grief. So, in cars, buses or whatever, no matter how hot or stuffy, when the speed and the altitude conditions demand it, the locals will close all the windows in the interest of health, safety and longevity.

Ultimately, I was glad we had not brought our car for this part of the trip. Some of the driving was hard. Some of the sightseeing was hard. I found some of it quite tiring and I was only doing the sightseeing bit - I could not have done both the sightseeing and the driving. Plus our 4Runner is small compared to the Landcruisers - we could not have coped with the extra payload, that is, carrying the guides, the gunmen and the cook.

National Geographic describes the Danakil as the harshest environment on earth. I think they could well be right and, incredibly, people live and work out here in such an extremely hostile place. We have had an absolutely amazing experience, although our operator and vehicles appeared to be a lot shabbier than any of the others we saw there – I think our man just made a living as some sort of tour guide driving people about in his beat up Landcruiser, but here he hired a man who had a car, knew the area and could cook, and cook he could. The food on the trip was excellent and, amazingly, in primitive conditions, it is the best food that we have had in Ethiopia. I still think it was expensive, but now I believe that it was money well spent. Absolutely incredible.

Back in Mekele, and after a thorough clean up, we go to a juice bar for a refreshing drink. The juices in Ethiopia are unbelievably fabulous, from simple, single-flavoured juice to exotic multi-flavoured drinks, the different juices are poured in carefully one by one, making a delicious rainbow. We walk into this bar and ask for a juice. Instead of asking us what flavour we want, the girl looks at us a bit funny, walks this way and then that way and then leaves the room. We sit down and wait and wait, and when the girl comes back, she starts fiddling about with the tables. After quite some time, we get fed up and, as we stand up to leave, the girl runs over to her boss in a panic. The boss then comes over and asks why we are not waiting for our chips. *Chips? We don't want chips, we wanted a juice!* The girl is despatched, presumably to cancel the chip order, while the boss, after asking us what flavour we want, sets about making us our glasses of juice.

In most of Ethiopia there are women who make coffee. We were a bit puzzled at first when we saw women who appeared to have set up their own business of making and selling cups of coffee in public places or within the realms of other businesses, perhaps on the patio or forecourt of cafés. As we venture around the country a bit more, we have seen more of this, even inside the dining rooms of restaurants and hotels, with leaves and grass on the floor, spread around their set-up. These, we have learned, are, of course, commercial enterprises.

One day we are lucky enough to get invited into someone's home for coffee and we get the opportunity to see the full and traditional process. There is a small box on its side with a small charcoal burner alongside it, as well as a very small stool for the lady to sit on. Small seems to be an important factor; the stool is no more than 8 inches high. First, a handful of beans are roasted in a pan over the charcoal. When the beans are done to a crisp, so it seems to me, they are then put in a long cylinder and crushed using a hefty piece of wood, as in a mortar and pestle, and pounded for quite a while. Then the ground coffee beans are put into a pot of water and put on the charcoal to brew. Every so often, some of the drink is poured into a cup and tipped back into the pot again. Eventually, the coffee is ready to drink. The liquid is strained though what I think is an old sock into various small cups. With that done, some herbs are scattered over the charcoal to give an aroma to the room and then the coffee is handed round.

It is delicious, but very time consuming; the whole process takes about an hour or more and, unsurprisingly, Ethiopians only drink coffee made this way two or three times a day. It was a nice experience seeing this ritual and having the process explained as it went along, so now, at long last, we understand the coffee stalls around the streets, in hotels and restaurants and on the forecourts of cafés.

We continue on, taking a roundabout route down to Addis Ababa. I was hoping to go to the area where 'Lucy', the prehistoric mummified girl, was found, but that plan turns out to be fraught with too many problems. It would seem that she was found in three different places, depending on where the information comes from, and it might be too difficult for us to get to, as one or two of the possible locations appear to be somewhere near to the border of Ethiopia's unsettled neighbours. So we abandon that scheme and continue our detour route to go through a wilderness park. Many wilderness areas that we have been to have been interesting and beautiful, but this area is drab and boring with nothing to see; a real desolate area. It was originally set up to aid the survival of the Abyssinian ass. Alas, I believe that these days the ass no longer exists, or at least no longer in this area, so the bleak wilderness park is just a bleak wilderness.

We have sometimes seen young boys at the roadside waving an empty bottle and we have taken that to be a signal that they are in need of water. A couple of times we have even stopped and filled up a bottle. We now find out that some gangs of bandits use the ploy of a young lad standing at the roadside begging for water to lure unwary drivers to stop, thereby making their targets easier to get. Needless to say, we do not stop for anyone now.

And finally to Addis. We need to spend some time reorganising and doing some minor repairs to the vehicle, plus getting the all-important visas for our onward journey to Kenya. We book into a place called Wim's. Wim is a Dutch guy who has travelled a lot in Africa. He has been settled in Addis for some time and runs a hostel-cum-campsite, and has built up quite a reputation. We thought we were heading to a slice of Holland in Africa, but were disappointed; we have been allocated a small space to put our tent in between a load of parked up trucks, the ablutions are 'African' at best, and Wim is drunk or arguing with his wife most of the time. But the food is good – most definitely the best food that we have had in a long time. Even better than the food in the Danakil.

Bright and early, we start on the visa saga. We take a taxi to the other side of the city, find the Kenyan embassy, fill in the appropriate forms, pay our money and are told: 'Come back in four days.' *Why so long?* I have to wonder. I thought about driving here in our own car, but, on arrival, I see that there are several embassies together, which is fairly normal, and it would have been unlikely that we could have parked anywhere near here, so ultimately I think the cab was the way to go. We catch another taxi back to the embassy at the appointed four days later, and the staff are pleased with themselves, as our passports are ready and waiting. It must have taken them all of two minutes to put the sticker in and sign it. But at least we have our visas.

Back in the UK, I had tried to find out what I could about malaria in Africa. I now know that it is a particularly virulent strain and can kill within a week. Neither of us like taking pills, and some of the anti-malarials can have adverse side effects - in some cases these can be worse than the disease itself - and we will need to take them long-term. While we were waiting for our visas, we went to a few pharmacies to try and get some local information. I have long ago learnt that the information in England, although good, provides too much blanket coverage. I have tried to narrow down the specific areas affected by malaria on our route, in order to minimise our pill intake, whereas the advice from our local GP at home indicated that practically the whole of Africa is at risk. We do not get a lot further in the pharmacies; they cannot recommend or stock any prophylactics, but they do sell the cure, so we buy two boxes of those. Maybe not the best option, but it is a start, just in case.

Here at Wim's we also meet again two of the three Spanish motorcyclists and for our next leg we will be accompanied by Marc. We first met Marc in Egypt when he and his two amigos were loading their motorcycles on the same barge as us in Aswan, and again in Wadi Halfa where we stayed in the same hotel. Due to them not paying a fixer 20 Dollars to get their bikes through Customs, they were not able to get their bikes out until late, so they left Wadi Halfa the following day. Their story is a bit long, but, for the moment, Gepi has gone home, Aurelli is going home, and Marc, who at the moment does not have his bike, is coming with us. Tomorrow we will head south into the Omo region and out of range of the internet, phone signals and all communications again. Not that that makes much difference to us, as we have been wandering around Addis going into several phone shops trying to get our sim card working but we have had no luck. We bought our sim card five weeks ago and, despite several attempts in towns along the way, we still have not got it working. In another week or so we will be out of the country.

Ethiopia is yet another non-camping country, but we have found a few places. We have managed to spend fifteen nights in our tent and the bedroom in the back of the car has been used a couple of times.

Mountain roads give Helen the jitters

Mountaintop church for really committed parishioners

Nerve-racking bridge crossing

Getting out of a hole with a little help

Other road users

Desert camel train

ADDIS TO NAIROBI
1 March

Our route to Kenya is a bit problematic – we have a choice of three routes, and they all have their own problem, but which one will be our best option?

Option one is the main road. The A2 goes all the way from Addis to Nairobi, and it is shown on our map, which is a good start. This route was our original plan; back home I had looked at a map and seen this road going all the way from Khartoum to Nairobi and just assumed it would be the route that we would take. But now I find out we have more options. The most we have found out about this road since being here is that it is boring, tyre-wrecking, suspension-busting and has been named the worst road in Africa. Also there is a risk of Somali bandits, which doesn't sound great.

Option two is the Turkana route. This route is hard, very remote and we are told there is no fuel for over 620 miles. The maximum amount of fuel we can carry will last us 440 miles on a good road, and this route is apparently a long way short of a good road. It is also recommended that you travel in convoy. Whilst in Addis, we were hoping to meet up with some other travellers going our way and I suppose we did - Marc -

but if we need towing out of a disaster, a Yamaha trail bike will not be of much use. This area is also not guaranteed to be devoid of bandits.

Option three is west of Lake Turkana. This appears to be the easiest route and the quickest way to tarmac, but it runs very close to the borders with Uganda and South Sudan, which we have been told would be best avoided, and it involves a 250 Dollar ferry trip to cross the Omo River. There is a bridge somewhere a lot further up river, but our map does not extend to that level of detail and it is remote country up there. There is also some tribal conflict - cattle rustling - going on, and now the natives are no longer armed with spears but have AK47s, which makes it a lot less safe for everyone. I heard a tale where someone had an armed policeman in their car as a security measure and, apparently, they were held up and the policeman was robbed of his gun.

We decide to go with option two; the route with no roads and no fuel. But, at least we do have a better map to rely on; we bought a road atlas of southern Africa on a previous trip and it extends to the top of Kenya. Although this more detailed map generally shows more roads, we have chosen a route that has none. Some you win, some you lose. Marc also has a map and there are a few dotted lines on both, but they do not tally with each other. We'll have to take it as we find it.

In Addis, when we met up with Marc and Aurelli, the Spanish motorcyclists, again, we got all the news of their journey so far. Aurelli has looked at these three options and has decided that he doesn't like the potential risk in any of them, so he has opted to try and sell his bike in Addis and go home. Marc doesn't actually have a motorcycle at the moment; he and the other one of his amigos started on the Turkana route some three weeks or so ago but, just short of the Kenyan border, Gepi fell off his bike and broke his leg. With little or no help from the insurance company, Marc got his friend and his two broken bones back to Barcelona in four days.

At the time of the accident, Marc got on the satellite phone to the insurance company and they insisted they needed a doctor's certificate before they could do anything to help. Marc told them he was in a desert with no doctors about, but they only repeated their requirements for a certificate, and Marc desperately repeated he was in a desert where there were no people, no e-mail and no fax, and he didn't know where a doctor could be found. I would imagine, in absolute exasperation, he was using every Spanish expletive he could think of to convince somebody sitting in a comfortable office in Europe that he was in a desperate situation. All to no avail. Then, luckily, someone came past in a pickup truck; they put Gepi and his motorbike in the back and took him to Omorate. This small town has some missionaries living nearby and they arranged for Gepi to be flown to Addis and for the two bikes to be left in the police compound. From Addis Ababa, Marc then got him on a flight to Barcelona. So it was four days before Gepi got any proper medical attention, although along the way they did meet a medico who wrapped some cardboard around the leg and bandaged it – an African version of a splint, I suppose.

This sort of thing winds me up; I assume that Gepi has been repaid his out-of-pocket expenses, but that is not the point. When you are lying on the floor with your leg broken in two places, you need help now and getting your money back at some time in the future is the least of your worries. Insurance companies up the premiums for any reason they can think of and then decline to help in your hour of need. I have to pay more because it appears that my age makes me a bigger risk, but to me it seems that the biggest risk is the insurance company saying something to the effect of: 'Sort yourself out and we might look at the bill when it is all over'. I feel that is not good enough. Luckily, after two operations and some steelware, Gepi is now on the mend. Both of the bikes are in Omorate where Marc now needs to go. As do we.

Kenya has just had a general election and we have no idea what has happened yet. But after the last general election one-hundred-and-thirty people were killed and thirty-five-thousand people were made homeless, so we would like to delay our arrival for as long as possible in the hope that, if there are any problems, they will have settled down by the time we reach anywhere with a lot of people.

Our proposed route has numerous river crossings. I am hoping that most or all of them are dry at the moment, but the rainy season is due to start any day now, so I am keen to get Marc's bike back and make tracks as soon as possible.

Passing through the town of Alba Minche on the way to Omorate, where we need to stop for Marc's bike, allows us to reflect on, and rectify, a bad decision we had made at the last minute before leaving home. As we had plenty of room in the car, we had decided to change our thermo-rest beds for full airbeds. We had two doubles, so we brought them both along. We have so far managed to get three punctures in one and can't get them satisfactorily repaired, no matter how many times we try. The second one always deflates overnight and we can't find out why. Alba Minche has a lot of shops selling foam mattresses, so we bin the airbeds and buy two single foam jobbies. Naturally, being Africa, these are made of cheap foam and they are great for a couple of weeks, but then start to lose their posture and, within a month or so, they are only slightly better than laying directly on the ground. For now we have to keep them until we can replace them with something else. This turned out to be around four months.

The town features in our guidebook with a recommended place to stay. We drive around in circles looking for this hostelry and, after finding it, opt to look elsewhere. It is a dump. But it turns out that everywhere in this small but bustling town is full. Eventually, we find a place on the outskirts. In the evening we walk into town to find somewhere to eat. Just as we get our beer the lights go out, the whole town is in darkness. Our food turns up with some candles to eat by, and by 9pm, soon after we finish eating, the lights come back on. The following morning, Marc spots a bank and, as he has some concerns as to whether he has enough money to see him through to wherever the next ATM may be, he wants to pop in and change a travellers' cheque. It only takes a few moments for him to come out disappointed; it would seem that travellers' cheques are a foreign language to this bank. So we leave town and continue on our route, with the thought that we may need to become Marc's 'bank' if he does run out of cash.

On our six day journey south from Addis we drop out of the mountains. Fortunately, Marc has been this way before and has got a good route on his GPS. It is getting a lot hotter and a lot more remote, but all is going well so far. Then, as we cross a bridge, we burst a tyre. The side wall blows out and I am a bit upset as there is still a lot of tread on it. We are right on the edge of a village, something actually not to be celebrated as an event like this is guaranteed to draw a crowd. In no time at all, we have an audience of twenty to thirty bodies, some wanting to help, some wanting to just look, and some wanting to see if there is anything they can fiddle with or take away. Those who want to help but have no ability, no common sense and are at it like a bull in a china shop are more likely to do more damage than help.

In order to change a wheel, I need to un-padlock the spare wheel on the back and a spanner to get the wheel off, un-padlock the jack at the front of the car and spanners to unbolt it, plus the wheel brace to get the wheel off. With the crowd we have around us we cannot leave any of the tools or padlocks lying around, so anything not actually in our hands goes back into the car. With all the doors unlocked and the car surrounded by onlookers, I station Helen around the far side to keep guard. Marc and I, with several helpers, then change the wheel. With my mind totally on security, the padlock off the spare wheel had been hung on the jerry can mount, as is my habit, but this time, when I come to lock the wheel back on, the padlock is missing. Someone has taken it. I look around at the sea of faces and, luckily, a lad points to the urchin who has my padlock. Even when I am careful I am a bit sloppy. When we are finally done and everything is stowed away, a few of the crowd ask for money, apparently for the help they gave us, although, from our point of view, they were just a hindrance. A few of the others want sweets. Some of them ask for the old tyre. I lay the wheel on the ground but even with a great number of them jumping up and down on it, they cannot break the seal between the tyre and rim so, unfortunately for them, none of them get anything as we climb aboard and continue our journey. These jobs are so much easier if they happen in the middle of nowhere and there are no locals about wanting to help. This time Marc was able to assist with controlling the willing helpers as much as possible.

When Marc's friend, Gepi, had his accident and Marc had contact with the American church missionary, he found out that the son, also a missionary, is a motorcycle enthusiast and he may be able to help with sorting out what to do with Gepi's motorbike when we rescue it along with Marc's in Omorate. One of the villages we stop at on our way is apparently quite near where the missionary's son lives, so Marc gets in touch with him and we are invited round. It turns out to be about 30 miles away and, after getting directions, we set off. One vital piece of information was left out of our instructions though, so we sally straight past the turning we need, heading off in the wrong direction. We ask several people if we are going the right way to

Maki and they all say, 'Yes, straight on'. One even claims to be a local guide and wants to get in the car to show us the way.

After 25 miles or so, we are told in one village that we are in completely the wrong area. We had happily believed all the people who sent us the wrong way. But we don't want to believe the guys who ultimately are right, as they say we need to turn around and go back. They look at our map, stab a grubby finger on it and say 'You are here in this area. You need to be here' pointing to a different place. We need to go back to Jinka and take the right road. We have just driven up a really terrible dirt road in really bad condition and now we have to go back to the start. My spirits are pretty low.

When we find the right road it is in much better condition than our wrong route – still only dirt but in a much better state of repair. 26 miles of this goes much quicker and then we find our little turning 'on the right next to a big Acacia tree', just as we had been told. The first few miles have been bulldozed, so the road is quite good, then we get into very rough ground with bushes and trees brushing either side of the car. We are worried that we may have gone wrong again, we can't see anything but the next few metres of the track, but there is absolutely no possibility of turning round. Eventually we reach a river, which is in our instructions, and there is a village the other side. It is looking good after all – if it is the right river. Although crossing the river looks like a bit more of an adventure than I want. There is a bit of a drop off at the bank, and as we get close it all disappears out of sight, with the bonnet blocking my vision. I creep forward very slowly, fearing that we may be about to drop into disaster. There is a drop into the river, but it turns out alright, and coming back will be even easier now we know it is possible.

We find our missionary and, after a very late lunch and arriving a lot later than planned, they offer to put us up for the night. Marc is able to thrash out some vague possibilities as to what to do with his friend's motorbike. We have a quick look around the local jungle, enjoy a swim in the river and meet some of the tribe in the missionary's local village. The missionaries have never been to the village. I have to wonder exactly what their role here is and I assume they are living on donations from the US to help the Third World. These particular missionaries are only sitting in for six months, but I would have thought they would have at least had a look at their temporary domain; it is only 100 metres away. The next day we make our way back to Jinka, fill up with diesel and fill our spare 20 litre can, which we wrap up very carefully and securely as it will live inside the car for the duration. Fully loaded, we carry on south.

On leaving the village, we are confronted on the track by a group of women coming back from the river. As we approach, they crowd around the driver's window, my window that is, asking for money. They are from the Mursi group of people, a tribe where the women cut their lower lip and insert wooden plates. They are from one of the tribes that we really wanted to see, and we have just been staying right next to their village, but had found it too difficult to go in and 'invade' their privacy just to gawp and to take photos. But now they are invading my space, so I think I will see if I can get some photos. On my side I seem to have all the old crones

121

with saggy breasts and without the wooden plate, the very saggy bottom lips dangling somewhere below their mouths, as they only put the plate in for special occasions. I do take a couple of photos, but nothing very good as the women are continually fighting to try and get some money. When I look round, Helen is feeling the breast of a young woman who has a very handsome pair. I am definitely on the wrong side of the car. Later, Helen explains the young woman in question had patterns all over her body. I believe this is done by making small cuts and then rubbing ash or something into the wound, which heals with a raised scar. Helen tells me she was only checking to see if the scars were hard or soft. *I could have done that.*

As we progress south, further into the Omo region, it becomes very tribal, with up to ten different tribes. There is also a lot less in the way of roads, a lot less in the way of traffic, and quite a bit less in the way of clothes. We had heard from a number of people and read in the guidebook about the markets and the strange and unique customs in a number of local villages in the area. Some of these customs include running across the backs of bulls, and whipping young women. That is mainly the Hama and the Banna people, who are also known for their extravagant and colourful dress. Nowadays, there is a charge to enter the village to see these events and a fee to take photos. I appreciate that it gives the locals a chance to upgrade their income, but to me it smacks of turning their culture and traditions into some sort of village zoo. I feel a bit sad about it all and am not sure what we should do. Our chance encounter with the saggy-lipped Mursi women was good, but we really would like to see some of this tradition in full swing, so to speak.

When we had first heard of all these tribes and their customs, it sounded quite exciting, so it became an aim of ours to get there and see them. But the closer we get and the more that we read, and the more travellers and tourists we speak to, the more it puts us off. Now we feel we have to give it a miss. I am a bit sad to miss out on these cultures, but I read on someone's tourist blog: 'I felt a little bit of my soul sliding away with every photo I took'. I have to think, *Why did you keep on taking photos then?* But this comment has helped us to decide to give the circus a miss. I now think that the best thing to do is to seek out the tribes that do not live on the tourist route and visit them in their 'natural habitat', but when we were at the Mursi village, we did not have the front to go and stare at them in their homes there either.

Apparently, giant foreign agricultural companies and the Ethiopian government want to turn this lush fertile area into plantations for sugarcane and palm oil. If it goes ahead, this could displace many, many thousands of people, with their traditional ways of life and culture. There are pressures from all sides, I guess.

Along our road we see a local market, so we pull in to have a look. We park next to the ox carts and hand carts and go for a wander around. In one corner of the field is a beer tent. Well, something more like an old wooden shack with some extremely rustic fencing, creating something of a beer garden. Marc and I are pondering whether to try this local brew, but with seventy or eighty semi-naked natives in various states of inebriation staring at us, we opt not to. Helen buys some carrots, garlic, onions and potatoes from various stalls, and we leave. I had been worried about staring at the natives, but we were the centre of attention everywhere we went in that market. As we wend our way south, I wonder what all the other villages have had to put up with until they hit on the idea of charging tourists for the show. We have just been stared at all the way round the market, which I did not really mind, but I am actually so glad that we have decided not to go to the village 'zoos'.

As we near Omorate, we see that there is a collapsed bridge. A new route is apparently planned to aid regional development on the other side of the Omo River, but, during the construction of a new bridge across the river, this huge span collapsed. The scaffolding holding up a ninety metre section of the bridge over the water gave way and the whole thing came down. This bridge was due to open in 2010, and was more than a year behind schedule when it fell down. We are here two years after it fell and it is still lying there in the river in a very sorry state. It would seem that regional development west of the Omo is on hold for the moment. Progress is very slow in Africa.

At Omorate, Marc can collect his bike from the police compound and we can continue to Kenya. Here, also, the missionary father lives. Marc collects his friend's motorcycle. There is some small muttering about money, but that is put off until we return to collect his own bike. We take Gepi's bike down to the river and, with a board and a lot of struggling, manage to wheel it up on to a small dinghy and take it across the Omo to where the missionary lives. Here Marc parks the machine in a shed, where it can be stored until something else can be sorted for it. On the return trip to get Marc's own bike, there is a bit more muttering from some police officers hoping to have some silver popped into their pockets. As Marc roars off down the road, the police round onto me for some money. I say 'It is nothing to do with me, you should ask him' as I point to the dust cloud disappearing in the distance.

Where the missionaries live the river is only about 50 metres wide. It makes me wonder how wide the river is where the ferry that charges 250 Dollars crosses it. I also think perhaps the powers-that-be should have built their bridge here, and then possibly they would not have 90 metre lengths of it laying in the water for two years. But, who am I to judge?

We are invited by the missionaries to stay the night again. Our host, Dick, tells us that after the famine in Ethiopia, foreign aid and religious organisations installed water pumps in every village in the country. Not one of the users maintained the pumps, and if they break, no matter how simple the breakage, the pump is not repaired, it is just abandoned and the villagers go back to the old ways of walking down to the river for water. Carrying 20 litres of water for half a mile or so is no easy task. Even young children are involved, but they only have to carry 5 litres, maybe less if they are very little.

Dick is involved with making and installing windmills. Some are for pumping water and some are for driving simple machinery, i.e. millstones, grinding wheels, or pumps. He has a lot of problems trying to convince the locals that they *need* a windmill. A lot of those he has installed are unused; he has no idea if they are just unused or broken but, judging by the story he has just told us, I think I may know the answer to that one. But he pushes on with his project. Dick and his wife are insistent that these people need their help. The fact that they are healthy, fit and happy, and have been successfully living this way for thousands of years (admittedly, not successfully as in the 'American way') seems to have gone straight over their heads. I must say they are kind, generous and helpful, but I cannot help thinking that their vocation is more of an egocentric invasion of other people's lives than is really needed. They have a nice house on a beautiful acre or two of ground and, apart from making his windmills for unwilling recipients, I do not know what else he does. I ask him about the village that is close by, but he does not know much about it, as they try not to invade the lives of the local people too much. I can just imagine fundraisers in the US paying for this. It appears that when missionaries in Africa have children, they go to a missionary boarding school, learn the missionary way, meet their future spouse at the same school and so carry on another generation of tunnel-visioned missionaries. Caleb, Dick's son, is at least a third generation missionary.

One of the main tribes in this area is the Dassanech. The men of this tribe carry a little stool about with them at all times. These stools are carved from a single piece of wood, are flat at the top and bottom, and slim in the waist, hourglass-shaped. At the slim bit in the middle, there is a handle, which is never let go of, unless they are sitting on the stool. The 'little' in the description of the stool means six or seven inches high, and about four inches in diameter. We have seen a lot of men carrying these things around. Dick tells us that he has had men helping, but only using one hand as they need to hang on to their stools with the other one. This is beyond my comprehension; the stools are so small and so low, that I think it would be easier to sit on the ground and not risk this slither of a tree trunk disappearing up the backside. Anyway, I suppose in their culture the men wander about, stool in hand, to tend the goats, which is easily done one-handed, and the women, without the responsibility of carrying a stool, have both hands free to do all the work in the house, in the fields, and fetch the water.

Now that Marc has sorted out his and Gepi's bike, and after a pleasant stay with our new missionary friends, we make preparations for leaving the country. I fill the car with diesel, buying it from a man who has a shed full of cans of fuel. After a lot of negotiation, we pay his first asking price. Marc fills his bike up with petrol from another man who has his fuel stored in two litre drinks bottles. He has the same negotiating luck as we did. This is a fair way past the last claimed fuel stop on the supposed 620 mile fuel-less route.

We complete all the exit formalities in one place in a compound on the edge of town but a long way from the border. In a large office, there is one desk with a load of clutter on it and an immigration officer from a Monty Python sketch. When we finish filling in forms, he can't find his desk keys or his ink pad. This is not the busiest office in the world - I would imagine they get one or two people a week through here - but obviously there is

127

long enough between customers to forget where things have been left. Having found the keys to his desk, the drawer does not contain what he wants. I do not think that there is even anything worth locking up in there either. Another search gets underway for the required tools of his trade, buried somewhere in all the clutter lying around. Once all these bits are found, it is all systems go. Until he cannot find his rubber stamp, so maybe not quite all systems go. After another failed search, he borrows one from the Customs man next door, which seems to be the easy, even if only temporary, solution. After getting the stamp and doing several test stamps on some blank paper, we get our passports done. Then we move on to the Customs office for the carnet. This goes like clockwork. The Customs man seems to be a bit more organised, at least until he cannot find his rubber stamp and has to go next door to get it back. I wonder if there is only one rubber stamp and it has to do the rounds for the whole compound. But now we are all finished, and Marc has all his paperwork stamped too. We set off in convoy for the remote and difficult route.

The daily chore of water collection

THE TURKANA ROUTE
7 March

Leaving Omorate, we have to double back more than 10 miles to find an un-signposted side turning, which is the start of our no-road route. Fortunately, Marc has been this way before, so he already knows the turning, and has it on his GPS. About 50 miles down this track, at some little known and unmarked place, we leave the country and enter Kenya. *Wow, Thanks Ethiopia, what a fantastic country.* As there are no Customs or Immigrations Officers here, it will be when we get to Nairobi in eight or nine days that we will get our entry formalities for Kenya sorted out.

With a change of country comes a change in having to drive on the other side of the road but, as we are not really on a road and are just following in one pair of wheel tracks, it is a bit difficult. Where we can, though, we will drive on the left.

Our first day is spent driving through sand – some of it quite soft, but most of it fairly firm and not too difficult. This is real wilderness - no people, no traffic, and no real roads, just tracks - we have to make regular stops to drink water, as it is important to keep our liquid intake up. We also need to keep in touch with Marc, as our two machines, his and ours, are handling the conditions very differently. We keep pulling apart as we go on ahead in the car, so every now and then we stop for a while and wait for Marc to catch up. After a chat and a drink at each stop, we carry on. On two or three stretches of easy road, Marc roars ahead and then enjoys the role-reversal of waiting for us.

We cross a number of dry river beds and I am thankful that we have managed to get going ahead of the rainy season. Even so, some of them are tricky, with soft sand or rocky bottom. With water in them so you could not see the bottom, it would be really difficult. A part of me would have loved to cross when the rivers were full, but really I am glad they are dry for us.

So easily, after sufficient trials with the driving for one day, we pull over somewhere in the desert and just put our tents up. Firm, flat, sandy wilderness for miles in every direction. *Fantastic*.

Next day, whilst we enjoy our morning brew, a Dassanech tribesman walks up, complete with stool. With a lot of sign language, we work out that he spotted us whilst tending his goats and so came over. We ask him where his goats are and he points to somewhere that must be just over the horizon as we can't see them. Not having a lot in common, in particular language, we start to pack up and he just stands watching. When we are loaded and ready to go, we turn to wave goodbye and he says, 'Shirt'. At least, I think he said shirt. I have a look and find an old shirt to give to him. He is as happy as a kid in a sweetshop. He and we are smiling as we drive off down the road. Apart from the fact that I only had three shirts to start with.

In our first four days on this route, we have not yet come across one other vehicle. We come to a road junction. I should qualify this term 'road' as any track that goes somewhere; they may be well defined as a track or just faint wheel marks through the sand or grass, or even a faint change of colour over rocky ground. Here we are at this junction of wheel ruts and, with the use of two maps, a compass, a GPS and a lot of discussion, Marc and I opt for the left-hand turning. 200 metres down this road, we meet our first other vehicle, a lorry coming the other way. We ask the driver if we are on the right road to Loyangalani. He shakes his head and laughs and then gets us to follow him for about 4 miles down the other road, the one we ignored, to where he shows us the correct left-hand turning. One piece of advice we hear time and again is, 'If you see anybody, ask the way'. If you take the wrong set of tracks it is very easy to get very lost in the wrong piece of wilderness. Experience has shown that you cannot always trust the answer when asking locals the way, but what else can you do?

We decide to head down to the shores of Lake Turkana, some miles over to the west, camp there for the night, or more than one night if it is good, and then take the lakeside road to Loyangalani. After finding the right turning, or at least what we hope is the right turning, we set off down it. The state of the road is awful; the whole area is just loose volcanic lava pieces. I also realise I do not like the general direction of this road.

132

We are heading north-west and we need to be going south-west. Even though we have been told there is a post with a sign on the junction, we just keep wondering if we are actually on the right road. There is a post with an arrow, but no writing on it. I do not like this so we stop and wait for Marc to catch up. When he doesn't appear after quite some time, we turn back and find Marc standing in the road with his luggage all over the ground. He had fallen over. I am beginning to think that these Spanish motorcyclists are not up to much. He could not lift his bike up on his own and so had emptied out his panniers and unloaded the bike to get it upright again. At least he did not break his leg, but he is definitely going to have one large and very colourful foot.

The driving here is tough going, even for our 4x4. The whole area is part of the Great Rift Valley and, a very long time before I was born, volcanoes spewed millions of tonnes of lava over an enormous area. Then, time and weather have broken the lava flows into boulders, making very tricky driving situations, and even trickier motorcycling conditions. We give up on the camping by the lake plan, and turn back to the main track, heading south and straight to Loyangalani. For the next few days, we carry all of Marc's luggage and equipment, in the hope that it will help his bike handling on this terrible ground. We do not want a repeat performance of Gepi's antics. Not anywhere, but definitely not out here. It is bad enough that he has a colourful foot and is limping somewhat. We later find out that we had been on the right track to the lake, but that it was an awful drive, so I, for one, am glad that we turned back, even if it did make us a bit wimpy.

We spend a few nights in this surreal, lonely wilderness and it is fantastic. Since the last truck we saw full of people, we have only seen four tribespeople. There are long stretches of lava, long sections of sand, and many areas of rock. All of it is physically demanding to drive on. We continue each day until we have had enough, which is generally after a hard drive, but not a lot of mileage. We are managing about 65 miles or so per day. I am a bit surprised at how little a distance we are able to cover, and I put it down to my age and lack of stamina. But Marc, who is about half of my age, is just as knackered as me. I suspect that driving on this terrain is a lot harder on a motorbike than it is in a car, which compensates for him being younger and fitter. Each evening when enough is enough we just pull over somewhere, anywhere, and put our tents up in absolute tranquillity.

Spending all this time bush camping, it is important to drink as much as possible to keep hydrated in the heat. Helen and I are dressed in shorts and T-shirts and we are feeling the heat, but poor Marc is head-to-foot in leathers, helmet and armour. I suspect he must be pretty warm as well. But luckily we can carry enough water in the car for all of us.

At last, we reach Loyangalani - an absolute Eden in this wilderness - a camp with green grass, palm trees and showers. Luckily, we arrive at our chosen campsite at exactly beer o'clock. We have not had a beer for almost a week, and here we turn up just in time. Helen's first priority is to have a shower, but she takes the time to order two beers on her way and has them sent over to Marc and me. *What can we do?*

We take a day off to recover and do some minor repairs to the car and bike. Marc spends some time trying to lighten the load on his bike. Mind you, as we have all his gear in our car, I suppose he was really lightening our load, *Thank you, Marc*. In Omorate, he had quickly sorted out what to take from Gepi's bike and now, having gone over a very rough route, he is of the opinion that his bike is too heavy. Going through his tool kit in more detail, he finds some odd bits of junk that he passes on to me. Although his rear tyre still has a lot of tread on it, he puts the brand new spare tyre on and ditches the other one.

I also have to mend a series of punctures for him. Two days ago he drove over a twig of acacia, which has very long and very vicious thorns, and now the tyre decides to go down. So, off it comes, with a lot of struggling with inadequate tools. I find the puncture and mend it, test it in a water butt, and find another one. There are three in all. I wonder why it is me mending his punctures. *What is he going to do when he is on his own?*

Going through his medical kit, he finds that he has the anti-malarial pills for the whole of his group, so he passes some of them on to us. Unfortunately, at least I think it is unfortunate, they are Larium, which for me seems to be the one pill that has the most and the worst potential side effects. But they are here and they are free, so we will give them a try.

We make a bit of space in the car by putting the diesel from the spare jerry can in the tank, and giving the can to the camp owner. I am still hoping our fuel situation is going to work out and we will find sufficient fuel stops to see us through.

We should really stay another day, the camp is comfortable and in a great location, and we could have a bit of a wind down, but the call of the punishing track is just a touch too strong. We find out that the general elections in Kenya were peaceful, so now we can venture into populated areas without fear of getting caught up in a riot.

We seem to be moving away from the volcanic area and the track is becoming more and more sandy, with rocky areas. Most of the rocky bits appear like ridges. We clamber up rock strata, sometimes almost like going up steps, and then as we go over the top it's a bit of a hair-raising drop down the other side. In a couple of places we come across a boulder in the middle of the track. One of them makes it a tight squeeze to get around. I suspect most of the vehicles using these tracks are great big trucks with a vast amount of ground clearance, so they just go astride these boulders. It is only Johnny Foreigners like us in our smaller vehicles that have any problem. Generally though, the driving is becoming less stressful, although we are still not really travelling any further each day. It doesn't matter; it is just fantastic with only us out in this relatively uninhabited wilderness.

A few days later, just south of Maralal, we say goodbye to Marc, as he heads west to Uganda, via a DHL office so he can renew his carnet, and we go south-east to Nairobi. We are sad to see him go. He was good company and I was very glad to have another man around to talk through any problems on this exciting stretch of lonely wilderness. Despite Marc and me really enjoying the drive, my navigator has not been quite so enthused.

We fill up with fuel in Maralal for our two-day drive to Issiolo where, supposedly, we will find the first fuel station on this 620 mile fuel-less route. By now, though, we know that you can always hunt diesel down in people's sheds, although the deep-seated worry of running dry and getting stuck never fully leaves me.

This stretch of road gives us our first glimpse of proper African wildlife. There are hundreds of zebra all over the place and it is all getting exciting.

Archers Post and finally onto tarmac. After seven days of hard driving we have covered 494 miles. Bits of the car have broken or fallen off. Some of the bits are things that I made and I did not ever realise how much shaking, bumping and jarring they would have to endure. The other bits are what Mister Toyota fitted and he appears to know about as much as I do. The tyres on the drive wheels are fairly well chewed - I think we have knocked about 6,000 miles off their lifespan - and the fuel consumption has gone through the roof. But we did it, and it saved us going the easy way. We drove an average of 70 miles per hard working, hard driving day.

We have a recommendation from some fellow overlanders for a community camp somewhere outside of town. When we find it, we change our minds, as 20 Dollars a night for a bit of wasteland with a pit toilet and no water has no appeal after the amazing free nights we have spent recently. In the town, we find a hotel with a clean room, en-suite, no frills for 10 Dollars. We get some bits of welding done, a puncture repaired, and the first of what would turn out to be many trips in several towns to try and get the local sim card working in our phone - taking the opportunity to avail ourselves of amenities whilst they are within reach again. We also get the car cleaned, or as clean as we can. I have never seen dust like it here. The car is always full of it; it gets everywhere. If I have to do any maintenance, lift a carpet, take off a door panel, I find dust under or behind it. I don't know how, but it even gets into closed boxes and closed bags.

A few miles outside of Archers Post is the Samburu National Park that was recommended to us by a man in Addis. It is only 20 Dollars to go in, so off we go for our first safari of this trip. Exciting! At the gate, we are told the price is 70 Dollars each, which takes the wind out of our sails a bit. We do not have that sort of money on us. The last ATM was in Addis, Ethiopia, nearly two weeks ago, and it will be another day or two before we get to the next one. We have to decline and turn around. Sometime later, we find out that these prices are the going rate, but at the moment we are not prepared for that sort of cost and are rather taken aback. We also heard later how good this park is, but for the moment, that disappointment is in the future.

Further south, just past the town of Meru, we cross the equator. We are now in the southern hemisphere. It catches us a little bit on the hop so, unfortunately, the celebrations for this momentous event will have to wait.

The area has suddenly become more verdant; after the last week or two of aridness, the greenery here is a pleasant change. There are trees, bushes in flower and banana plants everywhere.

Two days later, we reach Nairobi on the last 150 miles of tarmac. *God, I love tarmac*. We finally arrive into town and find our camping place. We have been in Kenya for eleven days and tomorrow we must go to Immigration and Customs to get ourselves and the car officially stamped in.

Immigration is not too bad. First we go into the wrong side of the building and, despite it being signposted for Immigration and there being a lot of counters, none of them are what we want. We get sent round to the other side of the building, where we are told, 'Go out of the door, turn left, at the end turn left, and go in the front door'. We follow these instructions and, when we reach the front of the building, and just yards away from the front door, we are stopped by an armed guard and told we cannot go that way. We must turn around and go all the way round the building to get back to almost where are now. Sometimes I get on my high horse, but one of my rules is: 'Never argue with a man who has a gun'. So we turn around and go back the other way. After waiting in the queue for a little while, we finally get to the window, and almost immediately we are asked to go the end, through the door and come in to behind the counters. We meet a man who has a bit of space in a small corridor as his domain. Our immigration approval starts with the small query as to why we are so late doing our formalities, but when we mention that we came in via Turkana, all is understood.

Then the process is very smooth up until the point when the official cannot find a rubber stamp. I am amazed; officialdom is ruled by the rubber stamp. It would seem that sometimes these people cannot even pass wind without getting permission rubber-stamped, yet they always seem to lose the bloody thing.

Customs is not quite so easy. There is no parking anywhere close to the Customs building. *But do they need to see the car?* I drop Helen off with the paperwork and almost immediately see what I think is a nifty and very handy parking space, right next to the building. But I am very swiftly moved on by some uniform-wearing, gun-toting official. So I just drive around in circles. Helen is sent to the tenth floor, which is apparently wrong, so from there she is sent to the fourth floor. Wrong again. Sixth floor? No. First floor, and bingo! Finally, she finds the lady she needs. Again comes the query as to why it was not done at the border. Helen says that there was nothing at the frontier, and the Customs lady replies, 'Rubbish, there is Customs at every frontier'. Once again, Helen says that we came in 'via Turkana' and that explains everything.

Once the paperwork is sorted out, they come out to inspect the car and, as luck would have it, I am driving by as they come out of the building and can stop long enough for the vehicle inspection and to explain to the Customs lady which numbers she needs to look at. She does not want to get too close to our dirty car, so she declares that all is OK and we get the clearance papers stamped. This has taken the best part of a day, but now we are all done. We have visas and stamps and are officially and legally in Kenya.

Car camouflage

Tackling the Turkana route with Marc the motorcyclist

KENYA
16 March

In our camp in Nairobi, I do some servicing on the car and effect a few minor repairs. Unfortunately, all the crawling around under and over the car uncovers some fairly major work that needs doing urgently, including some welding to the chassis, which hopefully will wait until I find somebody competent and cheap enough to do it. I go through the weekly checks - oil, water, tyres, bang all the sand out of the air filter. I thought the snorkel was supposed to stop this sort of thing, but then I wonder how much sand would be clogging the filter with the original air intake only a foot or so above ground level.

We get our sim card for the phone working at last. We are not techno whizzes, but for this trip we are geared up as never before: we have a basic GPS, a very basic mobile phone and, of course, the netbook with a dongle, which allows me to record everything as we go. We bought the sim card at the first opportunity, in Maralal, about a week after entering Kenya. Then we had to wait until we got to Archers Post before we could get an agent to register it, and, after he failed, we tried again at Isilolo, with no more luck. Now in Nairobi, seven days after buying the card, we finally get it registered and the phone working. This sort of thing will happen again and again. Sometimes we decide not to bother - in Ethiopia, we thought we were only going to be there for about two weeks, but after more than a week of to-ing and fro-ing we were still in Gondar, so we did buy one. Ultimately we were there for six weeks, but never managed to get the thing working. But the dongle is the worst problem; it does not want to work on a lot of countries' networks. Our low tech equipment is not clever enough for Africa.

Customs and Immigration all done, the car has been looked over, and now for a long-time dream of mine: we are going to the Masai Mara. Sadly for us, gone are the days when thirteen-year-old boys were sent out to kill a lion, armed only with a spear, in order to prove their manhood, and bare-breasted women wandered the Mara. Now the bosoms are on a strictly pay-to-view basis - you have to pay an entrance fee to go to the village and see a facsimile of their culture - and the thirteen-year-old boys have to find some other way to prove their manhood. This is not the first time on our travels that I am looking for a world from many years ago.

But, to get there, I still have to prove my manhood behind the wheel of our car. The Mara is a long way from anywhere. According to the map, we head up the main road, turn left and away we go. Some way down it gets more complicated and we have to ask the way several times. We reach a junction of a dirt road and a tarmac road - somewhere near the Mara, I think – and,

143

while we are pondering which way to go, an old boy comes running over and asks if we want the Masai Mara. *Yes!* So he starts going on about being a guide there - he was there only yesterday - all the stories we have heard a load of times, everybody seems to be a guide. But, with a pen and paper, he draws us a map, giving all the road junctions and distances. He demands a lot of money for his services. We give him a few Kenyan shillings and pull away. All we can hear as we drive off down the road is him shouting that we are robbing him and depriving him of his livelihood.

Our new map matches the roads and distances in only a few places, so we still have to frequently ask the way. It starts to rain, and I mean serious rain. The dirt road becomes rather slippery. Whilst looking at the map at a cross roads, a car comes along and it turns out he knows where we want to go so we are to follow him. He obviously knows the road and drives like a professional - or an idiot, depending on your viewpoint. In some places, the flood water on the road is so bad he drives up onto a bank and then along the edge of a field. The field is just as slippery as the road but now we have a three foot drop on our right. I am still thinking what an idiot he is, then remember I am still following him, and at the same speed. The bank has a slight gradient sloping towards the drop, so I keep as far left as I can, so much so that I have the two nearside wheels over the lip of the compacted dirt in the hope that we won't slither to the edge. After a while we are off the bank and back on the road and in the flood waters again. The next time we need to make a trip up onto the bank, it is not so terrifying. Now, after a long drive and a lot of struggling to keep up with our guide, we come to a junction where he indicates we are to turn off.

We get a brief respite from the rain and the going is temporarily better, but then it rains again and a lot worse than before. In places, I can barely see the road and we get ourselves into a slight panic, we have no idea where we are, or how far we have to go. *Should we stop? What if it rains all night? We cannot just sit here in the middle of the road!*

I opt for carrying on and hoping for the best. As luck would have it, the best does happen; it stops raining and we find our way to the Mara at last. At the camp, we mention the rain to a couple of employees but they tell us there has been no rain here. They then add, 'It always rains over there', waving an arm in the general direction from which we have come.

The next day I am realizing my dream; we are about to enter the Mara. I find, however, that the lions are preserved as bait for much bigger game: the tourist, particularly those with a fat wallet. That doesn't include me; I do not need guides, trinkets, help, or any other thing that separates me from my dosh. But I am stopped in my tracks when I get to the park entrance and find out the price – 80 Dollars each and 300 Shillings for the car (I like the way some things are priced in US Dollars and others in the local currency). But this is my dream, somewhere I really want to see. Yesterday was a hard day's drive on diabolical roads, through rain so thick I could barely see beyond the bonnet of the car, thunder, lightning, and floods. I was a bit worried at some points, but my navigator was in a state of near panic for quite a while during and after this treacherous journey to get here so we cannot just turn round and go back. I have to put on a brave face and pay up.

We are rewarded with a fantastic first day. Herds of all sorts of antelope, hippos, giraffes, a lot of birds and our first ever cheetah - we get two good sightings of it during the day - amazing. It is a great place to drive as well; it is driving in a wilderness with no real roads through wide open spaces. It is the dry season now and a lot of animals have probably migrated elsewhere, south of the Mara to the Serengeti and Tazania where there is plenty of room for them to wander, but there are still enough here to keep us happy. No lions though. Yet.

Day two is good as well. We add a big herd of elephants to our growing list of animals. There are not a lot of other tourists; we have the savannah almost all to ourselves. But still no lions. We make it all this way for the famous lions of the Mara, and no lions. I think the boys must have stopped doing whatever it is they do now to prove their manhood and have gone out chasing lions away. Apart from that, the savannah of the Masai Mara is all I had hoped for. *Fantastic*. We leave by a different gate and a different road - a long and dreadfully corrugated road - which is more uncomfortable, but maybe a bit easier and probably a lot safer than the route in that we had taken.

Back in Nairobi for a day or so to work out some sort of a plan for going east. I think it would be a good idea to go down to the coast so Helen can get some time on a palm tree-lined sandy beach and have a swim in the

Indian Ocean. On our way, we stop the night in a place called Voi, adjacent to Tsavo East National Park. This park, according to our guidebook, is one of the places where it is necessary to have a prepaid gold card. We have yet to find out what this is. We get the chassis on the car welded up, having spotted a workshop-come-garage advertising that they do welding, and, in no time at all, the car is in, jacked up, and metal is cut and bent ready to be welded on. While we wait, I find out that this workshop specialises in converting tuk tuks for African use. *Tuk tuks! And I am letting them loose on my four-wheel-drive Toyota!*

Once the welding is complete, and it seems to be a reasonable job, we go down to the park gate to get a gold card. I still can't work out why we need one of these cards to get in when we have to go to the gate to buy it. *Why not just pay the cash and go in?* But our plan is not to go in here but from the other side on our way back from the coast. Gold card in our pocket, we set off down the main highway to the coast, through a very crowded and congested Mombasa, turn right and along to Tiwi beach. What a fantastic camping location; a palm tree-lined beach on the Indian Ocean, a lot of seabirds and waders on the low ebb of the tide, and hornbills in the trees above. All very tropical and relaxing. There are even fruit deliveries every day from a man with his bicycle. It lacks pedals, has flat tyres and worn out wheel bearings - he has to push the thing along - and it is laden with baskets and bags of mangoes, pineapples, bananas, all sorts of fruit. Someone else comes round with fresh fish for sale. Helen is in heaven, swimming in the warm sea and eating fresh fruit. And with a bar just yards from the tent, life cannot get much better.

Real overlanders debate the pros and cons of coil springs or leaf springs as the best method of suspension in this rugged terrain. I have always been a fan of the coil spring - it is light, simple and bouncy - but as Helen is laying on the beach sunning herself and I am laying under the car surveying a broken rear coil spring, my fanship is waning fast. I have noticed my rear end drooping a bit recently, but I put that down to being overloaded with Helen's clothes and gubbins. Now I can see it has nothing to do with Helen at all. I know we have been in some places that have tested man and machine, but I was hoping that it would not break the machine. Before we left home I put some spring assisters in to, err, assist the springs. These are moulded rubber thingies that fit in amongst the coils. They looked good in England but now they look like tatty bits of rag and rubber and in worse condition than the broken spring they are hanging on. I have just had a large lump of steel plate welded onto my rusted chassis, and now this.

After our enjoyable lay on the beach we leave Tiwi to head up the coast, taking in a few ruins of ancient Arab slave trading centres, until we reach Malindi. We are lucky to find a place to camp, as it is out of season and everywhere is closed or under reconstruction. Lucky as we are to find a camp that will open to let us stay, we then find out that the owners' son is getting married, in our camp site if you please, and we are now invited. I am not a big fan of weddings and, in this case, we do not know anybody and they are Islamic, so the strongest drink flowing will be Fanta. It is a very quiet and fairly short affair, the whole ceremony and celebrations taking less than two hours. There is a huge crowd of people and a general segregation between the sexes. Even the bride and groom are separated throughout most of the event. We go back to sit by our tent in a corner of the site out of the way, but still get supplied with more food than we can eat, and we are supplied with drink until our cups runneth over. With Sprite, not Fanta.

As luck would have it, one of the wedding guests knows where we can get our car's spring problem sorted out. The next day we find the garage in question, but after several hours chasing about, that hope fizzles. After a couple of phone calls, we are told they can get the springs and how much they will cost. The garage will need some money up front, so we wander off to find an ATM. After a long while, we find one that will pay us out. Back at the garage, we hand over the cash, they phone for the springs, but then we are told they cannot get the springs and give us our money back. Two wasted hours of walking about looking for ATMs.

From Malindi, we take the inland road and leave the glorious Indian Ocean behind us, making our way up the rough dirt road to the east gate of the Tsavo National Park. We come across two Dutch guys in a Land Rover - or, more correctly, sitting on the ground next to a Land Rover - and they appear to be in some sort of trouble. They had managed to turn the Land Rover right onto its roof - as I said, it is a rough road - and they had finished up dangling upside down in their seat belts. A passing lorry had already towed the vehicle the right way up, but was going the wrong way to be of any further help so they are still sitting, dazed, trying to work out a plan when we find them. It seems that the engine was not too keen on being upside down for a while, as it now refuses to start. And here we are in our car with broken suspension. We tow them 12 miles to a safari camp which, luckily, has a mechanic. After a drink and swapping e-mail addresses, we leave the men, who still appear to be in a state of shock, to their own devices, and we carry on to the park.

At the gate of the Tsavo National Park, we present our gold card. We also ask about camping where our new Dutch friends have just recommended. I now find out why we need this card; it would seem the powers-that-be do not trust the staff at the remote gates with the money. Understandable, I suppose. So, we cannot camp where we would like to, as we have not prepaid for that; our gold card has only enough money on it to allow entrance. There are no facilities for handling cash here, so to upgrade we would need to go round to the main gate, pay and then come back. There is no chance of that happening. So all we can do is drive through the park, all the time bearing in mind that we are not sure how long it takes, and we have to be out or in a camp by closing time. Maybe sometimes it is better to do more research and planning than I normally do, and then we would not be in predicaments like this.

We manage a fair bit of wildlife spotting; it is very difficult trying to rush along when a load of magnificent beasts present themselves for viewing. We see hundreds of elephants - a lot of herds of between twenty and thirty animals per group. At the gate on the way out, we check that we can come back in the next day for the remainder of our twenty-four hours, and are told this is OK. So, back in Voi, we settle in for the night at the B&B we stayed at before, which has breakfast and internet, and is a fraction of the price of camping in the park. The next morning, we return for a bit more of a wander around to use up the rest of the time on our ticket.

We have several hours in the park and, as always, we live in hope, but once again the big cats fail us. But we do see a lot of antelope, giraffes, and a great variety of birds, as well as upwards of three hundred elephants, there were groups of them everywhere. They all looked amazing covered in red dust. Elephants seem to spend all their time eating, washing or covering themselves in dust. In this area, all the dust is red. Herds of red elephants wandering about, how absolutely amazing.

After leaving the park, we head back towards Nairobi on the main road. In one village, looking for somewhere to stop for the night, we find three guest houses that are too grubby, and the fourth place, a hotel, is way out of our price range. The whole village is dirty, complete with scruffy urchins running around, and, in the middle of it, is a hotel with rooms at 300 US Dollars a night! We carry on and further up the road there is a hotel that looks OK. I send Helen in to check it out and she returns, saying it is and the price is right. Inside, we find the two Dutch Citroën 2CV drivers whom we met in Egypt. They have flown from Holland to Kenya for a week's break, and we have just crossed paths, as tomorrow morning they are flying back to Holland. It is a small world.

As we near the city of Nairobi, we see a place that does suspensions. We spotted it a bit late and we are on a dual carriageway, so I stop on the roadside just past their entrance and walk back. They have the springs we need and cheaper than in Malindi. Now I need to negotiate how to get the car back to them, having passed the entrance on the dual carriageway. We'll have to go up to the next intersection to turn around.

Just before we reach the intersection, Helen spots another spring shop and this time I react quickly enough and in we go. They check the car and the computer. They have the springs in stock and the price is cheaper than the other place down the road. Quite excitedly, I give them the go ahead and, in no time at all, they have the car up on the lift, my broken springs off, and the wrong springs ready to go in. It takes quite a bit of computer-checking and stock-checking, while the car is hanging in the air, half-dismantled and springless. I am in a bit of a flux - we are a bit stuck without springs - but, after a while, they find the right size springs. Now I think we are on the home leg, but it would seem the fun is only about to start. The two men start by trying to manually force the spring into position. Absolutely no chance of that happening; their efforts of trying to force the long coil spring designed to hold up about two tons into its limited space with a tyre lever and a hammer is purely farcical. Next they try a whizzy spring compressor, except they cannot get the spring into the machine. Eventually, they manage to get a couple of coils in the machine, get as much compression as they can, tie the coils with some tape, and then, with a lot of brute force, levers and hammers, finally get the springs into place.

Then there is a lot more work trying to get back together the bits and pieces that only took a few minutes to get off to work on the springs. With the job done, I get the final shock. I am expecting that the springs they fitted, being bigger than the springs that they quoted for, will cost more, so I am ready for a bit of an argument, as they have already given me a price, but it comes to much less than their first quote. I am so happy, we pay up with great haste, just in case they realise they are wrong or something. We drive off down the road bouncing all over the place. Being this buoyant is going to take some getting used to, and we realise that the suspension has not been up to much for quite a while.

Only later do I find that they have not put the anti-roll bar back properly, so that needs remedying, but it is no big deal. Luckily, the firm that did the springs was one of those 'quick fit' type of chains, and as we come across another branch of the company, they agree to rectify the problem straight away. *Great*. Whilst I wait for the car to be done, Helen goes off to the pharmacy across the road to talk about her ear, which is painful. The outcome is that we immediately stop taking our Larium anti-malarial drugs, as it seems that one of the potential side effects is ear problems, so the pills have to go.

We are now back in Nairobi. We have been here twice and previously were here for over a week, but after we got some 300 miles away, Helen said she would like to go to the former home of the late Karen Blixen of 'Out of Africa' fame. This is one of Helen's most favourite films, so here we are on the outskirts of Nairobi yet again. We camp somewhere in the area of the said house and take a trip to and around the house and grounds, and learn some of Karen Blixen's history. The house is of quite a modest size, but the grounds are extensive and beautiful. We will have to look at the film again when we get home. She was well-revered around here, so much so, in fact, that the town here is called Karen.

Back in our campsite, we spot a parked car that belongs to the Italian we met on the ferry from Turkey, and with whom we then spent an anxious two days as we struggled to get our cars out of the docks at Port Said. There is no sign of him though. We raise him by e-mail and find out that he is doing his trip to Cape Town in stages. During a return trip to Italy, he and his girlfriend got married, so best wishes to them. Although we only saw their car and not them, this encounter does once again make it seem like a small world.

Our last night in the campsite at Karen is a bit of a disaster. There had been rain, so we had looked for the highest piece of ground when pitching our tent. There is not a lot in it, as the whole area is pretty flat. On this last night, we wait for the expected evening rain, and it comes, a bit heavier than usual. We sit waiting for it to finish, after its normal run. Tonight, though, there is no stopping. We get a bit worried about cooking our dinner; the rain is getting heavier, water starts gathering in the campsite and the tent starts leaking, very slightly, but leaking none the less. And now it is getting dark. We take a quick vote, the unanimous decision being that we should eat in the bar and see if they have a room. All is well, they have food and they have a spare room. The bathroom is down the corridor and it is huge, we could move our bed into it. In the morning, we go out to inspect the tent and, lo and behold, it is on the only piece of ground not under water. The water is just gently lapping at the edges of the tent and it is completely dry inside. It turns out it didn't have much of a leak after all. I have to wade through a couple of inches of water to get to the car, but I drive it round to the car park, which is above the flood level, and can make it really close to the tent - just the other side of a flower bed.

We had been dreading the rainy season but have actually experienced very little problem with it. Only two days and one night so far that have caused us any hassle. That is not a big deal considering the three months we have spent in the region during the long rains. When it does rain, it seems to be for a short while in the early evening or overnight.

We have not used the tent very much yet but already it is showing signs of wear, and we will have to replace it at some time, but at least, for the short term, we will be putting a tarpaulin over the tent at night. When you buy one of these things at home and it gets used on the occasional holiday, they last years, but here we seem to have already crammed years of usage into two or three months.

We decide to take a bit of a detour to Lake Magadi. The Great Rift Valley is littered with lakes and, as it is volcanic, a lot of the lakes are soda lakes. Some of them are freshwater and there are also hot springs and geysers. Lake Magadi is apparently the biggest soda producer in the world. I am not sure that is a good reason for going to see it, but the area is supposedly nice to see, and a number of interesting birds are attracted to these rather disgusting lakes, so we will give it a try.

It has rained a lot in the Ngong hills, just to the North West of Karen, and in several places lower down the slopes, this rainwater is using our road to Magadi for its own convenience as is rushes to the lower ground. It makes our driving a bit more interesting as somewhere alongside the road is the stream, which is the real course of the water, but at the moment the water level is high enough for the road to be about one foot under water. The murky, muddy water covers a wide swathe and we hope we can stay on the tarmac and not drop into the unseen river course on one side. After more than a mile of driving through the river it becomes a good drive and eventually we come to the village of Magadi and the soda refinery. The largest soda producing lake in the world is not really worth the hassle of getting there. There is a thermal spring in the area but it is not possible to get to it at the moment. After a quick look around and a good lunch in the workers' canteen, we head back to Karen, via the flood water route.

From Karen we are heading to a small game park called Hells Gate. Our first stop is not too far up the road; we go for breakfast with the two Dutch Land Rover drivers as they live here and work in the city somewhere, for some overseas aid agency. Although they are without the Land Rover at the moment - it is still in the garage in Mombasa being assessed after its rolling over adventure

- the Dutch themselves seemed to have recovered from the shock. They cook us a superb breakfast, we swap a few stories and get some travel advice. Leaving them, we carry on to the town of Naivasha and camp at a site on the shore of the beautiful Lake Naivasha, which is a freshwater lake.

Down the road is Elsamere, the former home of the late Joy Adamson of 'Born Free' fame. It is another modest-sized house, also set in beautiful grounds. This is not the place where 'Elsa the lion cub' was raised - that is further north, somewhere near Meru, I think. Both this house and Karen Blixen's are now set up as museums, and give a window into the life of ex-pats in days gone by. It is a little awe-inspiring, walking around these homes of people who wrote themselves into some of the history of this country. Joy and her estranged husband, George, did a lot for the wildlife and its conservation, lions in particular, all in the face of public and political opposition. It was by some strange quirk of fate that they were both shot and killed, at different times, in different places, by different people and for different reasons. But the legacy of their work is now probably the biggest business in Kenya, that is the wildlife and the tourism that it generates. I have to admit that our meagre contributions will not do much to help the economy.

The Hell's Gate National Park is only a small park, but our guidebook waxes lyrical about it. It also recommends a camp to stay in, so off we go. At the gate we lose some our joviality when we find out the cost. Once more, the camping is 50 Dollars. Down the road we were only paying 10 Dollars to camp on the lakeside

157

but, in great anticipation thanks to our guidebook, we pay up and go in. It is small and, although very pretty, almost completely devoid of wildlife. There is a huge area of geothermal activity but unfortunately this is also accompanied by a vast amount of Chinese industrial activity, which does seem to take the edge off the beauty of it. I assume it must help the people in some way, but it does little for the views. Our campsite, highly recommended by the book, is bit of ground with a toilet - a flush toilet, admittedly - but no water and, therefore, no actual flushing and, of course, no showering either. Luckily, we have water in the car, so we can cook our food and make some drinks. It annoys me that a park ticket is valid for twenty-four hours, but if you want to stay in the park for the twenty-four hours, you have to pay four or five times the rate a normal campsite charges, and you get a lot, lot less for your money. We would have done a lot better to ignore the guidebook and stay in our camp across the road and just come here for a day trip. I always learn something after I cock it up, and also, if I had not done any research - like read a guidebook - I would have probably done it my way, which as it turns out would have been the best way. Sometimes lack of research can lead you astray, but sometimes research is of little help with poor advice, and sometimes it points out some great things that you may have missed otherwise. I suppose you pay your money and you take your pick.

We drive further down the road past Joy Adamson's house to a place called Crater Lake. On our way we see giraffe, buffalo, zebra and antelope just wandering about by the road - a lot more than we saw in the park and this is free!

In the town of Naivasha, we are held up for a little while because of a traffic accident on a stretch of dual carriageway. Most of the hold-up is on the opposite carriageway to us. One tanker driver who is not too keen on being held up, turns through an intersection, carries on down the wrong side of the road, passing by very closely to a number of police officers who are standing in the road by the crashed cars. He then goes through another intersection back onto the right side of the road and carries on. The police take absolutely no notice of him; it would seem that this type of driving behaviour is absolutely normal.

We cross back across the equator into the Northern hemisphere. First to Lake Balingo, another freshwater lake, and here, after putting our tent up, we find we are camped only about 15 metres away from a couple of crocs just basking at the water's edge. *I hope they don't eat campers*. At night, hippos wander around the tent, grazing. There is an incredible amount of bird life in the area, including birds like the Red-chested Cuckoo, the Bristle-crowned Starling and Verreaux's Eagle Owl, and a whole host of others. We spend a couple of days here before moving on to Lake Bogoria, which is a soda lake and makes a change. We almost abandon it, as the price to go in is, in our opinion, ridiculously high; the cost of entry for the two of us, the car and one night's camping is over 150 Dollars. The man at the gate phones his boss and we successfully negotiate the price down to 100, which is still a lot but we have driven a fair way to get here and are pleased with that.

The best-placed campsite is unavailable as the high water level in the lake has made the road to it impassable. In recent years, the 'powers that be' have been trying to control the water. First they used too much control and almost dried the lakes (Balingo and Bogoria) and now their counter measures have caused both lakes and two other swamps to flood, drowning vegetation and houses. This is why the crocs were so close to our tent in the previous camp. When we get to the second choice camp, we find an untended patch of ground with grass that has gone wild; nothing that could be remotely called a fifty-dollar-a-night campsite. The toilets are another matter; from the outside the two toilets look very shabby, and the inside? Well, the inside remains to be seen. Due to the high water level these toilets now reside on an island and we are unwilling to swim or wade across to inspect or use them, so we are never going to find out what they are like inside. I am glad we got a discount at the gate, but it no way compensated for the lack of everything in the park. There is a thermal spring here, which the gate staff used as the reason for the prices, but to me a dirty brown puddle, faintly smelling of sulphur with steam coming off it is nothing to shout about and is no way worth paying 100 Dollars for.

This will be our last time in the Rift Valley, so we think we should try and make the most of it. Our main reason for being in this area is birdwatching, and it has not been disappointing. The valley itself carries on down through Tanzania, Malawi, Zimbabwe and Mozambique, but now we are taking a more westerly course.

We stop in Eldoret to get a couple of jobs done on the car. It is a bit of a dump of a town, so we plan not to stop for longer than necessary. I ask around for a garage and, after a while, am given directions to somewhere that turns out to be an area of workshops. Most of the work being done is outside, which is not so unusual. I ask about my CV Gaiter. 'No problem'. Two men get the car jacked up, the wheel off, and then look around for some cardboard to lay on under the car. It is still the rainy season and everywhere is muddy. I have a touch of worry as they dismantle the front suspension in all this mire; I know it is just normal in these parts, but that does not stop me from worrying. I am provided with a chair, so that I can sit and watch, which turns out to be very necessary as several times I have to say, 'No, not that way!' At the end, when they are refitting the brake pads, they cannot get them back in, so they are going to grind them down a bit. They don't seem to understand that they came out so they must go back in, and I have to actually show them the right way round to put them in. After I just easily pop them in, I am elbowed out of the way so they can get on and finish the job. Getting repairs done this way is probably the main cause of my worry on the whole trip.

We continue the hunt for anti-malarial drugs. In one pharmacy we are told that the one they sell is 130 Kenyan Shillings (£1) for three pills, and that would provide three months' protection. This seems a bit far-fetched and too cheap, but all the pharmacies have the same story, with the same product under different brand names. We search the internet and cannot find anything about this product, which is not too reassuring, but as it only costs a pound, we will give it a try. This is a bit of a cavalier way to try and avoid one of the biggest killers in the world, and, here in central Africa, we are in the land of the worst malaria in the world. This is not the recommended attitude to take, or the way to act. Also, if these prophylactics are so cheap, why are there so many people in Africa dying of malaria? Assuming that they do really work.

As we drive around this country, and other African countries, we are amazed and amused at some of the businesses and their names. The missionaries of old must have worked hard, as the country is very religious. Some of our favourite business names are: 'God Is Great Coffin Makers' and 'Jesus Loves, Motorcycle Mechanic'. Also, all the coaches, minibuses, delivery vans and big lorries have all manner of slogans in front and rear windows: 'God Will Guide Us', 'Jesus Saves', and so on. Most of them drive like they are fully protected by these logos and, unfortunately, all too often, we see the aftermath of lorries that have missed a bend, going downhill too fast, and have either hit a rock face or gone over the edge. Many vehicles have toppled over as a wheel or whole axle assembly has come off. The minibuses and coaches do not seem to fare quite as bad, but they have their fair share of mishaps. I am amazed that they do not suffer more, as these small minibuses, which would hold a maximum of twelve people in Europe, take in excess of twenty people here; the handling must be dreadful. I personally think these drivers would do better to improve their driving habits rather than rely solely on divine intervention. All the time I have to bear in mind that I am driving on the same roads as they are. We have seen quite a few cars rolled over, but then the car drivers do not seem to go for stickers in the windows.

The other motoring phenomenon we have come across is the 'broken down vehicle warning system'. There are very few triangles here; the local method is to pull some branches off of trees or bushes and spread them out on the road in front and to the rear of the broken down vehicle, or, if there is no greenery, they use rocks gathered up from the area. All breakdown repairs are carried out where the vehicle has stopped, whether it is a minor repair, gear box strip down, or major welding repairs. One of the apparent advantages of using local materials for warning signals is that, when the repair is finished, you can just drive away and leave all the rocks, branches etc. all over the road. What was once a hazard warning system is now merely a hazard for the following vehicles to try and avoid.

We love all of this quirkiness. Kenya is an absolutely fantastic country and tomorrow we enter Uganda.

The following morning, on our way to the border to leave Kenya, we take a bit of a roundabout route to look at some birds at a place called Saiwa Swamp. This involves taking a number of small roads, probably better described as dirt tracks, and getting lost. As in other places, we ask a number of people the way and they all say, 'Yes, yes, you carry on'. *Lying wotsits!* After a while, the road deteriorates a lot; in some places it is impossible to drive on the road itself and, in one or two places, we are straddling the ditch on one side of the road or the other. This becomes a bit awkward when we meet someone coming the other way doing the same thing but, despite all the local advice, we decide we were on the wrong road and turn around.

On our way back to the main road, it starts hammering down with rain. As the road is a bit iffy with all the water on it, we wait a while. As we sit waiting, we watch the water building up in the gullies either side of the road, forming torrents. These dirt roads have a steep camber on either side, so the road itself is a big hump in between two ditches. Once the rain abates a bit, we carry on. Then the car starts sliding sideways into the gulley. I frantically try to point the wheels up the camber only to find, when they do get a bite, we fly up the slope in a bit of a rush only to start sliding down the other side. We continue like this, slithering down one side, then down the other, all the way fighting like mad to stay on top of the hump in the centre. Then I manage to let go of the wheel for half a second to get into four-wheel-drive. This helps stabilise us a bit - not much, but the slithering is definitely more controllable.

After negotiating this slalom for a way, we reach some flatter stuff and it is easier to drive. I turn to my navigator, 'That was a bit of fun!' Only to realise she is frozen with shock or fear, and she doesn't speak for the best part of an hour. It might be worthwhile going back there!

When we do find the right place, we realise we should have turned right early on in our drive. The birding is not that good, certainly not worth the terror that Helen went through. Mind you, I cannot help thinking if she had navigated me to the right road, we would not have been lost, and she would have not been so terrified.

Needless to say, this took a lot longer than planned and we will not leave Kenya as expected. We stop for the night at a hotel on the road to the border and set off for Uganda the next day. Some three miles out, there is a queue of lorries. I am not African but I have started to pick up a few of their driving habits, so when there is a queue, you just drive around it. There is always a big queue of lorries at the frontier waiting for Customs clearance and it is quite normal for cars to drive passed them. So, on the other side of the road I go, until we come to a line of lorries that have also already done that, until they met a row of trucks coming the other way. Total blockage. But I can get around the lot of them by putting the two nearside wheels on the edge of the road and the other two down the bank. We are leaning to one side quite a bit but not enough to warrant the language my navigator uses. Or the kittens - why does she want us to have kittens at a time like this? Even with this inventive piece of driving, we come to a stop with yet more traffic.

It turns out that a lorry driver had been robbed, and he will not move his truck until the police, press and TV crews turn up. So he has locked his cab and is creating a commotion and a huge traffic jam. Most of the police and reporters seem to be there by the time we arrive and it is this that is causing the chaos. I investigate other ways to try and get through and spot a minibus going across the fields, coming from the direction of Uganda. Ding! That looks like my route. By the time I get back to the car to make tracks, two more minibuses have come up behind us and are blocking me in. I implore them to back up so that I can get out. This is not in their nature: 'Never back up for any reason' seems to be the motto. But when I manage to explain there is no way through and our only hope is through the fields, they back up and are ploughing through the mire themselves before I even get back to the car. As fast as I can, we are in hot pursuit. Unfortunately for them, they get stuck in the mud and need the passengers to get out and push - that is another common African duty for minibus passengers - but luckily, I have fat tyres and four-wheel-drive. With a bit of weaving in and out, straight through a bush, up the embankment, a bit of manoeuvring through a couple of gaps in the trucks to the right side of the road, we make it down to the frontier and Immigration. Driving in England will never be the same again.

If we had not got lost and left yesterday, we would have missed all this fun. Relatively quickly, we are all visa'd up, passports stamped, carnet stamped and we are in Uganda.

Road or river?

Stork in camp

Providing a Hornbill grooming parlour

Crawling under the car for maintenance is a regular activity

UGANDA
20 April

I am often baffled by the immigration process. It never ceases to amaze me when they consider providing an exit stamp in your passport with the question, 'Where are you going?' We are on the frontier between two countries, with one side for entry and one side for exit; there is no way they cannot know from where you have come or where you are going. And then again, after crossing the frontier, 'Where have you come from?' A smile, mention the name of the neighbouring country only metres away, and they seem happy, but I sometimes wonder if they know they are working so close to another country and, if so, do they actually know which country it is?

Our first stop in Uganda is the town of Jinja, which, so the blurb claims, is the source of the Nile. Rwanda also claims to have the source of the Nile and so does Burundi, but Jinja is where the White Nile actually leaves Lake Victoria.

Our guidebook is six-or-so-years-old, a fact that does not worry us. We rarely stay in any of the recommended hostelries featured in the book, as we can usually find somewhere better and cheaper. And anyway, things change, places come, places go, but the mountains stay, the pyramids stay, geographical features do not move or change. We walk down the road to look for this spot where the Nile exits Lake Victoria, but the ground around the area is now owned by a hotel and there is a fairly hefty charge to see the outflow area. We were hoping to see the start of the longest river in the world, but now we think, *it is only water, there is nothing spectacular to see.* So we decide to give it a miss. Anyway, we can see it a few hundred metres downstream.

We do a bit of shopping in town, including getting a new sim card for the phone, but we are not able to get it registered. So, back to the campsite where we are able to get some more welding done on the car. Most of the sites, especially the bigger ones, have a number of vehicles and their own maintenance workshop. Even small sites often have some sort of general repair facility. But here there is a man in one corner of the carpark who seems to have a small boat and trailer repair business. Luckily, he also has a welding plant and bits of scrap metal that we find useful for repairs.

Satisfied, we move on to a place down the road, or rather down the river. Bujagali Falls. Here, we do stay in a camp that is recommended in our book so that we can look over the falls. Whilst Helen puts the tent up, I get the kettle on. Then, as we sit enjoying a brew and the tranquillity, we realise that camping next to a waterfall should not be tranquil; we should be hearing the sound of raging torrents. It would appear that the falls are no longer there. Bang goes my theory about geographical features staying put. It seems some fool has gone and built a hydroelectric power station downstream from here, which has put these once spectacular falls under water. Apparently, at one time, as the Nile left Lake Victoria, it was via a waterfall, but this has also succumbed to the needs of electricity. We have plans to include Murchinson Falls Park on our route; I hope those falls are still there.

But first we are off to Kampala. There are a number of things we want to do and see in the city that, apparently, has it all. Quite a few miles outside of Kampala we join a queue of very slow moving traffic. Not that we can drive fast anyway; even though it is a mettled road, it is in poor condition. As it turns out, all the roads in Kampala itself are dreadful. Huge numbers of pot holes - some almost the full width of the road - and they are all deep, even the smaller ones. With everybody weaving about, bumper to bumper, it is difficult to see them. And, on top of that, there are bloody great speed humps. With the amount of traffic and the holes in the road, it is impossible for anybody to be going fast anyway.

After two days, we have had enough and abandon any thoughts of doing our bits here. Once again, in no time at all, a city has got the better of us. I do not know what happens, but we come in from the wide open spaces and, all of a sudden, we are overwhelmed by the city and feel the desperate need to get out as soon as possible. But we have got the phone working, so all is not lost, and we head off northwards.

It is quite a job getting out of town through all the traffic and not really knowing the way, but now on the open road it is virtually traffic free. Once again, we pass some townships that do not feature on our map, and we pass some areas where towns are marked on our map but are not there on the ground. After quite a long drive of flat, boring nothingness, we end up in the town of Misindi. We find a cheapish hotel and, fortunately, it is almost next door to a doctor's clinic. Helen is still having a problem with her ear, so we give the local quack a try. Sitting in the run-down waiting room with the paint flaking off what appear to be temporary partitions made from second hand timber, and sharing wooden benches with a load of women dressed in a variety of tribal costumes, is a far cry from the health centres back at home. Helen is diagnosed with an infection and is given some antibiotics and some other sorts of pills, and away we go. We wander around town and eventually find two things of interest to us. I get another clamp for the anti-roll bar on the car and we find the National Parks office. Unfortunately, there is only one very drunk man in the office and he is not a lot of help to us, but eventually we find the information we need elsewhere, and so the next day we set off.

On reaching Murchinson Falls National Park, the first thing we need to do is find the falls and see if they are waterfalls or power generators. Thank God they are still waterfalls, and pretty impressive they are. Not huge, but definitely impressive as the River Nile is forced through a narrow gorge. The power of the water is incredible. I believe this is the last waterfall on the White Nile as it winds its way northward to the Mediterranean Sea.

This is a game park, though, unfortunately, not as good as it apparently used to be. It is a beautiful area, but, during Idi Amin's rule, the Ugandan economy took a dive and the tourist industry also went to wall. Despite all this, he started to build a huge tourist lodge on the banks of the Nile, until the money ran out. Then, in order to feed his army, they had to go into the game parks and shoot their own food. They also went into rural areas and robbed the peasant tribes of all their food and harvest causing a famine in the country. Then things got a lot worse after he started a war with Tanzania, as, besides shooting Amin's troops, the Tanzanians also shot the wildlife, partly to feed themselves as they waged their war on Amin's troops, but then after the war they slaughtered elephants, rhino and other game to take tusks, horns and skins back home with them.

But things are on the mend now; the wildlife is recovering, if a little difficult to find. We find herds of buffalo, giraffes, antelope and a host of exotic birds. Maybe here we will see the rare, elusive and much sought-after Shoebill. I see some birders with a guide, so I stop and ask if they have seen a Shoebill, which we understand has been seen in the area, but they have had no luck. After a few more minutes, I stop our car again to look at a couple of hippos, and, as I scan the reeds, I spot a Shoebill, or at least I hope it is a Shoebill. Against all the rules, I have to get out of the car to get a closer look, feverishly swapping binoculars and camera, and saying to myself continuously, *it's a Shoebill, it IS a Shoebill,* looking at it with the binoculars and photographing my prize as I get closer and closer. It is only a bird, but it is a knicker-wetting moment for me. I am one happy bunny. I found it myself and I have seen a Shoebill. *How good is that?* For those who have never heard of a Shoebill, it is a stork-like bird, standing nearly 5 feet tall, and it has a very big and bulky bill that is suitable for snapping up fish, baby crocodiles and any other similar foodstuffs that wander its way. It is a one-of-a-kind species and a great oddity. What a privilege to have found one.

We spend a couple of days wandering around the park and, on the day we leave, we opt to go out of the North Gate, which makes a longer way round, but we will get a chance to see more of the park. As we wend our way through the savannah, a pair of grown lion cubs cross the track right in front of us. We stop immediately to watch them. They, in return, climb a rock to survey us. After a moment or two of looking, they then start cavorting about, as cubs do. We sit watching, enthralled, for half an hour or more, as they play as if they have not a care in the world. *How exciting is that?* It is a spectacular park, although still a little short on wildlife. According to our book, there was a time when elephants roamed in their thousands, but now the herds are very small. For me, it is well worth the visit, we have enjoyed a good time here.

Leaving the park, we turn right onto a tar road and almost immediately are stopped by the local constabulary. My seatbelt is not fastened. We are in a village of about ten tin sheds, we are the only car on the road, and we have been stopped by the only policeman within 100 miles and he wants to give me a ticket for not having my seatbelt on. I try pleading all the mitigating circumstances I can think of. Unfortunately, that does not amount to much - only that I have only just come out of the park and only been on the road for a few metres. He is not impressed. So then we start on negotiations for the cost of the fine without him writing a ticket. Once we agree on a sum, we have to go through a secret routine for handing over the money. There is nobody in sight in any direction, but the officer of the law leans through the window with a folded newspaper in his hand and I slide some banknotes up under the paper into his grubby little mitt. I take the precaution of doing up my seatbelt before handing over the money so that he has no reason to come back on me. Once our James-Bond-like transactions are concluded, our man stands back, salutes us and wishes us a pleasant journey.

After this little episode, we continue on our way to see some more Nile falls at Karuma. These are like huge rapids, and this will be our last look at the Nile as it flows north and we flow south. So now back to Misindi for a day off and time to check the car over before we hit the road again.

We are still a fair way from Misindi and civilisation, but we are keeping our eyes open for a petrol station. We spot one in a small village and, as usual, we are a bit hesitant about going in as we are not sure if they are open. There are some men on the forecourt area, so I point to the pumps and one of them gives some African hand signals. The Africans use a lot of hand signals for all sorts of things. Unfortunately, I do not know the meaning of any of them. I signify that I am none the wiser. He probably does not understand my signal, so that makes us even. He then points to the pumps, so I drive in next to the diesel pump. He comes straight over and says something like, 'Surely even you can see this is not working!' He then points to an area of ground and says, 'Look, it's got weeds.' I now realise maybe it was these weeds he was pointing at and not the pumps. I am afraid it still does not mean too much to me; we have been to a lot of petrol stations with weeds and, as I have said, a lot of them do not look like they are open. Some of them have pumps that look abandoned and derelict, but they are still in business, and one had to start a generator to work the pump. For me, weeds come a long way down the indicator list of signs of openness. We carry on and find diesel further down the road and, I have to own up, this place does not have weeds; not only does it look open, it is open.

Back in Misindi, we check back in to the same hotel, Helen goes back to the same doctor, as she still has a problem, and I crawl under the car. This is a somewhat regular exercise, crawling around to see what has come loose, or has come off. But this time, I come up against a real disaster.

Back home, when I got the extra spare wheel, I had to make a gate to go on the back to carry it. That works a treat, but I did not make the latch strong enough and had to get that strengthened and welded a while ago. But I am only an amateur, not a professional vehicle manufacturer. The professionally made Toyota spare wheel carrier is underneath the rear of the car, or should I say *was* underneath the rear of the car. It has gone, broken and gone, and my wheel - with a brand new tyre - has gone with it. The tyre that I was saving, which has not yet even been on the road, well, apparently, it is on the road now, but not with me or my car. I had never liked the design of the carrier but had not known what to do about it. Now I am seriously thinking about it; I need something that is capable of handling the bumps that we go over. *Toyotas, huh!*

But first, I have to try and find a wheel, and then a tyre. I have already tried to get a tyre in two countries and as yet have not been able to get the same size as we already have. *Toyotas, huh!*

It looks like I may well have to consider Helen's suggestion and take the easy, safe(ish) tarmac roads, and not do the interesting routes. That said, we need to get from Misindi to Fort Portal, which means we are now on a six-hour drive on poorish dirt roads. This is the only practical route. We go through a small town that does have tarmac roads, but there are more holes than tar and is in a lot worse condition than the rural dirt roads. There are quite a lot of dirt roads in Uganda, but, since leaving Kampala, all of the tar roads we have been on have been excellent; there is generally little traffic and good surfaces in rural areas and, therefore, easy driving. Most of the country's traffic seems to be in and around Kampala.

In Fort Portal, I manage to get a second hand tyre for my remaining spare wheel. It was expensive, the wrong size and largely lacking in tread, but at least we have a workable spare wheel.

Now we can get on with our next plan, going to Semliki Game Reserve. We make our way out of town and across the Rwenzori highlands out into the hinterland.

We think we are doing well, but, somewhere down the road, we find that we have missed our turning off of the main road. Seeing a National Parks hut at the roadside, we stop to ask the way. Alas, the road we wanted was 5 miles back. We turn around, find what we think is the right road and we are away, following the signs until we reach a rangers' gate. Here we are required to fill in a visitors' book, and then we are asked who we want to see. I am a bit lost at this question. 'Lions' , I say. 'Lions and the Shoebill' . This reply confuses the ranger; it would seem that we are at the gate of some sort of ranger training station and not the park entrance. We need to go back a bit, turn left and carry on down the dirt road that is not signposted for Semliki. But first, we need to sign out, even though we have not actually gone in; the paperwork must be kept in order.

Unfortunately, a couple of recent heavy downpours means the dirt road is not in the best of condition, so we are slipping and sliding about quite a bit. But with my amazing driving skills we manage to stay on the track, unlike a couple of locals. We come across someone who has slid into the ditch. In order to be of any help, I need to turn around. It is a very tight space, the road is narrow with steep, muddy, waterlogged banks on each side. After a bit of slithering and sliding I manage to get our car facing the other way and get a tow rope fixed. Time to start a bit of towing. How exciting. His car slides along the bank instead of coming up it. I need to change the angle of the tow by getting as far across the narrow track as I can without going down the other side and getting myself stuck. Helen, in her usual panic mode, thinks he is going to turn over. Eventually, I get him out of the ditch and on to the road.

The driver thanks us profusely, and he is off, leaving us facing the wrong way on this little track. *C'est la vie.*

Further down the track, we see another vehicle a bit awry. Somehow the centre of the back axle is on the ground, leaving one rear wheel down the slippery slope and the other wheel in the air. Four people are trying to rock, push and drive the thing out of its predicament, totally without success. Along comes 'International Rescue' to drag him to safety. They want me to pull the vehicle backwards out of its sticky situation, maybe so the driver can have a second attempt at getting stuck. After a bit of a walk around to test the ground, I manage to squeeze past the stuck vehicle so that, after I pull him out of his predicament, I can undo the tow rope and clear off. Our second successful rescue mission. You would think that people born and bred on these roads would be able to drive on them.

This park, although highly praised, seems to be in a bit of a flux. Once we reach the camp, we manage to get away without paying the 150 Dollar foreign car fee - not by some subterfuge on our part, but the temporary ranger phoned her boss who volunteered the offer for some reason. It would be rude not to accept!

We take a couple of walks, accompanied by the temporary ranger for one, and there are no animals around, but we do see a plethora of colourful bird life. We decide to use some of our 'saved' money, hiring a very expensive boatman to find the elusive Shoebill, as we would love to see another one. Unfortunately, this bird is more skilled at being elusive than our boatman is skilled at finding it. After failing to find us one, the boatman tells us on the way back that the Shoebill's habit is to stand at the water's edge, on floating reeds, looking for food. When the water is a bit choppy, the Shoebill will generally move away from the edge into the calmer, denser reeds and, as it is a bit windy today, that must be where all the Shoebills are. Of course, the next day, there is no wind and the lake is flat calm, but there is no way I am paying that man any more money, so we call it a day on Semliki.

We had camped at the northern end of the park, and had been the only ones there. We saw in the brochures that there is a very upmarket safari lodge at the southern end, where the tents have Persian carpets, four-poster beds, en-suite bathrooms - the works. As we will be passing on our way out, we think we will have a sneaky looksee. Driving down the long track, we wonder if we can afford to have a coffee there. But it is all to no avail as they are closed for renovations. So, as it turned out, we two were the only customers in the entirety of this highly-praised park. Maybe it is low season.

On our way out of the park, we come across a big articulated lorry at a precarious attitude; all the nearside wheels of the trailer have slid into the ditch, tipping the cab in such a fashion that its offside drive wheels are in the air. He is a professional driver! No way am I going to try and pull that thing out.

Back in Fort Portal and wandering the streets, we notice some shops have a board with about twenty different types of phone charger cables hanging out of it. We have seen this sort of thing a lot, particularly in small towns, and we only now realise - not being too quick on the uptake - that these are for people who are without electricity at home. For a small fee, they can come in and charge their phone. There are many, many people living in homes with no drainage, no running water and no electricity, but they are all connected on their mobiles, and, not only that, but most of them own smart-phones. For most of them, their only means of transport is walking, although some have push bikes. Consequently, everybody they know is just around the corner. I personally do not own a mobile phone as I do not see the need for one. Helen has one, but it is a bog-standard phone. I cannot imagine why a number of these people would want or need one here.

We visit the Batwa pygmy village. Unfortunately, it is as disappointing as we expect it to be. The pygmies have always been at the bottom of the social scale in Uganda - everybody looks down on them metaphorically and physically - and they do not have much in the way of stature to do manual labour, so now they spend much of their time tending goats and trying to glean money from tourists. We had hoped to find out a bit about their culture and life, but all the time there are hands out demanding money. Although I can sympathise with them, this is too in-your-face for us, so we don't stop long. It is a shame really, but that is life.

We wend our way south and there are a lot of rather beautiful lakes in this area. We find a local community camp for a few days. It is very basic but very clean, very well maintained, and in a fabulous location - on the rim of a crater, which is home to one of the lakes. We visit some of the other crater lakes. One of them has a beautiful old colonial house perched high on a cliff edge, which is now a lodge, so we go in to get a coffee. Sitting on the terrace with trellises of colourful flowers, and overlooking the lake, with a nice coffee. *Can life get any better?* Yes it can, because on top of all the climbing flowers, there is an amazing display of colours from the weaver birds, sunbirds, bee eaters, and others.

Whilst in the area, we book a trip to Bigodi swamp for a bird watching walk. This is also something that is operated by the community, so our money will go directly to the locals. We are issued with brand new wellington boots and we set off. One of the first birds we see is the magnificent Blue Turaco. We see many other birds, including Black and White Flycatchers, Crowned Cranes, and the African Green Pigeon. Twelve species are totally new to me, eight I have seen before but are new for this trip, and there are a lot of others that I have already seen, but how fabulous. We also see a few different monkeys, including the Red-faced Colobus. We walk for nearly four hours, mostly over dry ground or on boardwalks over boggy areas. I wonder why we are wearing wellingtons until we reach a stretch of boardwalk which starts to dip below the waterline. Typical Africa - do not fix the boardwalk, give the punters wellies.

Our camp is all refurbished and waiting for the next season, but at this out-of-season time we are the only ones here. Helen's task after putting the tent up is to make a cup of tea. This may seem like Helen has to do everything, but she only has to put the tent up, do the washing and scrubbing, car cleaning, cooking and navigation, which leaves me doing all the planning and worrying. So, after putting the tent up, Helen wanders around the camp looking for a power point and the only one she can find is in the staff kitchen, so she plugs the kettle in there, switches it on and leaves it. On return, she asks the staff if it has boiled but they do not have a clue what she is talking about, so with a small group watching, she switches it on again. The water boils and the kettle switches itself off. The kitchen staff are dumbstruck, completely amazed. It would appear that they have never seen such technology in a kitchen before. They are used to hanging a big black pot over the stove. And the camp has smart rooms and a posh restaurant to go with this outdated kitchen.

Generally, whilst camping, we have better control over the food we eat, although this obviously depends on what we can buy in the shops. Helen brought a big supply of dried soya mince with us, so we can do a variety of mince dishes. Buying meat depends on if we find a decent supermarket. Many of the local butcher's shops are just a wooden shack on a scrubby patch of dirt on the roadside, with various bits of meat hanging out in the sun with flies all over them, and often with a goat or two tethered outside, just in case there is a rush on for goat meat. Needless to say, we are not buying meat from any of these establishments. The local general stores also do not inspire us with confidence in the food line. So we either fall back on our soya mince option or eat out at a restaurant or hotel. Not being the brightest sparkler in the box, it takes me a little while to realise that these local establishments are probably buying their food from the same undesirable shops we turn our backs on.

After this stop, we make our way to Queen Elizabeth National Park. On the main road south, we know there is a line across the road and big signs denoting the equator. As this will be our last time crossing the equator on this trip, we plan to stop and share a bottle of warm Sprite or something to celebrate. Unfortunately, we end up not on the main road but going down very poor dirt roads, passing numerous delivery boys with seven or eight hands of bananas piled high on their push bikes, pushing up hill, struggling to stop them running away downhill. They do actually cycle the bits in between these ups and downs. The road is terrible; I certainly would not like to ride a bike on it, even without the bananas. So, being on this road, we bypass the white line marking the equator and actually forget all about it until three days later. Too late to go back for a photo now.

Our attention is drawn to a great big hawk - five foot plus wingspan - seemingly raiding weaver birds' nests. Most weaver birds are roughly sparrow-sized and weave amazing nests hanging on small branches, twigs, or even a few strands of grass, with a tunnel entrance at the bottom. We watch as the African Harris Hawk (according to my book) flies from nest to nest, hanging upside down on these delicate structures, trying to get its head into the small tunnel to catch whatever food it can. What an incredible sight, and as good as any other animal we have seen yet.

We stop at Kasese to stock up for the park. The town is a bit of a dump and not a lot of good for us. It is definitely a good place to leave. The guidebook claims that the Queen Elizabeth National Park is the 'Jewel in the crown of Uganda's parks'. It also claims that the elusive Shoebill can be seen at Lake Kikorongo in the park. This lake is our first destination; the local bird guide there tells me that the Shoebill has been seen there three times in the last five years, and he is not sure when it will be back. I am not sure I can wait for the next off-chance sighting. He also tells me that the bird is seen at Lake George, northeast of the park, and at Edward Flats in the south of the park, over 60 miles away. But - and there is always a 'but' - it is not easy to see the bird at Lake George; they are more often seen at Edward Flats. The savannah next to Lake George is a good spot for lions though, which are also on our list.

Yet again we are the only ones in camp. During the day, baboons and warthogs patrol the area and we have to be sure to leave no food in the tent when we go out. We even remove the lemon-flavoured washing up liquid and the peach-flavoured shower gel. I am not sure if these things would really smell of food to these animals, but why take the chance? If there is any whiff of food, the animals will rip the tent apart to get to it. At night we have elephants and hippos. The elephants are browsers and chew the bushes and trees. The hippos are grazers and munch grass - they grip the grass with their lips and pull it - and they have big lips. The sound of hippos tearing up the grass just outside the tent in the middle of the night is scary, so Helen tells me.

There is no electricity in camp and, for just such occasions, we have a 12 volt electric travel kettle. This is our first opportunity to try it; we fill it up, plug it into the car and wait. And wait. After some time, I tip half the water out with the plan of boiling one cup at a time.

After yet more waiting it seems like the wire to the kettle is getting hotter than the water in it. I am not too keen on that, so I unplug it and throw it away, getting out the trusty petrol stove. I do not mind too much about the kettle - it was cheap - but I have just carried it over 6,000 miles before finding out that it is no good and throwing it away.

We decide to visit Lake George and check in with the local wardens as we enter the area. They cannot confirm any Shoebill sightings, but they wax lyrical about the lions. As predicted, it is too difficult to get to the lake and the Shoebill areas. So we drive round the savannah to look for the 'regularly seen' lions. After two hours, not one lion. The grass is quite long and easy enough for the cats to stay out of sight, but by now I am in desperate need of a wee. I stop, scan all around, get out of the car and do my business, all the time looking, looking. It would be just my luck, after all that time searching and seeing nothing, that one would come out of the grass while I am standing there with my, er, my... standing there in a compromising situation.

Two days in the north of the park and not a lot to show for it, so now we are heading south. Along the track, we spot an elephant right next to the road. I slow down and then switch off the engine to coast to a quiet stop. Helen gives me the camera and, as we draw close to the magnificent beast, I see he has his ears flared. This is not a good sign, but it will be a good photo. But then the silly thing starts to charge at us. I thrust the camera back to Helen, opting not to take a photo of the elephant as its urge to charge and my urge to get away take over. I start the engine, fumble with the gears - it is amazing how all composure goes out of the window when an elephant is attacking you - and try to make a smart getaway. Amidst all this panic, Helen has the presence of mind to get a photo. Not the best composition in the world, but any photo in a panic will do. As we drive away, I glance in the rear view mirror, and the elephant is chasing us down the track, actually running after us. Feeling a little childish - I have got the upper hand now, I can go faster than him - I adjust our speed to that of the elephant and he chases after us for one or two hundred metres before giving up.

As we book into the riverside camp at the southern end of the park, we decide to have a cup of coffee at the canteen (shed). While sitting, drinking, and watching weaver birds at work, the tranquillity is suddenly broken by the roar of worn out diesel engines, and two ancient tanks burst into view. Jokingly, I ask the manager of the shed if this is part of the anti-poaching patrol. He laughs and says it is the Border Patrol. It is only a fifteen metre paddle, wade or swim across the river from the turbulent Democratic Republic of the Congo. So there are armed soldiers and police patrolling the camp and environs day and night.

Having put the tent up, we venture out looking for the famous tree-climbing lions that inhabit this area. After a while, and seeing no lions, we get fed up with that, so we head for Edward Flats to look for Shoebill. This is a lowland area and rather muddy in places. We have been told that the water level is low and, therefore, far off. However, we have also been told it is boggy in places and to watch out.

Back in the UK I had fitted a winch in preparation for the trip. It was a bit of a whim; I didn't really think we would be going any place where we would need one, but I just wanted one. It is only a gizmo, a boy's toy. I have spent a fair bit of time crawling under the car repairing things so far and, during this crawling, I have found several serious design flaws in the way the winch is mounted. I have now worked out how I should have fitted it to be stronger and more secure. But none of that really matters as we are not planning on going into any difficult situations, and I am never going to use it. Until now. I am standing up to my knees in gooey sludge, outside the car, surveying the situation I have just driven into. The car is standing slightly more than axle deep in the same goo.

This is what I call deep doo doos, and possibly the only thing that is going to help us out of this disaster is the defectively mounted winch, but there seems to be nothing to anchor it to. I walk around but can see no trees, big rocks or anything that looks good or solid enough to use as a tow point. The only things I can see are just a couple of small bushes. Inspecting these bushes I find one is far too spindly and the other one, although small, may just be up to the job. The thickest part of the bush is quite a bit smaller than my wrist, and it needs to pull our two ton car up and out of the deep, mud-filled hole. It also has wicked thorns - up to two inches long - making it not too easy to get to the thickest part of the bush. We have to hope that we have enough cable to reach it, as it is a fair distance from the car. We start unwinding the winch cable and have to run out almost the whole of the 50 metre drum to reach the bush. I am franticly waving hand signals to Helen on the winch control, needing her to stop, but she is franticly ignoring me and scribbling down our GPS coordinates in readiness to phone for help. The fact that we have no phone signal or a number for any potential rescuer seems to have gone completely over her head. But, once I get her attention and manage to get her to stop before she unwinds all the cable off the drum, we then start to act a little bit more like a team, and our self-rescue starts to come together.

I get the cable around the bush right at ground level and we start our tow. I ask Helen to keep an eye on the bull bar; I am worried about my flawed design and do not want the bull bar being winched out of the hole leaving the rest of the car behind in the mire. With me driving and Helen pressing the winch control button, we manage, inch by inch, to pull our two tons of vehicle up the side of the hole and out of this quagmire. As we creep up the bank, I think the winch mistress forgets her duties of making sure the car stays with the bull bar and winch, as she shouts, 'We're going, we're going!' As we move, she gets louder and more excited, coinciding with her bouncing up and down.

After a heart-stopping pull, we eventually manage to get the two front wheels up onto terra firma just as the bush uproots. From there we manage to drive out; without stopping I drive over the winch cable until all the wheels are up on dry ground. Somehow I manage to get the winch cable wrapped round the suspension, but that is small fry compared to being stuck in the mud. It takes a little while to disentangle the winch cable and get it all back on the drum.

Helen wants to turn back but I point out that, as we are across the bog, we may as well push on. This we do, until we reach the next bog and I can see this one does not look good so I concede defeat. On the way back, I stop and walk around in the long grass to find a route around the two difficult boggy places. Hidden in the tall grass are bogs, large holes and logs. *Logs? There are no trees here, where did the logs come from?* We manage to navigate around the two difficult bogs and after them we just drive through the easier ones until we get back on the main track and Helen is happy again. I realise later that we must have been so wrapped up in trying to save our lives, that we never gave a thought to taking any photos of the mud enshrined car, or the winching operation. I suppose that logical thinking goes out of the window when faced with a panic situation. Thus ends our day of Shoebill spotting.

The next day we take the other circuit for tree-climbing lions. These are quite famous and this is supposedly the only place in Africa where the lions climb trees. After one and a half hours of driving around in circles, looking at what we imagine to be suitable - but unfortunately lion-free - trees, we decide to give up and leave. On the way out, I feel the need to vent my spleen, and moan about the lack of wildlife and the cost of the park. I know seeing game is the luck of the draw, but this park does not have a lot, and it is the dearest park in Uganda. For us, being foreigners, it costs 35 Dollars a day each, and our car, also being a foreigner, costs a whopping 150 Dollars. The only other thing that gets charged that much is an articulated lorry, and there are not many of them out lion spotting. It is even cheaper to bring a plane in. There is a scale of charges: a local registered car is 30 Dollars, an articulated lorry and foreign cars 150, and at various levels in between are safari trucks, buses, and plane landings.

All the staff are apologetic and say we should have seen a lion - they are all there. Perhaps we should have had a guide, as they previously suggested, but we had declined. As I am ranting, two people are just coming in with a hired a local guide, and so the gate staff tell us to follow them.

Two and half hours later, after going to all the secret places that the guide knows - and, I admit, places we would never have found on our own - nada, zilch, nothing. At the gate, I thank the staff for their help, even though it was without success. I also tell them about our failure with the Shoebill and they say we should have had a guide. I mention the very recent unsuccessful lion-guiding episode. Everyone laughs and we leave.

Feeling rather disappointed about QE park, we plan to go to a campsite just up the road as it sounds very good. It is signposted off the main track as being 1.5 miles away. After 3 miles of very bad road, lots of mud and some very big holes, we come to the last turning for the camp. It is a very nice place in a nice location, but the camping area is awful and it is expensive, and there is no hot water or wifi, which you would expect for the price. So we just have an expensive lunch and carry on. Back on the main track, instead of going the long way round, we opt for cutting across country. It looks easy on the map. Experience tells me this is a fool's way of thinking, but unfortunately this falls on deaf ears. The reality of our chosen route starts sinking in when we seem to spend hours going down weird tracks and lanes from one unnamed village to the next. In fact, we seem to spend hours at each village we come to as every time the road splits we have to ask someone the way. We need to head towards Bushveni, but, even if any of the people we ask speak English, they only know the way to the next village. None of these remote villages are on our map. Eventually, with a bit of help and a lot of luck, we make it to the tarmac road. Reaching Bushveni, we find a hotel and give up for the night.

We are making for Masaka, which is straight down the main road and where we are assured we will see the Shoebill. This is the last place in the country where we may see it, maybe the last place in this lifetime. We find a nice camp on the edge of town and are camped near to where the bird lives. For four days on the trot we pop down in the morning to not see this mystical bird. At least here we don't have to pay to not see it.

There is more time for me repairing the underside of the car. The anti-roll bar has gone again, one of the brackets has gone for the second or third time and this time the connecting link has broken as well. I used to wonder why the mums that run their kids to school in 4x4s don't mount the kerb stones. Now I know; the vehicles are not up to such treatment. Also, the steering guard - the bit that is supposed to guard and protect - is broken and needs repairing. That probably happened falling into the muddy hole in the QE Park.

I make a new spare wheel carrier, which I hope is at least as strong as the Toyota one. I would like it to be stronger, but there is only me, a multitool and an African tradesman. For African tradesman read 'someone who is quite willing and knows a little bit about his job but not much commitment to quality'. I do actually have a bit more than a multitool at my disposal and the very nice owner of the camp lends me a few tools, including an angle grinder. *It is so good to have the feel of power tools in my hands again.*

So, now I have my brand new home-made wheel carrier, but unfortunately I have to fit it to the remnants of the Toyota system. But now I have added a failsafe device - a piece of chain secured to the chassis, dangling through the wheel hole with a padlock on it. I should have had that idea before we left home, it would have saved me a lot of money, anger and grief. I always seem to have the best ideas just in the nick of too late.

After all this, we decide to have a few days of R&R on the Sesse Islands, a group of paradise islands on Lake Victoria. We catch the car ferry to the island of our choice. Although it is the biggest of the islands, it is only few miles long. We book into a camp that our guidebook enthuses about and claims the Dutch owners are friendly and helpful. Tranquillity it is, camping right on the sandy shore of the lake, with an endless supply of hornbills in the trees above and nice walks along the shoreline to other lodges or cafes for a drink. And a spectacular view. *This is what it is all about.*

I spend some time talking to the German owners - maybe the guidebook author got a bit confused over their accents, they moved here some twenty years ago and seem to have become part of the scenery. They also seem to be the main customers of their own bar and, during one of their ramblings, they reveal with some resentment that the current issue of the guidebook is now not so praising of their camp. It is fairly basic - but this is a small island and everything is basic - so I would not be surprised if the comments in the book are more aimed at the inebriation of the owners than the camp itself. Or maybe the authors found out that owners are not Dutch but German, and they don't like Germans. We enjoy our stay on the island anyway.

Back on the mainland, and as we travel up country in our meandering sort of way, I find a wheel. It is expensive, it is the same design as the other wheels, it is the right fit for the hub but it is the wrong geometry for the car. But things like that do not seem to matter in Africa. I bargain over the price and manage to knock the salesman down to lower than he wants to go, but for that price he wants to keep the tyre. The tyre is worn down to the wire and is useless to me but he will not let it go for that price. No matter, the wheel is what we need and a week or so later in Kabale I manage to get a tyre anyway. The usual thing: second hand, very little tread, expensive, but at least it is a tyre, so now we are all complete with two functioning spares again.

Just so that we do not overdo it too much, we are having a few days by the beautiful Lake Bunyonyi, dubbed the Switzerland of Africa. It is quite a spectacular area. Our camp has lush green grass and we have pitched our tent right on the lake shore. Fantastic. I also acquire a new friend, the camp guard. On his patrols, he spends a lot of time asking me about

England and how it compares with Uganda. The first thing I have to tell him is that in England it is not necessary to have AK47 wielding guards on camp sites, or anywhere else come to that. It is a bit difficult trying to describe to somebody who lives in a land of armed bandits, no fridges, very unreliable electricity, and poor roads, with even poorer driving skills, what it is like in England. I say that in England and Europe everybody drives on their own side of the road and they all - or maybe nearly all - obey the laws. Motorcyclists all wear crash helmets. He tells me they have the same laws in Uganda but they are difficult to implement as everybody ignores them. Say no more. It is Africa.

Winston Churchill once called Uganda the 'Pearl of Africa'. Many years later, Idi Amin put a stop to that, but, since his departure, things are on the up. Uganda is an absolutely fabulous country. When they grasp the concept of constant electricity and tarmac on the roads, it will be even better.

Murchison Falls – thankfully flowing with water

Shoebill!

Banana carriers – rather them than me on this rutted road

Elephant!

RWANDA
29 May

Le Pays des Miles Colines. The Land of a Thousand Hills.
That is Rwanda. It is a small, high country, and we need
to change to driving on the right. We might start with a
couple of days in Kigali, the capital. As we enter the city,
it looks modern and buzzing. We have an address for a
hostel, but no real idea where we are or how to find it.
We stop at a petrol station, show them the map and ask
for directions. 'Where do you want to go?' they reply.
'There', I say, pointing to the place on the map, only to
get asked again, 'Where do want to go?' After the third
round of this we just leave. Aha! The police station.
There will be our answer. Helen, being the navigator,
goes across the road to ask first. She finds chatting with
six or seven men exasperating and comes back nearly in
tears, moaning that she cannot get anywhere.

'Let me have a go', I say, and I pop over to ask a
policeman. In no time at all, I manage to collect a group
of four, all pointing to different places on the map, and
in different directions in the street. I have to ask, 'How
do you find your own way around?' I get silly grins in
response. I try another policeman, 'How do we get to

this road?' He is swiftly joined by three others. They engage in conversation, again with arms pointing in all directions. An officer joins in (very briefly) and all the rest of them stand to attention as they speak. In the end, I am led away, so to speak.

As I make my way down the road and round to the rear of the building, my new guide asks me something. I do not understand, so I ask him to repeat it. Second time around, I understand the word 'French' so I say, 'English, I speak English'. Mulling it over a bit later, I work out the other thing he said was Kinyarwanda, which, even later still, I find out is the local language. I realise that he must have been asking me if I spoke French or Rwandan. My answer is still the same.

Round the back is a traffic division. The first man to be asked is driving a police car, so it is looking good. He looks at the map, engages in conversation with my escort, and leaves. The next man knows where we want to go, but he needs to get some paper to draw a new map. Within no time we have three policemen drawing a map with one pen between them, arguing about where turnings are, where landmarks are, screwing up the paper and starting again. I ask my escort, 'What would happen if someone who lives on Boulevard de l'oua (the street we are looking for) phoned the police for emergency assistance? How would you find it?' But I receive no answer to that!

Eventually, after three attempts, I get a hand drawn map, and it has only been one hour since we asked the first policeman the way. Now all the directions are explained to me, full of phrases like, 'At the loundabout take the light load', and, 'At the end of this load is the UN building.' I think, *I am not particularly interested in the UN building, I am looking for a hotel.* But all I can say is, 'Thank you, thank you very much'. It is times like this that I long for a sat nav. I did vaguely look at sat navs before leaving, but had trouble finding maps for Africa. *Anyway, why would I want a sat nav when I have Helen, my own Sat Nag, to navigate?*

Things are not going too well, so we need a plan B. We decide to stay anywhere we can for tonight and leave town tomorrow. We stop at the first hotel we see and go straight in. It turns out to be a bit more expensive than we would like, but we will live with it. We are told it will take half an hour for the water to be hot. One hour later there is still no hot water. I inform the manager and we get a succession of people coming in to test the water. Then we are told it will be one more hour. We go for dinner and afterwards there is still no hot water. Once again, the trail of people in and out running the tap and feeling the cold water. Eventually, they bring in two buckets of hot water. Paying more money does not necessarily get you a better service.

The service at breakfast the next morning is dreadfully slow. Getting the bill is even slower; one night's B&B, plus two dinners takes an absolute age to add up. We are now all paid up, loaded and ready to go. We have waited long enough. However, while we have been faffing about with this slow service, some disgruntled contractor has put a big security padlock on the gates to the exit and we are now stuck on the inside of this financial wrangle. We sit in the carpark for an hour or so, waiting for something to happen. Eventually, money changes hands or promises are made - I do not know which - the padlock is removed and we are free.

Right from the beginning of this trip, the one thing I wanted to do was see Mountain Gorillas. As we are doing a bit of a circular route to fit in what we can as we go, timing can be very tricky. It was difficult for us to do, or plan, in Uganda, as everything has to be done in Kampala on almost the opposite side of the country to the gorillas. In the DRC, the prices are supposed to be good, but at the moment the security situation is not good. So, Rwanda is my last hope. Helen is very unlikely to go as she has a problem with altitude sickness and the gorillas live at, or above, her height limit. For the last week or so I have had a bit of trouble with an achy hip and am not sure how far I can walk at the moment. But, in the town of Ruhengeri, we happen to pass the ORTPN office - that is the Mountain Gorilla authority - so we pop in to check out the situation so we know. Here we find out that the permits are 750 Dollars each. I lose interest quite quickly. I do not want to pay that sort of money and then find that I am not able to walk far enough.

With the gorilla search totally abandoned, we finish up at Ginsenyi, the 'Riviera of Rwanda'. Not the description we would have used. It is on the northern end of Lake Kivu, a volcanic area on the edge of the Parc de Volcans. Fairly often, so we are informed, gases are emitted from the lake floor. On windless days these gases linger about on the lake surface and they are poisonous, so it is unsafe to swim. The general idea for tourists seems to be, if there are no locals swimming, do not go in. Not my idea of a Riviera. This is also the gateway to the DRC

- the frontier being less than a mile away - and the army is all over the place.

Our plan is to amble southwards along the lake over the next couple of days. Unfortunately, it looks like we will need to start with a big detour inland as the lakeside road is apparently closed due to a broken bridge. In the tourist office, every question we ask seems to require a group meeting. The query about the route, however, also requires phoning a friend. We are then told that the road out of town is closed. We try and get a second opinion by posing the same question at the police station, where first there is a need for the general bobby to ask a more senior officer, and then another mini conference is required, and once more the need to phone a friend. We are not sure if the opinion at the other end of the phone is a genuine second opinion or the same friend's opinion a second time. We decide not to risk it and accept that we will need to take the detour. There goes at least half of our amble down the lake shore.

At Kibuye, we look for a rather interesting sounding hostel, but we cannot find it, so we spend the night in a hotel and re-join the lake road in the morning. We continue south - our planned lakeside route only touching the shore two or three times - until we reach the town of Cyangugu. This is another gateway to the DRC and the crossing point is in the town centre. The locals seem to wander across the frontier at will and the army is nowhere in sight. I'd like to pop across and have a quick look but Helen gives a rather emphatic, 'No!'

Filling up with diesel in Africa really means filling up. As I mentioned earlier, in Egypt a tank is not considered full unless at least half a litre or more has run down the side of the vehicle and on to the floor. Elsewhere it is done reasonably carefully, but at least up to the brim. I have even been asked to inspect that it is properly full. I have tried to get them to stop before it is up to the top, especially with the jerry can, but, without resorting to physical force, it is a complete waste of time. Now I patiently watch them poking the froth down with the nozzle so they can see if they can get a few drops in. But here in Cyangugu, we see it taken to a new level. Some fuel stations have a little ramp so you can drive one wheel up on it and raise the corner of the car up, presumably so they can get an extra teaspoon of fuel in the tank. The mind boggles.

This area is really beautiful, making the so-called Riviera at the other end of the lake look like a dump. But, even so, there is not all that much to see, so I spend some of the time looking under the car. It would seem that, due to the bumpy road between the two places and a bit of iffy measuring on my part, I will have to make a minor welding adjustment to my new homemade spare wheel carrier before it gets its real test in Tanzania. Sometime later - I think probably after Tanzania - I find out that the problem was not due to iffy measuring on my part at all, but some failing on the Toyota winding gear.

Going east, we drop out of the mountains and through the Nyungwe forest. Somewhere just over to our left is the source of the Nile, at least the Rwandan source. There are a lot of genocide memorials in Rwanda and we read about one along the road we are taking. It was the site of a college and many people were sheltering there when the killers came. Hundreds of men, women, children and babies were slaughtered by gun and machette. After the conflict, the bodies in this building were preserved with powdered lime, and they are still there to this day. Should one have the desire, it is possible to wander around the classrooms and corridors to view these mutilated remains. Why anybody would want to do this, I just cannot imagine. Maybe it is an acceptable practice in Africa, but it is definitely not for us.

Driving through the Parc National Nyungwe Forest, we see some Angolan Colobus monkeys. We are not big monkey fans. We have had prior experience of baboons - the thieving wotsits - stealing stuff from us. In a lot of camps, they are always on the lookout for foodstuffs and we always have to be on guard. They also parade about, showing their bright red bare bottoms to the world, which probably helps to put them on the bottom of our popularity list. The Vervet monkey is another chancer when it comes to nicking foodstuffs and also has the habit of posing their privates as they strut around, showing off their bright blue testicles. They are also low on our list. The Angolan, the Red Faced and the Black and White Colobus monkeys all look nice enough though, as long as they stay in their place.

On one of our drives around the countryside, we come by a load of kids on their way home from school. Like kids the world over, they are all released the same time, but then they somehow spread themselves out over a great distance as they amble home. These kids, however, unlike most kids the world over on their way home, all carry three house bricks on their head. They have some leaves on their head and then three bricks on top. Don't ask, we tried and did not get anywhere.

By luck, or magic, but not necessarily good navigation, we make our way to the town of Butare, which is also known as Huve. We have three maps for Rwanda; our road atlas and two tourist maps. Many towns appear to have different names, depending on which map you look at, and at least one town has a name that is not on any of the maps. To add to the problem, most of the road signs only point to districts and not towns, but these districts are not marked on any of the maps. Helen is really beginning to hate being navigator and here I do have some sympathy for her.

We find a hotel that was in the past frequented by the Belgian royal family, Rwanda once being a Belgian colony. I suspect they did not stay in this room, it is not the best. The whole hotel is a bit run down and has definitely seen better days. We both opt for a steak at dinner. Mine is as tough as old boots, I cannot even cut it with the knife. I complain to the waiter, but he just shrugs his shoulders and walks away. When we have finished - apart from my steak - a waiter comes to clear our plates and I also complain to him. He promises to speak to somebody, and clears our plates away. Less than a minute later, he is back with the bill for the full amount. This leads to a rather warm discussion and, in the end, I pay what I think is fair and leave. I am sure the standards have slipped since the Belgian royals stopped coming here, or at least I assume that they have stopped coming. Funnily enough, this was the first hotel we had seen when we entered town and, although it looked a bit tired, we thought it looked too expensive for us. Having carried on down the main street, out the other side of town, turned around, up and down a few side streets, we found nothing else. It looked like the only place in town. Ultimately, I suppose the price was alright and our room was clean, although rather lacklustre. The restaurant was a dingy faded shadow of its former self.

After leaving here, we embark on a very rough dirt road. We have quite a long way to go and, on numerous occasions, have to ask the way from people who do not speak English, who are not sure where they are, and do not know where the next place is. Eventually, we are within sight of our destination; some wetland area, so I can do some bird spotting. We, however, are up a hill and the wetlands are at the bottom. I can see where I want to be, but I cannot find a way down. Again, I need the assistance of the locals. I point, 'I want to go down there.' And with lots of arm waving this way and that, they indicate I should take this footpath-width track. I indicate that I am in a car. *No problem*, is the indicated reply. So, off we go. The Sat Nag immediately bursts into 'We can't go down there' mode. But we criss-cross the hillside one footpath after another, following one set of directions after another. I am listening to the constant 'We can't go down there!' and thinking, *There is no point in having a go-anywhere vehicle if you can't go anywhere*. All the time I am hoping that we can get out at the other end, as there is absolutely no way we can turn around.

After an age of driving through sweetcorn, sugarcane, coffee, sunflowers and God knows what else, and seemingly getting no closer to the water, I decide that I have done enough bird-watching for one day, so we try and find our way out and back onto the main road. Once again, I am directed to a track narrower than the car, but several other locals appear to be in disagreement and are pointing down the hill, giving me some doubts as to what I should do. I opt to go up the hill on the narrow track and, as luck would have it, in a short stretch of time, we come to a small tar road. After a much longer stretch of time, we get back onto the main highway.

The Chinese have been busy building roads in Africa. The finished job looks good, but only time will tell; one road is only seven or eight years old and is already in a poor condition. They also don't seem to have mastered embankments; in several places where they have cut through some higher ground, the embankment is often not stable enough and has slipped. In one place, it has come down en mass, complete with trees, grass and bushes, so now there is a garden taking up more than half of the width of the road. Back on one road in Uganda, where they were still working, a landslide of hundreds of tons of embankment had slid down and blocked a completed section of road. The construction crew were just a couple of miles or so down the road, but they had to stop work and bring diggers, trucks, shovels and brooms, and spend a couple of days clearing all this slippage off the brand new road. Here in Rwanda, it looks like the Chinese are diligently working away with basically the same rate of success.

Having failed everywhere else in Rwanda, we decide, against our better judgement, to try the Akagera

National Park in the hope that it will add some brightness to our stay. I have found some information stating that the Shoebill is present in the park. We had previously decided not to bother coming here as during the period of the genocide the slaughter did not stop with the people, it also included the wildlife, so the area is reasonably deplete of attractions. But I am still looking for the Shoebill and I am willing to put up with the shortage of other wildlife and concentrate on the bird life.

We stop at a posh hotel for the night before reaching Akagera, as everywhere else we have seen so far is either full up, or rather run down. Although it is expensive, we are not taking chances, or so we think. Our meal on the terrace overlooking the lake, watching the sun go down, is spoiled only by the food. In the morning, we have breakfast on the same terrace and it takes an hour for the eggs and bacon to turn up. The waiter then goes to get cups and saucers. Then off he goes again and we are still just looking at our rapidly cooling food. Back he comes with all the condiments and then, on his third trip, he returns with knives and forks. The manager then actually comes over to ask if everything is OK. Needless to say, he does not get a good response; after my diatribe about the lack of staff training and their lack of abilities, he gives a grunt and clears off. Amazing. A further 10 or so miles down the road we find a small town with several hotels and I bet any one of them would have been better than this place. And cheaper.

Entry to the park is the usual routine of form filling, paying too much for too little, paying over the top to camp on a Spartan patch of ground, and nobody working there seems to have any information about the park itself. As we drive around, I get more disappointed by the hour. There is hardly any access to the wetland areas and it would seem with the lack of browsing animals that the vegetation has taken over everything. There are very few birds there of any sort, let alone my Shoebill. We set up camp for the night. In the morning, we think we will cut our losses, go and have a quick look at the savannah, then leave.

Due to some peculiarity in the layout, we have to pass through headquarters to get to the savannah and we have to show our receipt. This is taken to the office and, after a while, I have to follow it and am kept waiting. After what seems to me hours of standing, fuming, it turns out that my receipt is made out in US Dollars and silly me paid in the local Rwandan Francs. So, in the most complicated way imaginable, a new receipt is made out in Francs. As far as I am concerned, we are leaving and they can keep the piece of paper and fiddle about with it in their own time. I cannot understand why they cannot just lay the page in its original place, cross out the dollar payments and write in the franc payments. Or, better still, just write it out on the carbon copy and not delay me at all. But they have to write out another receipt on a new page further on in the book, and keep turning back to the original page - now placed loosely in its original place - to copy the details. So now, in their book, they have one receipt in dollars and one in francs, but only one payment.

I am livid, having to hang around all this time for such a stupid reason. But then we notice that my new receipt has got today's date on it, so is still valid. With this I decide to extend our stay and go to the north end of the park. After a three-hour drive, we get to a ranger station and take the opportunity to pop in and ask, 'Are there Shoebill here?' 'Can we get down to the lake area?' 'Is the north camp open?' 'Where is the best place to see any wildlife?' My questions flow like water. They do not know about the whereabouts of any Shoebill, or even what it is. They point to the lake and say it is over there, but give no indication as to whether it is accessible. One ranger then asks if we have a map. Out comes the map of the park and, with one look to get his bearings, he says, 'This is the north and this is the south, and we are...' His finger is roaming around the map. I point to the spot. 'Yes, here', he replies, and then carries on. 'This is the primary road and it goes all the way down here. Here are the headquarters' On and on and on. I lose interest, as he is describing the route we have just driven up, and all the small turning we took to get here. The only piece of information he gives us is that the north gate is closed. That we already know. But he knows nothing of the north camp. 'Thank you, thank you very much.' We give up and go back to the south camp where we stay the night, but leave the next morning feeling disappointed. I am sure that the awful experience is my punishment for stealing an extra day.

According to our information, Akagera in its heyday was nearly twice the size it is now. During the revolution - I am not sure if can be called a revolution, but for the want of a better word - millions of people fled the country. Then when refugees started coming back after the conflict there was a need for land to house them, so a large portion of this park was taken for this purpose. I am not particularly good at mathematics or logistics but millions of people fled the country, and hundreds of thousands were slaughtered. After the conflict maybe more than half of the refugees returned, and thousands of the perpetrators fled to the DRC, so the sum total of this is that the general population was reduced by nearly one quarter. Why, then, did they need extra land to rehouse them? There is no need to worry about this now as we are definitely going to leave.

In Kibondo, just a few miles short of the border, we decide to stop the night so that we can do the border crossing in the morning. There are two places in our guidebook for this small town. The first one we try is far too dingy. At the second one, we can't manage to make it understood that we want a room. Once again, we are mystified, *Do the staff know what sort of trade a hotel does?* The mind boggles. In the end, we find a really nice place - clean, en-suite bathroom, bar and restaurant - by using our own initiative. Coming out of the shower in the fully tiled and clean bathroom, Helen slips and goes down right onto her back. I think it hurt her, but it frightened the life out of me - she is my navigator, amongst other things - and starting tomorrow we have two weeks of bumpy, dirt roads.

There is not much in the way of camping in Rwanda so we have upped the usage of hotels. Admittedly, we are staying at the budget end. One of the things that amazes us is we get a double room and a breakfast for one. This seems to be an African thing. A double room costs more than a single, obviously, but breakfasts are issued per bed. So the rule is: one bed, one breakfast.

You pay for a double room but if both of you want breakfast that will be extra. *That's Africa*.

Rwandan immigration is easy. Customs for the car takes a bit more effort. Helen hands in the carnet de passage and three men stand around having a conference, with the look of never having seen one before. There is a line of traffic outside; surely this is not the first one they have come across. After a while, they get their act together and start filling out the bits. Then one of them wants to tear out the page we need to get into the next country. He stops, with Helen trying to squeeze between the bars shouting, 'No, no, no! That is for the next country!' He then tries to tear out the page that is our proof that the car has left Rwanda, the one that he has just stamped. But again, he stops when Helen is halfway through the bars screaming at him. Eventually it is all done, he signs the car out on one page and stamps the next blank page. The fool has no idea, or he just does not care how valuable each page of a carnet de passage is, or the potential problems we may have in the future with a stamped blank page. As it happens, we have a couple of pages spare, so we should be OK, but it could limit us changing our plans. Or would do, except we don't really have much of a plan.

Rwanda is a beautiful country; the scenery is great, but most of it is under agriculture and the wild areas that could attract tourists are all but abandoned or deplete of wildlife. Even though we tried our best, I'm afraid we found it boring. Unfortunately, we did not put our best efforts into seeing the gorillas. But such is life. Time to move on.

Leaving Rwanda, we are also theoretically leaving the rainy season. In this region, the official period for the rainy season is from the start of March through until the end of May. We managed to spend the whole of the long rains in this region. I am not sure how much difference it would have made, as this area has four seasons: the 'long rains', the 'short rains', the 'long dry' and, not unsurprisingly, the 'short dry'. Despite being in the region for the whole of the long rains - having entered Kenya at the beginning of March and left Rwanda on the eighth of June - camping almost all of the time, we had surprisingly little trouble with the rain. Had we set off on the journey on a different date, we may have missed these rains, but would have possibly caught some others elsewhere. So, we count our blessings for now.

Why *do* the children carry bricks on their heads?

TANZANIA
10 June

Getting into Tanzania is easier than expected. Well, getting the car in is easier than expected. The last car we brought into this country was the Volvo that had to be abandoned on our previous trip and the entry for that took quite some effort; our passports, driving licenses and all the vehicle documents were photocopied, and loads of forms filled in - somewhere they probably still have everything about us on record - and we had to pay out a small fortune to get a temporary import permit. Then we had to register with the police, and were told off because we had not already registered the car with Interpol. We were checked for fire extinguishers and emergency triangles. When we later had little choice but to abandon the car with its blown-up engine, we had technically imported the vehicle into the country. Possibly, we still owe two or three thousand pounds import duty. This time, however, we have a carnet, which apparently makes things a lot easier. The Customs man does not want to see anything - not even the car - he just stamps the carnet and gets back to his newspaper.

With another stroke of luck, we find there are money changers at the border. Somewhat strangely, none of the banks in these countries deal in their neighbour's currency; it is possible to get UK Pounds, Euros or US Dollars, but not the money of a country a few miles down the road or, in some cases, literally just across the road. At this frontier crossing point from Rwanda, there is a bank right on the border, next to the Immigration office - no town to speak of, only a few wooden shacks - but it does not have currency exchange facilities. *Why is it there?* We've had various issues getting money from ATMs; either the ATMs are not where we are led to believe they are or they don't accept our card. We have a Visa card, usable around the world, except for some of the places we go. We know, or at least according to an internet search we think we know, that there is an ATM at Kigoma, about three days' drive from the frontier, that will take our card, but our cash may not last that long so we are thankful once again for the street money merchants. There is often a whole line of them on one street, all offering the same deal with not much to distinguish between them. We have no idea what exchange rate we will get or whether we will be ripped off, but there is no alternative, so we accept whatever deal is on offer and change our money so we can carry on.

Our route is through a rather remote part of Tanzania. Having said that, Tanzania is big and the road system is poor, so nearly everywhere in the country is remote. We have no idea how we are going to get on. Some while ago I read a book called 'Jupiter's Travels' about a man who motorcycled around the world. This salient phrase after he had run out of petrol has stayed with me: 'I sat down by the side of the road and waited for something to happen, and it always does'. How absolutely right; we have experienced this sort of thing before, so we know there will be no problem. Or maybe that should be, we hope there will be no insurmountable problem.

We have been to Tanzania before, and this time we are only cutting a corner through this far west and remote region, to get to Zambia. We do not want to be too long in the country, just in case news of our presence reaches the ears of whoever dealt with our previously abandoned car, but judging by our experience at the border, I do not think we really have much to worry about.

An hour or two down the road, we come to a village and stop for a drink. The building next door advertises rooms. Helen takes a look and they are acceptable and cheap, with secure car parking, so we decide to stay. It is a little bit early in the day but who cares? Next to us is a man cooking goat, so we enjoy goat and salad for dinner and have another drink. Lovely. In the morning, a man comes up to us as we are packing the car readying to leave, and says breakfast is waiting. *Breakfast?* We only paid about two pounds for the room, which was clean, smart, en-suite, with hot water and electricity, and now we find out we have breakfast included. Wow. Our quite low expectations are exceeded.

Now getting to Kigoma is a priority. This is the town three days from the border with the cash machine. It is on the shores of Lake Tanganyika, the longest and second deepest freshwater lake in the world. The town is at the end of a railway line and has a seaport - maybe lake port is more correct. As it turns out, it is not as interesting as we had hoped. Our first hotel option - one that is in our guidebook - has unfortunately gone from budget to very upmarket and very expensive - several hundred dollars a night - since our book was printed. We find a campsite on the lake shore, but that is very expensive as well, with very little in the way of facilities. So we eventually find a cheap place on the edge of town, where the price includes breakfast. This is not much to write home about, but we do enjoy a huge glass of juice, which we think is called tree tomato. We have had this a few times before and it is really nice, but we still have not found out what it actually is.

Just a few miles down the road, in the village of Ujiji, we stand on the very spot - or probably somewhere in the vicinity of the very spot - where, in November in 1871, the immortal words 'Doctor Livingstone, I presume' were reputedly uttered by newspaperman Henry Morton Stanley, on meeting the famous missionary. It is quite emotive being in the place where such a world famous event took place, but there is nothing of equal standing here to mark it. There is a small museum and a plaque. But there are also a lot of plaques for people who have never even been here.

I am not religious and am not too keen on the effect that it has on unsuspecting tribes people, but I do feel that we ought to admire Livingstone. He made a name for himself as a missionary, explorer and an active anti-slavery campaigner. He travelled around many countries here, including Angola, the DRC, Botswana, Malawi,

Mozambique, Zambia, Tanzania, RZA, and Zimbabwe - although the geography and names would have been different in his day. And these travels would have all been done by ox cart, or on foot, as he transported his family and their belongings all over this harsh, Spartan wilderness. He died relatively young by today's standards, yet he had led a full life, and he truly became a legend in his own lifetime.

From Kigoma, we make our way back up to the main road. I had found on the internet that the Shoebill is present in the Moyowosi game reserve. This reserve is undeveloped for tourism and Kasulu, where we are now staying, is, according to two maps, only about 20 miles away, but nobody here has heard of it, or knows where it is. My navigator is not keen on me roaming the African wilderness looking for an undeveloped reserve in the hopes of seeing an elusive bird, and if the people living almost next to the place know nothing of it, then our chances of finding it are probably pretty slim. It seems I would need to do a lot more research and planning to go there, so I think we are just going to move on. Some months later, I found out what undeveloped, in the game reserve sense, actually means: 'real' wilderness with no roads, no camps, no rangers and no organisation of any sort; I suspect that we would never have been well enough prepared for it, so it is just as well we did not try harder to get there.

We are staying in a comfortable place, but it has no kitchen, so we venture out looking for dinner. We've had various success with eateries. At the first place we find, which looks like a shack, we encounter a language problem in asking about the menu. In this situation, our usual course is to wander around the cooking area to see what is on the go. This ploy has worked successfully for us on a number of occasions, as we can just point to something that looks tasty. In this place, one pot has a meat stew bubbling away so we opt for two bowls of that. A short while later, sitting looking at our bowls of chopped up intestines, bits of pipe and things in gravy, we suddenly lose our appetites. We pay up and leave to try and find somewhere less exotic. On our travels so far, most of the food has ranged from quite good to edible. Some could be put into the category of 'we are desperate to eat, so we will have to give it a go'. But only a couple of times have we come across something like this, where we are not adventurous enough or hungry enough to even give it a try. Thankfully, we then find a hotel restaurant where the food is acceptable. In fact, it even entices us back the following morning for breakfast. We ask for a milky coffee. For some reason that we do not understand the coffee is not available, so we ask if we can have black tea. After a while the waiter tells us that we cannot have tea as there is no hot water, but then he offers, 'Would milk coffee be alright instead?' Now that is Africa!

The hotel, as with most others we have stayed in, provides a mosquito net over the bed. The beds are all a standard size and all the mosquito nets are a standard size. Unfortunately the standard size mosquito net is just a bit smaller than the standard size bed. We frequently have a fight to try and get the net over all four corners of the bed, which is best done from the outside, but it then becomes near impossible to get into bed. One night, my slumber is disturbed when I realise that the net has moved and my arm is hanging over the side of the bed. Something brushes against my arm and I leap instantly from deep sleep to defensive mode, swinging my arm about to beat off whatever it is that has come into the room. A monkey? A leopard? I awaken fully when Helen shouts 'Stop! Stop, it is only me!' as she is trying to refit the mozzie net from the outside.

We have been suffering with a tyre with a slow puncture; every three or four days I have to pump it up. It is not a big deal, so I keep putting off getting the thing sorted, but here, on a corner just across the road from where we are staying, is a place that can fix it. There are places like this throughout the continent, sometimes on a bare patch of earth and sometimes with a bit of a shed or at least a roof over them. They usually have a compressor that looks like it came out of the ark. A lot of them use a homemade sledge hammer to break the seal between tyre and rim, and I have previously always avoided them for fear they may damage the wheel with their zealous swinging of the mighty Thor hammer. While they take my tyre off, I use their airline to blow the sand out of my air filter. I normally bang the sand out, but if I ever get the chance of using an airline, I grab it with both hands. The slow puncture turns out to be a four- inch nail; very little to see on the outside, but a lot of nail dangling inside the tyre. How amazing that such a big nail could have caused such a small leak, and how lucky we were that it held until we could get it sorted.

We continue along our remote route. As I have said, much of the road system is through remote areas but on this section we are faced with more than 600 miles of dirt track. Some stretches are reasonable and some parts are really rough. Looking at the map, the distances between places are not too great but it is not practical to drive very far each day on roads as poor as this. Thankfully, we are finding reasonable places to break the journey without breaking the bank. In Kasulu, a town that is given reasonable significance on the map, we stay in one of the many available hotels and are treated to a huge double bed, electricity, TV, hot water - all very clean and smart for only £6. Tonight we are in the very grubby town of Uvinza, staying in the best lodge we can find. It is very, very basic - water in a bucket, electricity only for a few hours in the evening - and it still costs £4. The eateries in town are particularly disgusting and grim. We get a Fanta and drink it straight from the bottle; the place in no way inspires us to eat there. But at least we can get some of our camping gear out and cook our own food, make our own tea and coffee, on the step of our room.

Uvinza straddles the road south and, according to our map, no turnings and no room for error. We make an early start and are surprised that, despite the fact that it is still the dirt road, it is in really good condition. We are making good time. One and a half hours later, we find that the sun is in completely the wrong place, which means that either there has been some cosmic shift, or we are going in completely the wrong direction. *How have we taken a wrong turning where there are no turnings?* We are on a road where, according to our map, there is no road. We try to find out where we are by asking some locals, but with no success, so we have to rely on the theory that the sun is in the right place and we are wrong. All we can do is turn around and go back to Uvinza to start again. Even though it is only

11am when we get back to town, it is now too late to start on the right route today. The locals think it funny that we should check out and come back three and a half hours later to book in again, but they helpfully shed some light on the road we need. It would seem that the road through the town is a new road that is not on our map - it is actually still under construction - and the road we want is an un-signposted turning off to the right about a mile before town. So, hopefully, better luck tomorrow.

From my school days and up until fairly recently, I imagined Africa as being mostly covered in jungle. I suspect this idea comes from the stories of Tarzan swinging through trees. I believe that there is jungle more to the west in the DRC and maybe other countries, but my new experience has shown Africa to be mainly arid. But here we experience the first dense forest. We drive for an hour or two down a lonely dirt road with dense forest either side. There is no sign of habitation, but then suddenly we see somebody walking, and someone else on a bicycle. It is still another two or three hours' drive for us to get to the next town. *Where have they come from? Where are they going?* There could be villages somewhere off to the left or right through the dense vegetation, but I cannot imagine riding a bike through the jungle. It would not be easy on this road, let alone through the trees, bushes and thickets.

Further down the road, at the town of Mpanda, is the entrance to Katavi National Park. We had planned to visit this park, but find out that it costs 40 Dollars to go in and another 40 for the car. If we want to camp, which we would like to, it will cost 60 Dollars extra. We then find out that the main road to Sumbawanga - our next destination - is closed, and that the detour uses a minor road that goes straight through the middle of the park, for free. We opt for not spending 140 Dollars and just drive straight through. We see a few animals - elephant, giraffe, hippos - but the most populous thing was the tsetse fly and, in our opinion, they were well worth not stopping to look at. So, money well saved.

On reaching the other side of the park, we find out the reason for the road closure: the Chinese engineers are busy with more new road build programs. I have noticed that a lot of these roads appear to be in remote areas and are, therefore, probably not destined for a lot of use. Hopefully, that should increase their lifespan. Sumbawanga is a town of some size. It sits on the junction of several roads; the one we just came in on, one to Dar es Salaam, one to Malawi, and two different routes to Zambia. However, along the road we have just travelled, we have only seen on average two or three other vehicles per day. Understandably, most of the towns are like grubby Uvinza, or Mpanda, and I guess they have little contact with the outside world - the outside world being the rest of Tanzania - but Kasulu, further along the same route, is a bustling place with what appears to be thriving businesses and a number of clean, smart hotels. The main road through that town is tarmacked but none of the side roads, neither before nor after the town boundary. *Why in this isolated town and not the others?* It does not appear to have anything obvious to make it more of a town than any of the other places along the same route, so who knows?

In Sumbawanga, we have a day off, having just completed seven days of hard driving. It has been dirt road all the way, something like 750 miles of difficult driving. One day we did as much as 120 miles - that was six hours of hard work - and I look forward to being back on tarmac. Today, we leave for Zambia on our last 80 miles of dirt road and from then on, everything will be easy.

ZAMBIA
20 June

We are entering Zambia in a remote corner of the country. We had used the internet before leaving Sumbawanga to check on a few things and help us plan our cash flow. According to the Visa ATM finder website, the nearest is probably eight or nine days away. We later spot a few ATMs that the website failed to mention, but as they were not actually working - probably to the lack of cash or something - maybe the website is cleverer than I give it credit for. There is some confusion over the current exchange rate, with two websites confirming that the Zambian Kwacha is currently 8,323 to the pound and another that the Kwacha was rebased as of the first of January this year, making it worth only just over eight to the pound. We are not quite sure what to expect; eight thousand or just eight - it makes quite a difference. We have a drive of over 55 miles to the border, where we hope there are some honest money-changers who will help us with this confusion - we always live in hope - but, if there are no money-changers, it means we will have to turn back and choose another route via a bigger border crossing. We have a big wad of Tanzanian Shillings that will be no

225

good outside of this country.

As we approach the border, the dirt road gets worse for the last 5 miles or so. There are no people, no traffic and not a lot of hope of money-changers. The Tanzanian border post is deserted apart from one man in the office. He is keen to do our paperwork, having probably not seen any customers for a while, but we explain our financial predicament; we need to change our money before we can do any Immigration formalities. Helpfully, he phones a friend, who also phones a friend, and after a while we have several friends all chipping in a handful of Kwachas until eventually they have enough to swap our one million Tanzanian Shillings for a wad of rebased new Kwacha notes. It turns out that some of my internet research was correct and Zambia had rebased its money in January, knocking three noughts off the end, so now the smallest note is one Kwacha instead of one thousand. The one hundred, fifty and twenty Kwacha notes are in good condition, the tens are OK, but the five, two and one Kwacha notes are all in a disgusting condition; they are really grubby, and they are only six months old. *How can the bank notes get into such a disgusting condition in only six months?* This is true of all Third World countries; the low denomination notes always get disgustingly filthy, and barely recognisable as bank notes - in such a short time, it is unbelievable.

With our stash of cash sorted, we complete our Immigration formalities and the carnet for the car. We hope that it is remote enough here for them to have no idea of our previous escapade with the illegally 'imported' Volvo. I am sure that our previous capers are all on the computer system somewhere, but many of the frontier posts do not have computers and, even if they have them, they either do not work due to being broken, or there is no electricity. Most likely, there is also no internet connection with the outside world, so maybe we needn't have been so worried about our old Volvo, but now we are out of Tanzania.

As we drive up to the Zambian border, we are surprised to find it shut; the gate to the country is closed and has a padlock on it. This is the first time I have ever tried to enter a country and found the door closed and locked. About 30 metres away is a brick shed with its back to the border. I slip through a gap in the fence to investigate and it turns out this is the Immigration office. The man inside, who also has his back to his domain, reading his newspaper, seems totally unaware that foreigners are getting through the fence he is guarding, even if it is only to see him. Once he realises we are in his office, he asks to see our passports and the carnet. I have to go back through the hole in the fence to get them and Helen out of the car. After inspecting the two passports and the carnet, our official says, 'The man that does the passports is off sick, and you need to go to Mbala'. That is 25 miles away! It also transpires that he cannot do the carnet, as that is not his job - *What exactly is his job, apart from reading the newspaper?* - and we will have to go Mpulungu, another 20 miles in a different direction, to get the carnet done. But, and this is a big but, he does hold the key to the gate, and he does disturb himself to open up and let us in. At Mbala we find the small Immigration office, get our visas and are stamped in. Mpulungu is on the shore of Lake Tanganyika and we have to go into the docks to find the Customs office. We get the carnet filled in and stamped, and are told we have to pay a carbon tax, but the man with the receipt book for the carbon tax is not there, so we will have to go elsewhere. *How far do we have travel to get two pieces of paper sorted out?* But at least we are in.

Our guidebook claims that entering Zambia from the north is like going into wild country and not the homogenised and neatly packaged tourist Africa that can be found elsewhere. Although it is nothing like as wild as the country we have just left.

We stay the night in Mpulungu and, as it is still fairly early in the day, we take the opportunity to try and clean the car out a bit. This is an on-going job, as dust gets into everything, everywhere. It is one of Helen's main occupations. While I lie under the car looking to see if anything has fallen off - I spend a lot of time under the car checking around, as quite often bits come loose, bits go missing, and nuts and bolts fall out - Helen mops around the interior with a damp cloth. On our previous trip, when we stayed mostly on good roads, we got the car vacuumed a couple of times. This time, we have spent most of our time in the dust and dirt, and we have not yet come across anyone who knows what a vacuum cleaner is, let alone owns one. It also amazes me that our clean clothes, after a day of just sitting in the car, get really grubby. The local school children in nearly every country we have been to so far, wear sparkling white shirts and we have seen them go home from school with shirts still sparkling, and yet they walk along the road to and from school through dust clouds sent up by passing traffic. *How do they stay clean?*

Cleaning duties done, and as much dust removed from the car as possible, we investigate a couple of interesting-looking areas on the lake shore, and the port, but there is not much else for us, so we will head back to Mbala which is at the head of the road south.

We stop to see the nearby Kalambo falls. Nearby, in this context, turns out to be a 45 mile round trip or, to put it another way, three and a half hours of hard work driving on a very bad track. But the falls are worth it; the river drops 230 metres and then winds its way through spectacular scenery to Lake Tanganyika. These falls are second in height - for a single drop - to Tugela Falls in South Africa and third to Angel falls in Venezuela. So we are told. There is a lot of work going on, building a new visitor centre, new toilets and other buildings, but the access road is dreadful and the nearest town, Mbala, is not exactly the epicentre of the tourist industry. I can only imagine what their expectations are.

Leaving Mbala, we are leaving the African rift for the last time. I know I have said that before, but what I did not know then is that the rift has a tributary, maybe more than one. It starts in the north of Uganda in (or under) lake Albert, runs down the Semliki Valley, along Lake Kivu in Rwanda, and along Lake Tanganyika and on to Lake Malawi where it joins the main rift. Or at least that's what I think from what I have been able to work out. This is something that makes you realise how little we know about the world and I do actually ponder, as I prove that I don't know much about where I am or what we are doing, that perhaps I should not be let loose on the world. But they do say that travel broadens your horizons.

On entering Zambia, we found a camping place for our first two nights, but now we are having to stay in hotels. We arrive to book in for the night and come across a little problem: the registration form requires standard information, like name, date of arrival, where from, where to, and what tribe. Strictly speaking, I do not know what tribe Helen is from or, come to that, what my tribe is! And there is not enough room to put in both of our tribes. We find that most black Africans are not happy if you do not fill in all of the boxes on the form. Hopefully, as we are white, they will understand our predicament on this one.

After a few days of driving in Zambia, we realise that nobody jumps out of our way. In the last several countries that we have been through, people walking along the roadside would leap off the road at our approach - literally bounding across ditches or jumping into a hedge. Even cyclists would leap off of their bikes or ride into fields. I thought this was a funny practice until I remembered how the average African drives and I realised that the pedestrians are seriously running for their lives. If only they had known that we are British! Also, in previous countries, a lot of livestock wander about freely, particularly goats and chickens. They roam all over the road and then run like mad when they realise that a vehicle is close by. We have chewed our way through a few very tough goats and chickens and now we can see how they build up that toughness. I am sure some of the chickens we have eaten could have gone ten rounds with Mike Tyson. But, as well as the seemingly better driving standards here, we are not getting the same wandering farmyard problem, so hopefully our meals will also get better.

Within minutes of this thought, we encounter a cowherd driving his charges out onto the road in front of us. We stop and watch the cows amble across the road as the cowherd runs back and forth, whacking them with a stick. One very small calf is particularly slow, all the rest have crossed, but this one is still on the road. The cowherd jogs around, kicking this small animal up the backside and laughs as he looks at us. However, whilst looking at us he doesn't notice that the calf has stopped still and he trips fully over it. He gets himself up, kicks the calf again, looks at us and laughs again, kicks the calf once more for luck, and they are off. We set off again too with something to laugh at as we continue down the road.

The herd of cows made an amusing change from some of the pointless road barriers we have encountered. Not just here in Zambia, but in many of the countries, we drive down the road and there is a barrier - a typical African affair, some sort of gate made out of scaffold poles, a pole across a couple of oil drums, or a rope with some tatty bits of rag attached and, as we approach, someone opens the barrier and we drive straight through. Sometimes there is a group of three, four or five people sitting there all day doing this, and some of them are armed. At the end of their shift, they leave the gates open and go home. We haven't yet worked out what this is all about, but I would imagine that, if there are any shifty individuals about, they could merely travel through at night, when the watch has knocked off for the day.

The sights and scenes along the roadside prompt some observations and reflections on the African culture. I have mentioned the fuel tank filling at petrol stations, where they do not consider it full until it is overflowing onto their feet. We notice here in Zambia, as in other African countries, that charcoal is used a lot and I think most of it is sold at the roadside; there are sacks of charcoal lined up for sale everywhere. It would seem, though, that nobody can find a big enough bag, as when the sacks get nearly full the vendors push some lengths of split bamboo or something similar into the edges of the sack and build up the charcoal pile until it is at least half the height again, before tying it in with raffia. Almost every vehicle on the road - lorries, buses, vans - have these overflowing sacks of charcoal stashed away somewhere. Obviously buying your charcoal at these roadside places is the thing to do, but unfortunately we have to get ours from the supermarket; these great overflowing bags may be a bargain, but we have nowhere to stash it. Vegetables and fruit are treated in the same way; potatoes are sold by the bucket and, once the bucket is full, potatoes are then neatly stacked until the pile comes up to a point with one single potato on the top. Onions, oranges and tomatoes, the same. It is possible to ask for a medium pot or a small pot, but they are served in the same way, even the small pot is piled high up to a point. It must be something in the African psyche that nobody will buy any of these goods unless it is piled high and you are perceived to get your money's worth. I must admit that I can't understand only needing a small amount of something, but refusing to buy it unless it is overflowing or piled high!

Way back in Ethiopia, we could stop for a coffee as often as we liked, but, since leaving there, all of the countries that we have been through appear to only have alcohol available. Towns only seem to have 'bottle shops' and even in small villages it is the same. As we drive through small shanty villages there are quite few sheds that are bottle shops; some people must walk for miles to get to these places for a drink, unless the people in the village drink an awful lot. Sometimes the bottle sheds seem to make up about one quarter of the apparent village. It's no good for the thirsty traveller!

Enough of the rants, after four trouble-free days of tarmac, we - or maybe I, really - are hankering for the old hardship again, so we turn right onto dirt roads to head for the Bangweulu Swamp. On the way we will go to Kasanka National Park, which is the administrative centre for the Shoebill Camp. We find a great campsite on the edge of a pond with a variety of birds and a few hippos. The camp has six individual sites, with each neighbour a bit of a walk away through the bushes, but at the moment, we are the only people in the whole camp. In fact, we are told that there is only one other couple in the whole park, and they are in a camp elsewhere in the reserve. The ablutions are rustic but great; the shower requires one of the staff to heat up some water on a fire and put it in a bucket suspended in and over a semicircle of bamboo, the toilet has a proper flush but with the same semicircle of bamboo for the rustic feel. In both cases there is no door, but the opening is strategically-placed, facing a bush so that no passing strangers - or passing wildlife - can see the occupant sitting on the throne. We take various self-guided tours around Kasanka to seek out more wildlife than we can spot from our camp – quite a few birds and some hippos. We find a lookout point, but Helen decides she is not going to bother to look; she is put off by the ladder, or sort of ladder - bits of wood nailed together in a rather whimsical fashion, which changes direction several times as it wends its way up and through a giant tree. I climb it and am rewarded with a view of a vast area of grass, but not much else. This appears to be the low season for animals as well as punters, and it seems the best place is around our campsite after all.

We sort out going to Shoebill Camp, which is one very long (or two shorter) hard day's drive away. We opt for the two-day drive and stop for the night half way at a cultural village. It has brick built huts, flush toilets and hot showers - not exactly my idea of a cultural village. I think the culture was paying for them to put on a song and dance show for us. We are able to camp here, so we buy some firewood from the locals and they end up cooking dinner for us, although Helen has to supply the potatoes. A couple from Holland joins us around the fire and we pass the evening sharing some Euro-culture. After making our own breakfast the next day, we go to the office to pay our bill, which seems to be very complicated. The firewood was paid for on delivery, so we just had to pay for two couples' camping and dinner, but somehow this process gets dragged out for the best part of an hour, putting entries in several books, and doing endless calculations. But eventually we get away, finally arriving at Shoebill Island. We spend the night in the posh camp - big tent, proper beds, a rustic en-suite shower and toilet - not as rustic as the one in the previous camp, nor does it work as well, but it is tiled. This is real wilderness country, and very exciting - dirt roads, six foot high grass, remote villages, vast open plains and driving through tens of thousands of Black

Lechwe, Zebra, Wattled Cranes and Tsessebes. It is also the very last outpost of the Shoebill. This *is* Africa.

The day of the Shoebill hunt begins and we have a guide in our car with us. For a long drive, off across the grassland through the antelope herds, our guide says, 'This way a bit', 'That way a bit'. It all looks the same to me, but I expect he has his eye on the sun or a tree or something! As we cross a vast open savannah, we spot a few birds along the way. Our guide is able to name them very quickly, which makes life a lot easier for me. *This is great!* We get into a routine - I see them, he names them and Helen notes them down. Then we come to some long grass, some three to four feet high, where luckily there are some wheel tracks to follow. They meander a bit, and weaving along the track, only being able to see the straight bit in front of me, makes the driving a bit interesting. There are also a lot of termite mounds in this area, which I know as I caught sight of some, semi-hidden in the tall grass at the edge of the track. I also know that they are as hard as concrete, as I hit one a while back. I decide it is best to stick to following the wheel tracks and not risk wrecking the front of the car on an ant hill. Even this is tricky though; where there is a bend in the track, it just seems to disappear with all the high grass around it looking just the same. You need to be right on the bend before being able to see where the tracks go. It is all great fun.

We drive as far as we can, which takes about two hours, and then walk for forty-five minutes through mud and water. In places, it is up to knee deep. Then the last leg is by boat to reach a very small hamlet - three or four huts with families living in them. How absolutely astounding that people can live here in these few huts on a patch of land surrounded by waterways and marshes, and this is the dry season – do they move away in the rainy season or manage to live even further cut off by wetland? Two boatmen from this hamlet pole us through narrow channels for the best part of an hour and eventually we come upon our Shoebill. It is a magnificent bird; unfortunately our camera is not up to taking a magnificent photo, but we really enjoy some spectacular sightings and are amazed as this giant and prehistoric-looking bird takes off to move to another fishing spot. We are very, very pleased, not least because last night Helen decided she was not going to come because of the mud, but this morning she changed her mind, and luckily she enjoyed it too. What a fantastic day out and the effort and journey to see this particular bird all formed part of the adventure.

On our way back, driving through the long grass, a ranger flags us down. Two others are with him and they have caught a poacher. They hope that we can take the three of them and their AK47s and the poacher and the poacher's rifle and the dead antelope back to somewhere. As much as I would like to help the rangers in their fight against poachers, fortunately, there is no way we can squeeze them all in. We heard a couple of gunshots from our camp last night, followed by the sound of presumably hundreds of Black Lechwe running through the water, although where we are now is quite some distance from the camp.

For us, it was an effort travelling through this swamp area, even in the dry season, but in April 1873, David Livingstone and his two helpers, Sussi and Chuma, crossed these swamps in the wet season. Livingstone was also very ill, and Sussi and Chuma had to carry him on a litter for much of the distance. By the end of the month, they had got to the village of Chief Chitambo, at LLala. The following morning, Livingstone was discovered dead by his long serving helpers. He died just a few months after his sixtieth birthday, having succumbed to malaria and dysentery. His two followers cut out his heart and buried it under a tree before preserving his body with salt and carrying it over a thousand miles to the coast. From there a British warship carried this great explorer's body back to England and he is now buried at Westminster Abbey in Explorers' Corner. We have come across a lot of places in southern Africa where Livingstone has worked, lived, camped, or even just had his name given to, so I have taken some interest in him. As we drive to Bangweulu, we pass a turning with a big signpost indicating the Livingstone memorial. 'Another Livingstone memorial', we mutter, as there a lot of them all over the place. Sometime later we find out that this one was for the actual place where he had finally come to the end of his African mission. And we just drove past it.

After five days in this delightful piece of wilderness, we are back on the tarmac and heading for Lusaka. We have plans to get some things done in the city, but we usually find that our enthusiasm for these noisy, smelly concrete jungles wanes ever so quickly, and the call of the open road becomes too irresistible. Whenever we park the car there are ten people vying for the job of looking after it, and parking in an area where there are no harassing parking attendants is not always advisable. This is not true of every city, or indeed of every country, but it is one of the niggles that helps hurry us on our way. We want to get a couple of bits for our car, but the Toyota garage fails us in this quest - no big deal at this stage, we will just keep an eye open. We stock up on some other essentials and decide to leave the city after just one day.

We head off to South Luangwa National Park. This is a three-day drive for us, as we do not cover big distances in a day. Our last stop is in the town of Chipata, where we take a day off to stock up on food, diesel, money and try and get our internet dongle sorted out. A failed attempt though and, ultimately, we never got the dongle or the phone working in Zambia. From Chipata we have a 75 mile drive on what was labelled the worst road in the country. Most of it is now under reconstruction and the whole drive is a lot easier and a lot quicker than expected. As we drive down to our chosen campsite, which is outside the park, we encounter two herds of elephants and several antelope. Even in the camp, we see elephants, giraffes, and antelope. But our main aim this time is leopards. We have been to a number of parks that claim they have leopards, but we have yet to see one. I am pinning all our hopes on Luangwa to rectify this situation. I know they are secretive cats and very hard to see, but we remain ever hopeful.

We plan to stop at a place called Wildlife Camp; we have been to this park before and know this camp just outside the park boundary, across a river. It gave us a fantastic experience last time, with elephants wandering through our camp day and night. On our previous visit we did not have the car for the job, or the knowledge to know what the job was. This time we are better equipped and better educated. The 4x4 has paid off; we can drive around a much wider range of terrain than we could do before. As we drive around, we ask other people if they have had any luck. One man says he saw the back end of a leopard disappear into the bush. Two other cars of people say they saw a leopard and we wait with them for it to reappear, but with no luck. Someone else shows us a photo he took of a leopard's backside before it disappeared. We are getting closer but are beginning to despair - it would seem we are always in the nick of too late. But at least we know they are about.

As we now have the right car for the job, we think we might venture further into the park to camp at an even more remote spot to up our chances of leopard spotting. We ask the owner of Wildlife Camp if he can recommend anywhere. 'Lots of places', he replies, but it turns out that there is no camping allowed at any of the camps - 'camp' being a generic title - and the cheapest lodges are around 600-1,000 US Dollars per person per night. That is a tad outside our budget, so we will stay put and go in and out of the park on day trips. We are camped right next to the river with good views and lovely sunsets, so we shouldn't really complain.

Eventually we find our leopard; it has just killed an antelope and is in the throes of dragging it to a tree. We have been looking up trees to see if any leopard is there - always looking for trees where the main trunk has a good incline and a good horizontal branch for the cat to rest on, that being our impression of the perfect leopard tree. However, this tree that the leopard is heading for is very upright and the first branches are some four metres from the ground. The big cat has to climb this with twenty or thirty kilos of dead animal in his mouth. We watch, absolutely fascinated, for almost an hour, but we're not sure it is going to climb this tree and decide to go further into the bush to find a tree that better fits our perceived ideal. So we were not lucky - or patient - enough to see it climb the tree, but next day by some miracle we find the same tree and the leopard is up there with its kill. It is amazing to see it again and we are astounded that it managed to climb this tree. I just cannot believe it, which shows that my theory about the perfect leopard tree is a load of rubbish.

In two days on our own and a night drive with a safari company, we see leopards, and yet more leopards. On the night drive, we watch one for half an hour, stalking in a gulley before it got dark, then it came out onto the open plain. Fantastic! We have now had six sightings of three leopards and that should be enough to satisfy anybody. We are happy but, even so, we would like to see more. The rest of the wildlife put on a good show - herds of various antelopes, giraffes, zebra, buffalo, hippos, crocs, elephants, birds and more. No lions though, once again, no lions, but our day will come I am sure. On our previous trip, we had seen several prides of lions, but this time they are a bit scarce, which could be due to seasonal migrations. South Luangwa is a fantastic park that I had once read about in a low-grade travel book, written - poorly - by a newspaper writer and part-time ornithologist. Somehow his description of the park inspired us to come here. Now, on our second visit, we are equally happy that we did and just hope we get the chance to come again. We love it.

Now we have to retrace our steps down the T4 Great East Road, back to Lusaka, for a bit of shopping and to fill up with fuel for the next leg. In preparation for heading into Zimbabwe, we change our remaining Kwacha for US Dollars, but as we are checking out of Zambia, we are reminded that we still need to pay our carbon tax. Unfortunately, the man with the receipt book is here, so we cannot put it off any more and, according to the law of inverse probabilities, or whatever it is, he needs paying in Kwachas. I'm sure if we were paying for a visa they would want the money in US Dollars. So now I have to go out onto the street to find a money-changer to swap back some of my newly changed Dollars.

Zambia is vast, so there are a lot of areas that we did not get to on our journey, but we had a fantastic time and I would like to come back again someday. But for now, onward to Zimbabwe. We were going to take the main road all the way, but the owner of the camp we stayed at last night gave us a new plan.

Camp life

Bush shower

On the hunt for Shoebill across the grassland

On the hunt for Shoebill by boat

Leopard kill

Relaxing after a hard day's safari

ZIMBABWE
15 July

We take a short cut to get into Zimbabwe, down a small side road for about 40 miles to the village of Siavonga, where we camp for the night right on the shore of Lake Kariba. From here the following morning we drive across the vast dam that created the 68 mile long Lake Kariba. Customs and Immigration are at the top of the valley on either side of the dam. Entering Zimbabwe is very easy and quick. We are asked by an official if we have a present for them from our country, to which we reply no, as we know what he really wants. So he goes on to say, 'Anything will do, even any clothes'. Again we reply in the negative and tell him the only clothes we have are what we are wearing. The last and final try is a bit more blatant, 'How about a few dollars then?' To which we can honestly answer, 'We do not have dollars in our country'. And we carry on to the small town of Kariba.

In the sprawling, grubby town, wildlife comes out of the bush and wanders the streets. It is a bit unusual, at least for us, to see cars and pedestrians wander down the road in the company of zebras. On our way to the campsite, we see elephants at the roadside and we even have to sit and wait for one to move out of the way of the gate so we can go through to the camp. There are hippos wandering around the camp at night and crocs basking in the sun on the lake shore, just outside the bar, during the day.

Upon reaching camp, we pitch our tent in the shade of a Jacaranda tree. I just *had* to write that; it is so evocative of Africa to me. So many authors have written such a phrase in so many books and I have been waiting for an opportunity to use it myself. The tent may not be in the best of places - there is a water tap and a braii (BBQ) to hand, but not much more - and the shade of a Jacaranda tree is much the same as the shade of any other tree, as far as I can tell, but purely from the romantic point of view, that is where I just had to pitch the tent. Or rather, where I had to get Helen to pitch the tent.

We spend a couple of days in Kariba, looking at a couple of sights, walking over the dam that we have just driven over, and finding out where to go next. We are told that there is an area nearby with quite a good chance of seeing some wildlife, so off we go, following our simple instructions, probably exactly, but I think the directions must be wrong. After 'Go out the gate, turn right onto the track' nothing else matches. We give up on animal watching and head north to see if we can find the lake shore. Huge areas along the water's edge have been taken over by crocodile farms. We drive around these security-fenced areas housing thousands - or more likely tens of thousands - of crocs of all sizes, all just lying there, waiting. Waiting to become a handbag, or a pair of shoes. Some are really huge buggers, so they must have already been waiting a very long time. We cannot find a gap anywhere between these crocodile farms, so we give up on finding the lake shore and head back to camp for a brew.

From Kariba we go to the Mana Pools safari area. This is one of the places that I had on my wish-list to visit, but I have been put off. Our guidebook mentions it, but the review is written in such a funky way that I conclude that it is not for us. It is also another park where the booking and the payments have to done in the capital, Harare, which also helped to put me off. But the owner of our campsite really recommends it and says there is a parks office up the road where it should be possible to bypass the bureaucracy of the capital, so there we will go. At the parks office we manage to get booked in and a permit to enter the area. There is a bit more of a drive on tarmac and then a long and terrible drive on a dreadfully corrugated dirt road, but eventually we arrive. At the camp office, they show us the camp map and offer a whole range of sites, 'Take you pick'. We pick one, then another, and yet another, and at each one we choose we are told, 'Sorry, not there'. After a while, we are allocated a site, so off we go to set up tent.

We are now on the banks of the Zambezi and, for a change, we have hyenas, antelope and honey badgers as our night-time visitors. We take several drives around the park. You are allowed to get out of your car and walk around here, although you are advised to keep a wary eye out for lions. We dare to walk around in a couple of places, and I get neck ache from swivelling my head round a lot looking for lions. We don't actually see any from the car or on foot. It is a great camp and a good park, but unfortunately not a lot of game around at the moment. We need a lot more luck than we have with us.

We decide to stay an extra day and, back at the campsite office, they have to e-mail the head office in Harare to see if there are any vacancies on the site that is just outside the window here. We pop back to the office a couple of times to see if they have any news from HQ but no, so we pay for another night anyway and tell them to come and tell us if they need us to move. I do not think that I will ever get used to the pan-African working systems.

Whilst out on a drive, we see a guide in a safari truck, so we ask where is good to go. He tells us of a lion kill yesterday and says the lions should still be there if there is still meat left. We race off like bats out of somewhere, but, unfortunately, we only find a naked carcass. About one hundred metres away from this feast there is a camp of three or four tents. Wow, they must have a story to tell with a lion kill right outside their tent. *Why do other people always get the luck?*

We leave the next day and, as we head south, it is necessary for us to stay in a B&B or two en route. In the first town we try to get a room in, we spend quite a bit of time going from place to place for a vacancy. It turns out that there is a general election coming up and everywhere is full. I think the current President has sent his promotional teams out to the provinces to try and drum up votes.

We try and fail to find accommodation in Harare so we move on to Nyanga, to a one-time home of Cecil Rhodes, where we camp in his front garden, or there about. This place has a bit of altitude and the day time temperature reaches over 35 centigrade, but drops to below freezing at night. If we want to stay any longer, which we do, we will have to sort through our African safari luggage to see what we have that will be suitable for Arctic survival. I awake early, as usual, and, looking outside, I wonder if there is a frost. The winter grass is dead and a very pale yellow, but I decide that the frost is just my imagination, compounded by my weary eyes and the weak morning light. But the following morning, a nine inch high ice stalagmite building under the dripping tap confirms that it is very cold, bleary eyes or not. We manage to sort ourselves out sufficiently and stay for three nights. We keep a fire going just outside the tent at night, partly to cook our dinner on, but also to keep us warm while we sit around it and we hope that maybe some of the heat will drift into the tent.

I need to do some repairs on the tent. I have done a bit of patching, but now we are experiencing zip failure. In the past, anything that had a zip got thrown away when the zip failed, but now I see it as a bit of a challenge to fix them. With pliers and grips, I get the zips working again. I am on a mission to see how long I can make the tent last.

Camping in his front garden has given me a moment to think about Rhodes. To my mind, Cecil Rhodes was an amazing man. He was, by all accounts, a bit of a sickly youth and was shipped out to the colonies at the age of seventeen in the hope that the climate would do him some good. In a relatively short period of time, he became Governor of the Cape Colonies, the early name for present day South Africa. In the following years, he had two countries named after him; North and South Rhodesia. HM Government also asked him to look after Bechuawanaland - nowadays Botswana. He founded the world's largest diamond dealers, DeBeers, owned several houses in a number of countries, including the vast tract of land we are now camping on, which is not only big, but also contains the second highest waterfalls in Africa, three other spectacular falls and the highest point in Zimbabwe. At his peak, he was probably the richest man in the world and I have a feeling that he was not a modest man. He died at the age of forty-nine, but what an amazing achievement for a relatively short time, in a wild and hostile frontier like Victorian Africa. He had hoped to see a railroad from the Cape to Cairo and had put in a lot of railway himself. He also hoped to see British rule during his lifetime, believing that all countries would be better off under British rule. I have spoken to quite a few locals in Asia and Africa and they agree that their country was better off under British rule. On his death, he left all of his wealth in a trust for education of the youth of Southern Rhodesia, as it was then. That trust is still educating the youngsters today. Mugabe, I am sure, will only leave debt and poverty behind. I am not a fan of his.

We are now wandering south, down the eastern highlands. We make a stop in the Bvumba hills at a highly-recommended place called Tony's. We enjoy a really great coffee and a cake in a fantastic setting, but I have to send Helen in to pay for it in case I wilt at the price. We have not had much cake in Africa. One reason is that we are not big cake eaters, and the other is that the cakes in Africa all seem to be too colourful; the display cases in shops are full of a blinding array from lurid lime, bright pink and orange, to blue and yellow, plus most of them have over-the-top colourful decorations. They are painful to look at and do not inspire any desire in us to try them. But the cake at Tony's is delicious.

Tonight we are at 1800 metres altitude and are fed up with cold nights, so we book into a hotel. Helen tells me our dinner - rump steak, cauliflower, peas, carrots and chips, with two ginger beers each (we know how to live!) - is cheaper than the coffee and cake at Tony's. From our bedroom window, we have a view of Chimanimani National Park. We have been put off visiting; apparently the park was restocked and anti-poaching patrols introduced, but either African thinking or lack of money has prevented them from patrolling the park boundary that borders with Mozambique – even more rife with poachers than Zimbabwe - so, apparently, the park has lost a lot of its attractions to the Mozambique bandits.

Although we are generally ambling on our journey, we are also hurrying a bit at the moment because of the upcoming elections. Zimbabwean elections have never made it into the top ten of tourist attractions, as they have a reputation for being accompanied by violence and mayhem, so we want to be out of the country when it all goes down. However, we are now temporarily held up by some medical mayhem. In Uganda, Helen had a problem with her ear, going totally deaf. The first pharmacist we consulted advised to stop taking the anti-malarial drug. Later, a doctor prescribed some antibiotics and other pills. After ten days, she was still having problems, and on the third visit she got some stronger pills. Somewhere further south and still suffering, well, not really suffering, but still deaf on the left side, we visited another doctor in another town. This one was not keen on giving yet more antibiotics, and was not sure what to do, so he called in another doctor, and yet another one. Helen then had three doctors looking in her ear with the aid of a mobile phone torch as they could not find the proper gadget to do the job. They syringed the ear and said the best thing to do was to wait and see. I was not ever so happy at paying for the medical advice of 'wait and see', but this is Africa. Now I appear to have the same affliction, deaf as a post in the left ear. In Mutare, I go to a doctor. He takes my blood pressure and pokes around quite severely in my ear with the right tool for the job, although I am inclined to think that the torch on a mobile phone may have been a bit less painful. He also asks five times how my balance is, and five times I tell him it is fine. I am not sure what his diagnosis is but he prescribes some antihistamines, anti-falling over pills, and some eye drops to put in both ears. I drive down the road muttering to Helen, 'That is twenty dollars down the drain'. I have visions of having to follow Helen's route: one quack doctor after another. But 3 Dollars for the medication and a few days later and, amazingly, I am cured. It seems that eye drops in the ears was the right treatment after all.

Back on the road, we find a nice camp to break the journey to Mutare, which will be our last stop before leaving the country. The facilities are a bit run down, but serviceable. I take the opportunity to do a bit of maintenance and Helen catches up on the domestics, washing and scrubbing etc. We are still quite high here and it is a bit chilly in the evenings, so Helen is going to try and cook a stew on our wood fire. I am looking forward to it. I have never had giraffe stew before. That with jacket potatoes and a drop of red should keep the chill out of our bones. We're mostly cooking our own food and in many shops or supermarkets it is possible to get a huge range of meats - Kudu, Klipspringer, Zebra and Giraffe, to name but a few - and the quality varies between predominantly black and white shopping areas, with a much better quality and variety available in areas with large white populations. This has been the same in several countries. In indigenous areas, the meat is often frozen first and then cut by band saw - some of the cuts can be as big as a dinner plate and more than an inch thick. Sometimes there are chunks of bone in these cuts of up to fifty per cent, and it is still the same price as a cut with little or no bone in it.

Some while ago, the Mugabe Administration had a bit of a problem with inflation; people were spending money quicker than the presses could print it. At the time, Mugabe's answer to the financial crisis was to print more money, which obviously increased the crisis. I think the largest denomination note was ZW$ 100,000,000. He then decided to adopt the US Dollar as the official currency in the hope of stabilising the economy. When we came two or three years ago, we had to make sure all our notes were less than a certain age, as anything with the wrong head cashier on, or pre-2000, or whatever it was, was not acceptable. Now the one dollar notes are a scrungy mess and it is difficult to make out that it is a bank note, let alone what year it was printed.

And they still have a problem with change, as there are no US coins. If your goods come to 10.50 Dollars and you are very lucky, you will get some South African Rand in change. If not, you will get sweets or pens. In a pharmacy, Helen gets ten paracetamol as change; maybe they think I give her a headache. The thing that really winds me up is buying diesel. They always fill the car up to the brim, and won't stop when it reaches, say, 70 Dollars. They poke down the bubbles with the fuel nozzle and continue to squeeze a little more in, until it reaches 70.50 Dollars' worth, but then they have no change. I fume just a little. I ask why they don't stop when it reaches a round figure, so they could avoid the no change problem, but they just look at me as though I am stupid. Sometimes, I think I must be. I try paying the extra over the round number of Dollars with Rand coins, sweets, or whatever is to hand, but they are not very happy with that when the shoe is on the other foot. I just drive down the road, scoffing Helen's surplus paracetamol in an effort to try and calm myself down.

We reach Mutare and find a Toyota dealer. I hate main dealers but I decide to bite the bullet and get the bits we need for the car the easy way.

'I want a bracket like this for my anti-roll bar.'
'Just a moment… No, sorry, we don't have.'
'OK, I want two bolts like this.'
'Just a moment… No, sorry, we don't have. You can go to the auto breakers down the road, they have everything.'

We later tried a Toyota dealer in South Africa for a steering joint and, after a four hour wait, they came back with a list of jobs that needed to be done on the car, but they could not do any of them as they did not have the parts. *I am glad I bought a Toyota!*

We have just heard from Marc, our Spanish motorcycling friend, more than four months after we went our separate ways. He has reached the Cape, so congratulations to him. However, he is unable to sell his motorbike due to South African import restrictions, which is what we thought would be the case, and he has a problem with his temporary import permit, which we do not understand, and will not understand until we experience it ourselves. So Marc has elected to ship his bike back to Spain.

Approaching the border, we are dropping out of the highlands and it is getting warmer again. A day short of the border we come across a National Park called Gonarezhou. We have spoken to someone that has been here and it seems quite interesting, but unfortunately when we reach the gate, it is the old story; we have not booked and paid for entry in Harare, so we cannot go in. This idea of booking in the capital may work for a lot of people taking trips, but it does not work for us.

So, at the frontier, we go to find whatever system is operating at Immigration and then to Customs. It all goes well, even with the usual fiasco with the carnet, so off we go. On the way out from Border Control, we have to hand the gate pass in, only to be told it is not stamped.

'Not stamped by who?' we ask. 'The Customs.' So, back we go to Customs.

Us: 'You did not stamp our gate pass.'

Customs: 'When?'

Helen: 'Two minutes ago!'

Customs: 'I don't remember you. Let me see your carnet.' The carnet is handed over, followed by, 'Oh, yes.'

We get our stamp and away we go again. We get back to the gate man, only to be told that the police have not stamped it either and it is the police that hand them out. So, back to the police we go. He barely turns from his conversation to thump the stamp down - at least it is dealt with quickly - and at last we are done and through the gate. Across the bridge over the Limpopo, quickly through the South African Customs and Immigration and we are in.

Zimbabwe is a super country with a lot to offer but, under the present management, it is very run-down and disorganised. We found it difficult to get to some places and even more difficult to get any information. Due to the financial problems in the country, poaching is rampant; although it occurs a lot in a lot of Africa, most countries seem to be able to effect some sort of control, but Zimbabwe does not have the financial resources to give much protection to the wildlife that may attract foreign visitors and more income for the people. Even in 2013, herds of elephants are being slaughtered in Hwange National Park. And of course there are other animals and other places. Hopefully, one day, that will all change, but I cannot see it happening while Mugabe is here, as even now he is trying to implement new laws which, in my opinion, will impoverish the country even more. Prior to Robert Mugabe's claim to power, South Rhodesia (as it was then) was one of the richest countries in Africa, but under his rule, his policies have made Zimbabwe now one of the poorest.

But now, on to South Africa. I can almost smell the climax of our journey as we approach the southern tip of this vast continent.

Wildlife on the road

More wildlife on the road

SOUTH AFRICA
29 July

Entering South Africa is easy. Immigration and the carnet are simple and straightforward and, when we approach Customs to have the car searched, they just wave us through, saying that I look too old to be smuggling drugs. I am almost on the verge of arguing with him, not wishing to be considered too old for anything, but common sense prevails in the nick of time.

We are in Messina, or Maseena - a town that has two ways of spelling its name, and both are used frequently. According to the guidebook there is a campsite, but our search for it is fruitless; it would appear that the camp has been turned into a residential chalet estate, so we end up in a motel. Here we meet the 'box number problem'. Africa does not have much of a postal system; all the post goes to a local post office and anybody who is likely to receive post has a box number. We are required to enter our box number for room registration and have previously tried explaining to the staff of other hostelries that we do not have a box number because the postman at home delivers the mail to everybody's

260

own house. Here, they seem to wilt and visibly crumble as I try to explain our situation, but they just want a box number for their form. In a moment of minor inspiration I put in Box 123, Rochford. It is like they have been drinking from the fountain of the elixir of life, coming back to full size, big grins and all happy again. From now on, for all forms, we will live at Box 123. It's an easier thing to make up than the name of your tribe!

We have great hopes of getting some work done on the car, having accumulated quite a list of jobs. In two and a half days of driving around town, we try a Toyota main agent, but our Toyota, apparently, does not fit within their remit. This is the third Toyota main agent that does not have spares for our Toyota. They take four hours to tell us what needs to be done - which I already know - and then tell us that they do not carry spares for our car. Eventually, we find a non-Toyota agent to do half a day's work, leaving our jobs list largely intact. They do fit a new steering link for us – after telling us which part we need and sending us somewhere else to buy it ourselves. The mechanical work is the usual African style, that is, undo all the nuts then smack whatever is left with a big hammer until it falls off. After the new part is fitted the car goes into the high-tec tracking bay where the wheel alignment, camber and caster are all set up by computer-controlled, laser-guided four-wheel tracking equipment. This seems a little bit at odds with the hammer swinging next door.

Although we do not get as much done as we would have liked, Messina is the town for car repairs, with loads of garages and auto factors. The town borders Zimbabwe, which is short of everything, so the auto factors here are reasonably equipped for having spare parts for foreign cars and, apart from the Toyota dealers, everywhere is very friendly and helpful and able to find parts for imported cars like ours. After I get used to the way things work - having to trawl around the auto factors looking to buy the parts ourselves and taking them back to the garage to be fitted - I quite enjoy going around, having a laugh in some of the places. As we have a non-local car and have driven down from the UK, most of the people in the factors are keen to talk to us, and very keen to try and help us. We managed to source some shock absorbers and so we have a more comfortable ride, for a while at least.

I end up carrying out a few more repairs myself. One of the light fittings is breaking out of its housing and is not really repairable, but with a squidge of silicon to press the fitting into, we can call it another job done. At home, I have a large shed, I have a work bench and tools, and I have boxes and tins of useful bits. I have to say that I really do miss my shed. Here, on the road, I have a few tools; hopefully enough to be able to carry out minor maintenance and repairs. My kit consists of a bag containing cable ties, duct tape, epoxy resin and some bits of wire. I also have a cocoa pot of handy nuts, bolts, screws and clips etc. We had to drink a lot of cocoa in the evenings to release this pot for service so I could start collecting useful things. It is still a far cry from my shed full of goodies, but I have managed to wire and glue bits back together, and screw and fix things along the way. Usually larger jobs that I don't have the tools for require a garage anyway, or I have managed to borrow something from other - much better equipped - overlanders.

Preparing to leave town, we decide not to visit the Kruger National Park. We have been before and really enjoyed it, but we have now visited a number of parks on our way down, and we think that the Kruger is very sanitised, compared to some we have been lucky to experience in other countries; the roads are all tarmac, the campers sleep in cages - it is almost like driving through a zoo. However, on studying the map, we find we will have quite a difficult route if we want to head straight south. The Kruger is nearly 190 miles long and is easy driving all the way, in the right direction, so we decide that logic should take priority over our preferences, and that will be our route.

Leaving Messina, we miss the petrol station - not a real worry as, according to our map, there are several towns along the way. Our map seems to be a tad wrong though and we only come across a few Spartan little villages on our route. I start to get a little anxious about our fuel reserves, but then all is saved - before it escalates to panic - as we find a village with diesel. The pump is in a field behind a house, down a lane. Not ever so easy to find - even when a man around the corner has told us where it is - and not ever so cheap either, but we fill up and are back in confidence mode again.

On entering the Kruger, and after discussion with the reception staff, we decide to buy a wild card. We can go into any National Park in South Africa as often as we like, valid for one year - which does not matter to us - but the cost is only the equivalent of five days' entry to the park. Despite all their sales patter, however, they cannot actually sell us a wild card here because their computer is down. Apparently we will be able to get one at the campsite. On our way to the first camp we see loads of antelope and have to contend with giraffes and elephants on the road - the tarmac road which is supposed to make life so easy. Tarmac is so under-rated. At the camp they cannot process our booking because their computer is down as well. 'Come back tomorrow' seems to be the catch phrase.

The next day we venture out on a game drive, seeing lots of wildlife, bird life, and lions. *Lions at last!* We were beginning to think all the lions had gone somewhere else on holiday. We watch two females wander through the bush, only a few metres from the road.

Back at camp in the evening, and the computer is running, so we can pay for our camping, buy our wild card and are all set to roll for another year if we choose. We do not actually get a 'wild card', we get a wild piece of paper in lieu of it. Also, as we are foreigners, we have to pay twice as much for the privilege. Once all the paperwork is completed - after a considerable amount of time - the wild card is posted to our home address. We are here, they are here, the parks are here, but the wild card needs to be posted to the other side of the world to turn up several months later. Our wild piece of paper works OK in the most part, with only two encounters of staff, unaware of their own system, who are not happy with it. As far as I am concerned, that is their problem, not mine. *Africa or what?*

Our two day drive just to get somewhere becomes five days of adventure. It is brilliant. We tick off all the 'big five' - lion, leopard, elephant, buffalo and rhino - in one day. Four lions this time - the tide is turning. We also see giraffe, zebra, hippo, our first ever wildebeest - good gnus! The bad news is that there are only thousands of them, not the legendary millions during migration season, but still certainly enough to keep us happy. We stop whilst one or two hundred of them cross the track in front of us.

We join a traffic jam to see something - a common feature of the Kruger as, once people start queuing, it is impossible to get around them on the narrow road. This is one of the things that will dissuade us from coming back here. We eventually find out it is a leopard, but difficult to see, and we are stuck on this much over-rated strip of tarmac until there is a gap in the traffic to get away from the crowds. This is probably the homogenised Africa our guidebook mentioned - it is neat, tidy, over-safe and full of other people, but we do have a fantastic time. Much later, back at home, I read of two incidents of elephants in the Kruger rolling over tourist's cars - maybe it is not as zoo-like as I thought.

From the Kruger, we head for the Golden Gate National Park, on the recommendation of an Australian we met in South Africa about ten years ago. It is in the Drakensberg Mountains, so it is a bit high and it is cold, wet, and miserable. Not a nice night's camping. The birds and other wildlife seem to have left for sunnier climes so we decide to do the same. We pack up our camp, take a speedy whiz around the scenic drive and call it a day.

We used to have a friend in the village of Bulwer. I think we still have the friend, but he no longer lives in Bulwer, he is in the UK. But his ex-neighbours, Johan and Tazzel, still live in the village and we renew our acquaintance with them. Being nice people, they put us up for a few days and we catch up on some of the local politics and gossip. One evening, we go into the wilderness behind their house to race their dogs. They have three greyhounds and a few other dogs. A quad bike is driven away and two of the dogs are released to chase it. One of the greyhounds is apparently not much of a racer, but seems very keen to go, so all three dogs are let go on the next run. It gives up after about thirty yards. A greyhound that does not like running! It doesn't even look just a little bit embarrassed.

After a good time with our hosts, we leave Bulwer armed with information for our route. We make our way south to the coast, the so called 'Wild Coast'. We toddle around fairly slowly, stopping at some really nice places, including Port St Johns and Coffee Bay. Then, at Gonubie, we suffer a dead battery, or perhaps, more correctly, a dying battery. We have two high-capacity batteries and one of them is having a bit of a wobble. We have had to push start the car two or three times in the last month - not too easy with this weighty machine. I would have thought that one heavy duty battery would have turned the engine but no, we have to find a new one. Whilst getting the battery replaced, Helen spots somewhere across the road with a vacuum cleaner, the first we have seen in Africa. She immediately orders me across the road, but I have to calm her down a bit, as we need to go back to the camp to empty the car out first.

First thing next morning, the empty car and I are sent back into town and I get it cleaned out. Helen is now one happy bunny, although, I am not really sure for how long.

Further south we make a detour to the Addo National Park. It was originally set up as an elephant reserve and there are still some sections of the first elephant proof fence around - great lengths of steel and some really hefty timbers. Signs everywhere proclaim, 'Dung Beetles have right of way' and 'Do NOT drive over dung beetles'. Our normal modus operandi in game parks is to drive reasonably slowly, heads swinging from side to side trying to spot wildlife, with an occasional glance at the road to see if we are still on it, and a bit of an eye out for pot holes. Now we also have to keep a sharp look out for beetles rolling balls of elephant poo across the track.

We see quite a few elephants and our first ever meerkats, which is exciting. At night we hear lions roaring but they are fenced out - or rather we are fenced in - protected by a great electrified, elephant-proof fence. They sound very close, if the noise is anything to go by, but we do not see them during the day. A family of Ring-tailed Genets visits our camp; they must have sneaked through the fence.

Carrying on along the coastal road, we come to the famed Garden Route. Several people have said to us over the years, 'If you ever get to South Africa, you must go on the Garden Route'. Well, at least now we can say we have, but I'm afraid I find it dreary and we have to keep finding a way off of it to maintain some interest.

267

We stop at some nice places, including Knysna, Wilderness and Mossel Bay, but most of them are in river valleys and, although spectacular, the sun only reaches into the valleys for a short time each day at this time of year, so it is quite chilly for a big part of the day and definitely cold at night. I believe there is some spectacular wilderness to the north of this route. I wish had known about that earlier, then I could have looked for a more interesting drive. Sometime later, I read an article claiming that the Garden Route is so dreary it is inspiring people to drive faster to get their journey over and done with, and some of this driving is becoming reckless and dangerous. That is our sentiments exactly. Our friend Pete, ex of Bulwer, likes this area a lot - I assume he does not mean the road, but more likely the long distance walks along the wild coastline and the wilderness inland from the road. It is too late now for us, we have blown our chances of finding enjoyment in the remote wilderness of this area.

We reach Cape Agulhus, the southernmost tip of Africa and, geographically, the northern point of the meeting of the Indian and Atlantic Oceans. Standing on this wilderness tip of this great continent, looking out over the conjunction of these two vast oceans, is absolutely amazing. *Next stop: Antarctica.* But it is too windy and cold to stay too long. As we turn northwards from this point, I suppose everything we do now is theoretically on the way home.

But we are still seeking *the* cape, the peak of our journey. Through a bit more mountainous countryside and we get closer, setting up camp in the town of Muitzenberg on the side of the peninsular that is home to the Cape of Good Hope. Here, Cecil Rhodes popped his clogs at the age of forty-nine and his house is now a museum. We have a list of other things to see too, but our priority has to be to get to the pointy bit at the end.

We strike out for Cape Point first thing the next morning – August 26th. The Capes are magnificent. Very bleak, with huge waves crashing on the rocks. We ride up to the old lighthouse in a vernacular and enjoy the view from the top for a while, but it is very windy. Also, in the way of this pioneering journey, we find out that Charles Dickens made it here before us, and on horseback. But, although we have a more modern mode of transport, *We have done it - Rochford to the Cape!* A dream conceived many months ago, now realised, with nearly nine months of overland adventure under our belts. There are probably a lot of people who have flown to the cape but, without blowing my own trumpet too much, that is not quite the same. We will have a glass or two of red tonight.

We are looking forward to exploring more and hopefully tomorrow it will not be so windy. We wake to rain - not enough to put us off entirely, but enough to slow our gallop. Late in the day, it gets very windy and more rainy. We visit a local nature reserve at a bit of a run, trying to get round it and see whatever we can before the threatening rain starts once more. We pass some time in an internet café, mainly because it is warm and dry and they serve a decent coffee - perhaps the rain is putting us off after all. The next day, we wake to even heavier rain and the campsite is starting to flood. We pack everything away wet and decide to leave Cape Town to its own misery. We drive over the cape to the coast road on the western side, where it is very exposed and the rain cuts the visibility down to just a few metres. Water is flowing down the road in torrents and there is a rock fall to add to the hazard. Cape Town is awash as we pass straight through it and away. It wasn't even this wet in Kenya and Uganda during the rainy season, which makes us realise how lucky we have been.

In the town of Bloubergstrand, across the bay from Cape Town, we find *the* place where the iconic photos of Cape Town with the backdrop of Table Mountain can be taken. Our photo shows two cold, wet and miserable people and a car, standing in the rain, with a far-from-iconic dark grey - and very wet - background. Our 'been there, done it' photo does not look triumphal and glorious, and just serves to add to the anticlimax of completing our journey.

But it is not quite time to head home yet. We have a few more weeks of validity on our car's carnet de passage, and no reason to be back in the UK for a while, so we decide to try our luck further north to see if we can escape this rain belt. After days of driving, we reach the town of Springbok and the sun is shining. Hooray! We thought we would never get away from the rain. We settle down with a coffee to plan our next move. What to do? Where to go? Whilst we are thinking, it starts snowing. We look up and realise there is a blizzard out there. Then we get hail, sleet and rain.

This helps to form the plan. We will make a hasty getaway in the morning and leave the county. This rushed plan turns out to be a bit of a mistake as, a couple of months later, we find that there was a more interesting route that we could have taken, but such is life. We find a place to stay, indoors. At dinner - and at breakfast the following morning - we suffer the apparent Africa-wide incidence of rapid table-clearing. We have experienced it a lot and assume that it happens in other African countries as well. After sitting at a table for ages before getting a menu or being asked what you would like, and then waiting ages before being served, the clear-up starts almost immediately upon receipt of your meal. With a forkful of food halfway to your mouth, the plate is suddenly gone. Pick up your cup and the saucer goes. We have even had jams and spreads cleared away whilst sitting there with toast on our plates. Call the waitress over to order another coffee or a dessert and she slaps the bill on the table, and gets most upset when we order more, because they have already made the bill out. Generally, in Africa, service and organisation is slow and poor, but at table-clearing while you are still eating, they are world leaders. This has happened so often we should be used to it by now. Once we finish our highly-begrudged second coffee, we are up and off, ready to clear out of the country.

Our main aim is to find somewhere to sell the car now that it has served its purpose and safely got us to the Cape. We find out the problem that Marc had with his temporary import permit (TIP) - South Africa, Botswana, Namibia, Lesotho and Swaziland are all in a common Customs area, so it is not possible to just pop over a local border and renew the TIP. This dashes any aspirations of selling the car in Namibia or Botswana. We will head for Zambia and try our luck there.

But first, there is just enough time for a little more adventure.

Helen straddles her birth sign

Where the Indian and Atlantic Oceans meet

Cape Point – we made it!

Our postcard home

NAMIBIA
31 August

Leaving South Africa and entering Namibia takes us from rain to sunshine. As we cross the Orange River, we leave the green, verdant, wet countryside behind and venture into the arid, sandy and sunny Namib Desert.

Clearing Immigration is a piece of cake and Customs is almost as easy, once we find them. The road and buildings are under reconstruction, forcing us to take a roundabout route and then search the appropriate temporary shed.

At Customs, we have to acquire a cross border permit and the Customs Officer has to inspect the car and chassis number. Taking him out to the car, I open the bonnet and point to the VIN plate on the bulkhead at the back of the engine. He stands back and says, 'I think the car is too dirty for me to touch, but I am sure the numbers are right. OK you may go'.

We have been to Namibia before and there are some places that we will revisit but our main aim is to try and explore new areas. Our first stop is just outside the town of Keetmanshoop. Adjoining the campsite is the largest stand of Kokabooms - that is Quiver Trees to you and me - in Namibia. These are a weird plant of the Aloe family and a national icon. The camp also has four cheetahs in two fenced areas and 5pm each day is feeding time. We are not big fans of this sort of thing but we go along anyway, just for something to do. We are allowed into the compound with the animals, as long as we do not let them eat us! It is actually a great experience and one of the amazing things we find out is that cheetahs - those big, very fast, killing machines - meow, just like a domestic pussy.

Helen gets talking to a South African camping next to us and, during the cross examination about our trip, Helen reveals that we had no real plan, an out-of-date guidebook, no fridge, and no sat nav. The South African is dumbfounded; he just cannot believe that we have done this whole journey - all the way through Africa - without a fridge! Mind you, he is not the only one. We have crossed a number of agricultural control points at various border crossings. Some of them only want to write down the make, model, and number of the car, and ask us what country we come from and then wave us on our way. *How is that stopping import of disease and pestilence?* At two control points we had to walk on a wet towel whilst they sprayed the tops of the tyres with pesticide. I know it is easier to only spray the top of the wheel, but what is the point of doing it at all if not doing it thoroughly? But then, some check point staff want to see our fridge. Of course we have to tell them we do not have one. They are a little taken aback but then respond with, 'OK, can I see your cooler?' Upon hearing 'We do not have one of those either', they are amazed, but, with a very quick look in the car and seeing no electrical appliances, they wave us on our way.

After learning all we can about the lifecycle of quiver trees, the eating habits of cheetahs, and the travelling requirements of South Africans, we head off to the desert. There is a thermal spring at a place called Ai-Ais and Helen does enjoy a natural hot water dip so we will aim for that. We bypass the Fish River Canyon - the second largest in the world after the Grand Canyon, USA - as we have seen it before. But we do call in at the Canyon Roadhouse, which we had bypassed last time and now have the opportunity to right that wrong.

The place is littered with old cars and ephemera, indoors and out. Cars, petrol pumps, tools and other paraphernalia are interspersed with dining tables and the bar. There is a genuine-looking mock-up of a workshop in the dining room. Even the toilets offer no escape from this memorabilia onslaught with posters - one of a man in the Ladies', and one of a young woman in the Gents' - both scantily clad and with a door in the nether regions. Opening the door triggers ringing of bells and blowing of whistles throughout the building. There are a few sheepish grins coming out of the conveniences. What a fascinating place. I am glad we stopped.

We spend a couple of days at the thermal springs, but the main one is indoors in a tiled pool, which loses some of the magic. It is relaxing nonetheless.

From here, we wander through the wilderness for a few more days to reach a place called Sessrium, where we camp. Further into the wilderness is the National Park of Sossusvlei, a vast area of stunning sand dunes. We have been here before but it was very windy and the sand blowing about meant that my photos of this fantastic area were mediocre. This time, so far, there is no wind. So, up at 5.30am for an early start to capture my perfect photo.

There are a million stars in the sky and it is looking good. It starts to get light as we drive out to the dune area. The clear skies become a little murky and the lighter it gets, the cloudier the sky gets. This means that my wonderful shots of the bright orange dunes against the backdrop of a cobalt blue sky are, yet again, going to stay in my imagination. Even though we have the vehicle to be able to do more than we did last time we came, we do not stop for long. This is a bit of a shame, really, as it is a spectacular area, but my enthusiasm has waned now I know that the fantastic photos I had in mind are not going to become reality.

Leaving Sessrium, we move up the road and spend the night in a place called Solitaire and comfort ourselves with an apple strudel in a café famous for it. This is another place that has remnants of old cars scattered around. It is OK to leave old cars outside in a climate like this; they will last forever.

Then, we strike out into miles and miles of stunning wilderness as we cross the incredible lunarscape of the Namib desert to Walvis Bay. Somewhere along this rough desert road, we hear a peculiar sound. We come to a stop, and so does the noise. We have a flat tyre, which I hadn't noticed – it is impossible to get any feel from the car when it is shaking about so much on these roads. And the noise the car itself was making from all the shaking had drowned out the flat tyre sound.

We change the now knackered tyre for one that is defective and flat. Wheels changed and tyre inflated, we carry on to town. Gone now is my hope that the tyres would last for the whole trip, so in Walvis Bay we have to trawl the tyre shops looking for a set of matching tyres the right size. We do not find a matching set but, eventually, we do find some that are near enough, so now we have four new boots.

We try to explore a bit of the coastline, but some of the sand looks too risky and I am afraid of getting stuck with very little chance of help coming by. There are also vast tracts of land - hundreds of square miles in Namibia and stretching back down to South Africa - designated as 'no go' areas. They belong to diamond companies and they do not like wandering visitors getting lost on their land. This ends our visit to Walvis Bay.

From here, we move to Swakopmund, the second of Namibia's only two seaside resorts of any note. Walvis Bay is a port and has a salt producing area, but the town itself seemed like a grown up shanty town. Swakopmond, on the other hand, is a lovely old characterful place with many German colonial buildings. However, the Benguela Current, which comes up from Antarctica, gives this whole coastline a chilly atmosphere at this time of year, so we do not stay too long before moving inland.

Amazingly, the Benguela Current can create sea mists along this coastline that can reach up to 60 miles inland. It is probable that these sea mists are responsible for the many shipwrecks strewn up and down the famed Skeleton Coast – an occurrence that new technology has, in all likelihood, helped bring to an end. Ever since my school days, I thought it was these shipwrecks that gave this coastline its sobriquet, but there is a more likely - and less dramatic - reason for its name: in the past, the tribe, or tribes, that lived here mainly ate the thousands of seals that inhabit the beaches, and the occasional beached whale. Hence the coastline was littered with the skeletal remains of these animals.

This is such a desolate area, desolate beyond imagination. We have driven this section of coastline before – mile after mile of black sand, with mile after mile of bleak and empty Atlantic Ocean to our left. I cannot imagine what the unfortunate shipwrecked sailors thought if they managed to get ashore and were then faced with this black desolation for as far as the eye can see. It is an interesting experience to have seen the area, but in no way can I recommend it for holidaying.

This time, we choose a different route and venture further inland. We drive into the desert and find a visitor centre near some ancient rock art. After an hour's walk, we reach the Brandenberg White Lady. Some years ago, a French archaeologist, who did not seem to be able to tell the difference between men and women, called the white legged man in the centre of the art work, the White Lady. The name stuck. Our guide tells us there are a lot more examples of rock art in the area. They are estimated to be more than two thousand years old and pre-date the Damara people who live here today. They are attributed to the San, the first known people of Africa.

We also find out from our guide that Namibia is littered with many plants endemic to only one region in the country and the world. A number of trees and bushes are pointed out to us. It is a fascinating walk, but, as usual, I will never remember any of the names or usage of any of the plants.

A bit further up country from the White Lady is a large area of petrified forest. We missed this on our last trip and are not making the same mistake. We take a guided tour and get a thorough run-down on the local flora and fauna. Some weird cacti occur in this very arid area, but some of the plants are even stranger still. One plant - I can't even remember its name - is very slow growing and can live for two hundred years. All it has to show for these centuries of lifetime is a couple of straggly leaves. I feel quite emotional, standing beside it, thinking of its years of struggle to survive. I must be getting old, or sad, or something.

The main attraction here is the petrified tree trunks. According to our guide, these trees drifted here millions of years ago from an area in what is now known as the Democratic Republic of Congo. That is one hell of a distance for trees to wander overland. I get the impression that the trees had fallen before they started their migration, but I am not sure. *Did the petrification take place before or after their journey?* Maybe the fossilising process took place along the way, during a shifting of the land mass. This is definitely a land of wonderment and it doesn't really matter that we don't get all the answers straight away. A lot later, Google informs me that these trees are 280 million years old and were probably washed down in flood waters at the end of one of the Ice Ages.

Namibia is some 320,000 square miles in size, which is something over three times the size of the UK. Almost the whole of the country is desert, forming part of the Kalahari Desert. The population of this vast wilderness is only around 1.85 million. The towns and villages are rather spread out and the majority of the roads are gravel. Most of them are excellent to drive on, a few are not so good, but there are only about nine or ten main tar roads to help the long-distance driver.

We always seem to have the dirtiest car; if it is washed, it is always dirty again by the end of the day. It is quite rare to come across another car in the same state as ours. We drive for miles along some desert road, acquiring a coating of camouflage along the way, and then park next to a row of shiny Land Cruisers. *How do they do it?* Do they fly their cars in? Are the cars washed before anything else is done?

We stop for the night. After settling down, a noise outside our tent wakes us. I venture out to investigate and it is an elephant feeding on the bushes in the camp. He comes over to the bush right next to our tent, not three metres from where I am standing. Helen, who has joined me, takes several paces back, but I just stand, transfixed by this magnificent beast. *This is much better than being fenced in, as in South Africa.*

We continue northwards through some spectacular and beautiful wilderness, reaching the Kunene River and the border with Angola. This is home to the Herero and Himba tribespeople. These two tribes are related and speak the same language but they live and dress completely differently. Both of the tribesmen wear more-or-less Western clothes, although sometimes the Himba men wear a loin cloth with their jacket and T-shirt. The Herero women wear full-length Victorian dresses, with all the petticoats and puffy sleeves, even when working in the fields. They also wear a hat that has some resemblance to horizontal cow horns. The Himba people tend to live a more traditional way, the women covering their bodies with a mixture of red ochre and animal fat. They wear only a couple of squares of goatskin, one front and one back to cover their nether regions. The ochre and fat mixture is added to clay to create some amazing hairstyles.

The Himba are still mainly nomadic, following their goats and the seasons, and living in mud or wooden huts in different places as necessary. Some Himba stay in or near towns, the town of Opuwo in particular, and sell things to tourists. Seeing these women wandering about in town and even in supermarkets with their bosoms swinging about is a bit strange. Our local supermarket in England will not allow entry to women who get up late and need to visit the shop in their pyjamas, and they have not even got their boobs out.

We spot several signs in shops stating: 'No more than 10 kilos of lard per person'. *What an amazing amount of lard to get through in the average kitchen - we would not use that amount in ten years!* But then we realise -

or, rather, are told - it is used for body adornment, not cooking.

On the other end of the spectrum in fashion, we have seen many women in the towns and cities of southern Africa wearing very high heels and very tight skirts. That is OK, if you like that sort of thing, but many of the roads have huge pot holes, the kerbs are often broken or have bits missing and some of the pavements are a bit of an assault course with broken slabs, gaps, missing drain covers – a potential danger with every step. I have no idea how they cope in those shoes as I have enough of a problem in my sandals. Even Helen, who is not a high heel wearer, but is a woman so she should know, is amazed at how these women cope. I suppose being a slave to fashion is enough to overcome anything.

Back into the countryside and in another camp, we enjoy another nocturnal visit by elephants. I climb out of bed to have a look, grabbing a camera rather than my clothes. Unfortunately, it seems that scrambling about naked, in the dark, waving a compact digital camera, does not get David Attenborough quality pictures, but there you go. Of course, there is also the concern that someone else is up, looking at the elephants, carrying a light-up-the-world torch instead of a camera. Neither camera flash nor torches are advised for nocturnal wildlife watching though; bright lights at night can agitate the animals and should be avoided.

One of the things I like about Namibia is that the wildlife roams freely, rather than being enclosed in parks. We see elephants, giraffe, zebra and antelope. We have been told that leopard, cheetah and lion also roam at will and have heard stories of farm animals, chickens, goats and cattle being taken by these big cats. A couple of farmers near Etosha National Park claim that they have lost sixty to eighty head of cattle this year, all of which they put down to lions ranging outside of the park. Knowing that big cats are wandering, unseen, around us adds an extra buzz to the already exciting adventure.

When we arrive at camp in the town of Kamanjab, we discover that, as overlanders, we are eligible to stay for free. An offer we cannot refuse! Our photo is taken for the book and we decide to stay for three nights. Looking through the photo album, we recognise a few people that we have met elsewhere and exchange e-mails to update each other on our whereabouts. We met one couple four years ago, originally in a group planning to drive to Cape Town in five months, but they are still here enjoying life.

To help offset a bit of the free camping we have taken advantage of, we eat dinner in the bar for our last night. Zebra steak and chips! And the meat is not only very nice, but huge - we take our leftovers away for tomorrow's lunch.

And so to Etosha National Park. Unfortunately, according to some locals, the area is suffering its worst drought for thirty years. We expect all the wildlife to be crowding around the few watering holes, but, unfortunately, that is not so. I suspect that a lot of the animals have migrated to wetter parts of the world, or at least wetter parts of their world. But we do see herds of antelope, zebra, and a host of elephants, rhinos and giraffe. Maybe we are getting a bit picky now.

At one waterhole, we are lucky enough to see two rhinos – a mother and baby. The youngster suckles on its mother a couple of times, which is interesting to see. The baby probably weighs half a tonne or so and has a fully-developed horn. It must be uncomfortable for mum as the baby stuffs its horn up into her underside in order to get its lips on her teat. Some mothers have a lot to put up with.

At the same waterhole the next night, four elephants come in to drink. Two of them seem not to be on friendly terms, with one of them not allowing the other next to him at the water. As the group moves around, there is a lot of jostling for position to make sure another elephant always remains between the two antagonists. It is interesting and amusing to watch. Even some pachyderms want nothing more than to get into a fight when they go out for a drink.

Honey Badgers visit the camp every night. Any unattended food is snapped up in an instant, even from inside the tent of the unwary camper. They work as a team to empty the dustbins: two get together to prize the lid off, then one of them hops inside the bin and, with one inside and one out, they rock the bin until it turns over. Most other places we have been have animal-proof dustbins, some have even had elephant-proof water taps, but here, the bins are free-standing. Once the badgers have the bins on their sides, out comes the rubbish to be scattered around the camp, any discarded foodstuffs finding a new home in their tummies. Honey Badgers may have a sweet name, but they are aggressive and vicious, so nobody interferes with their rampage. Every morning, the camp staff have to clear up after them.

On our drive out of the park, we see white elephants. Elephants cover themselves with dust to help deter bugs and things. The ground in Etosha is a white chalk-like substance and the elephants are covered in it. We have seen White Elephants! And I thought they were only mythological beasts.

Further east, near the town of Grootfontein - well, only 90 miles from Grootfontein - we take a trip to see some San people in what is called a living museum. The San were, apparently, the first people in Africa. They are made up of many tribes - the Gana, the Gwi, and others - lumped together as the San, also known, colloquially, as the Bushmen. As a race, they are small of stature, standing at 1.5 metres on average. As other, more well-built, tribespeople moved in, the San got pushed to the more remote parts of the continent.

We would like to find out more about their traditional skills and lifestyle so we visit a mock-up of a traditional village. First, we are given a demonstration of how to start a fire with two bits of wood and some dry grass. The man doing the fire lighting then shows us his axe. It is like an early-day multi-tool. The shaft has a knife slotted inside it, the rather narrow axe head comes off to change the direction of the blade - lengthways it is an axe, crossways it is an adze - and the whole thing can also be used as a pipe. This man, who also happens to be the Shaman, puts something in the appropriate hole in the axe handle, lights it, puffs on it, and then rolls around on the ground rubbing his stomach. We are at a loss as to what this is supposed to signify, but it looks good. God knows what they smoke.

Then, it gets more exciting. Off we go into the bush – that is, Helen and I, the Shaman, an interpreter and some bare-breasted women. The Shaman explains in San language - and with mime - the uses of plants and trees in medicines and food, and the interpreter translates for us what we haven't picked up from the mime. At one plant the Shaman does a lot of belly rubbing and makes a lot of rumbling noises. Then he squats down and makes a lot of raspberry-blowing sounds. We do not need the interpreter to tell us that this plant is a medicine for diarrhoea. This medicine man is not only a Shaman, but also a consummate actor.

We also learn that scraping the bark of the Lavender tree and mixing it with rabbit droppings is what is used for tobacco. Helen and I do not smoke and knowing what he puts in his pipe is never going to tempt us to develop the habit. All sorts of other plants and their uses are pointed out to us. I really enjoy these nature walks, but they are always an information overload, and, afterwards, there is no way I could ever trust myself to remember which leaf, bark or berry comes from what plant, and whether it would save my life or kill me.

I then get to make a traditional San bow and learn how they extract poison from beetle larvae to use on their arrow tips. Bow and arrows at the ready, I follow the Shaman into the bush, tracking a fictional animal spoor: him in a crouched position, moving noiselessly through the bushes; me, in only a semi-crouched position due to my creaking joints, making more noise than a bull elephant. Our trail leads us to a bit of a clearing and there, in the open, is a bundle of dried grass. The Shaman looks round to check if I am ready. Being left-handed, I am holding my bow in a left-handed sort of way, which, apparently, is not the way the San do it. The bow is pulled out of my hand and put into the other one. Now the arrow is on the wrong side so that has to be corrected. All this is done in absolute silence, as we do not want to startle the bunch of hay. When we are ready, the Shaman takes aim, shoots and misses. Now it is my turn. I hit the grass target and kill it. Well, wound it at least – I am not allowed to play with the poisoned arrows. The Bushmen are living in a conservancy area, so they are not allowed to hunt nowadays and these 'hay stalks' just serve to preserve tradition for the tourists.

There is a lot of singing and dancing to finish off the day and then we go back to our camp and the San return to their modern village. Modern, that is, if living in wooden huts instead of grass, but still with no electricity, no drainage and water from a bore hole, can be considered modern. We had a bloody good time, learned a lot and provided a bit of income for the San.

From here, we go back up to the Angolan border again and along the Caprivi Strip. This narrow strip of Namibia is a result of some negotiations by a German named Leo von Caprivi to acquire some land from Botswana, then Bechuanaland, so that the then German West Africa could have access to the then Northern Rhodesia.

We look for a camp that we have stayed at before, only to find that it has gone out of business. We find somewhere else to stop, which is still in business but nowhere near as good as the one we wanted.

The next day, we carry on to the town of Katima Mulilo. As we drive along the strip, a herd of elephants crosses the road in front of us and then a herd of buffalo comes out of the bush, reminding us that this is a wild country.

Tonight we camp on the banks of the Zambezi River and tomorrow we leave for Botswana.

We have been to Namibia before and, therefore, expected this visit to be a short one - maybe about two weeks – but, unexpectedly, we have just clocked up six weeks. We love it. What an awesome country.

We will miss the sand

San Shamen with his pipe for smoking rabbit droppings

BOTSWANA
9 October

Botswana is a real 4x4 country. We have been here before as well, but then we only had a two-wheel-drive car and were very limited in what we could do. We did not know about the wild driving options available. This time, we have the right car for the job.

As we cross the border from Namibia, we are straight into Chobe National Park. We had tried to change some money in Katima Mulilo in Namibia, but one bank did not offer foreign exchange and the other did not have any money. So then we hoped to change our money at the border, but, again, no joy. Although the park goes right up to the Chobe River, and the country's frontier, the actual entrance gate and the pay desk is nearly 60 miles down a very sandy track.

After a long, hard drive, we arrive at the park gate, but we have no acceptable dosh to pay the entrance fee. They will accept GB Pounds, Euros, SA Rand and US Dollars and they point to the list of currencies and exchange rates, but this list does not include the currency from their next door neighbours. Actually, that is not strictly true, as they will take South African Rand, and that is next door - the SA Rand and the Namib Dollar are the same value and are legal tender in each other's country - but our Namib Dollars are of no value here. We offer a credit or debit card, but they cannot process a payment. They point, once again, to the list of acceptable currencies and their exchange rates. Once again, we tell them 'We only have Namibian Dollars'. They suggest that we go to Kasane, where there is an ATM. That is all the way back up the sandy track, turn right and drive a few more miles. There is no way I am doing that and then coming back again. Then, after a while, one of them has an idea and, after a phone call or two, it is agreed that we can pay in the park office in the town of Maun in the south, after leaving the park.

Once away from the office, we start off stuck behind a convoy of four cars – two South African and two Namibian. Unfortunately, they had all the right paperwork and the right money, so, whilst we we had been mucking about trying to get in, these four had sneaked in front of us. The track has a lot of deep sand, and is not easy to drive so they are making slow progress. Despite the fact that they are locals, so to speak, and they have outdoorsy trucks full of outdoorsy gear, I manage to overtake all of them.

My all-wheel-drive gearbox has two gear levers: one to go through the gears and one to go from two-wheel-drive to four-wheel-drive, high range, and then to four-wheel-drive, low range. We are racing along, sort of, on firm ground in 2WD and, suddenly, Boofff! Into deep sand. We need 4WD and low range as quick as possible. We continue to travel along, eyes glued to the track, trying to spot the hard sand from the soft, with me gripping the wheel for dear life whilst fumbling about with two gear sticks. This is really hard work. By the time we reach a camp - 70 miles later - I am knackered, and then a full two hours after us, the convoy of locals turns up.

Arriving at the camp, halfway through the park, we are a bit shocked - or maybe a lot shocked - to find out it costs 100 US Dollars a night to stay here. They are, again, unable to accept Namibian Dollars or credit card payment. My first reaction is to drive on, but there is still a very long way to go to get through the park and I am now tired. We have got to stop, no matter what.

I remember that we have some US Dollars saved in preparation for our next visa, so we bite the bullet and pay out one hundred of our precious dollars to stay the night. We had planned to spend two days here, but, having a very low opinion of the camp and an even lower opinion of the price, we will move on after just one night.

The toilet block is surrounded by a huge fortress, or stockade, that appears to have been built to keep out the biggest and strongest of animals. We cannot even find a water tap anywhere. But then I see a man get down onto his knees and reach through a very low hole in a concrete block and water squirts out of the side of it. Apparently, these concrete blocks - which I had seen before but not understood - are the elephant-proof taps that I have heard of. And tourist-proof as well to the uninitiated.

Leaving, we continue on the same sand road. We had met someone in the camp who came in this way and they said that it was a dreadful road. It runs along a sand ridge through the park. After a while, as a bit of a distraction, we turn off to look at a marsh area. It is laden with game and it also turns out that we can continue this way to the exit. This route is a lot longer but much easier driving and so we avoid the rest of the sand ridge road.

When we reach the exit, the woman at the gate starts laying into me about not paying on entry. I explain our financial predicament to her and she says we can pay here and now. *Great.* We follow her into the office and then we go through the same process of acceptable currencies and their exchange rates. I remind her about our lack of acceptable of money. She gives me some more stick about not paying on the way in. I tell her that we had agreed with the people at the other gate that we would pay at the parks office in Maun. 'What other gate?' is her response. She does not even know that there are other entrances to the park and still berates me for not complying fully with their system.

For the second time in almost a year, I lose my cool. The African mentality is a real wind-up for me. Nice people, but so difficult to understand. I give her my opinion on how they should operate and actually do some work, but, most of all, actually know something about the job they are supposed to be doing.

Surprisingly, we make it away unscathed and, in Maun, we successfully pay for our visit to Chobe. We also decide to book and pay here to go to Mabuasehube, one of the parks in the central Kalahari. However, we need to tell them the dates we want to be there. For the last year (or maybe a lot longer), I have not known what the date, day or time is. Now I need all my fingers and a lot of help to work out when we will be at Mabuasehube, as we have other places we want to visit as we wend our way there. This is a big problem in Africa, at least for us. The need to book and pay for things ahead of time and a long way from where they are does not suit our meandering style of travel.

From Maun, we move on to Sepupa Swamp on the Okavango Delta. We have been here before and know it is a good place for birding, but, unfortunately, it is very dry at the moment and the birds are few. A boat trip might enhance our chances of seeing things. However, a bush fire has been raging across the countryside, so, before booking, I ask about the effects of it. 'No problem', they say. 'The fire is a long way back from the river.' I am, therefore, somewhat disappointed as we motor past a lot of fire-ravaged riverbank. The fire may be a long way back from the river now, but a day or two ago, it clearly was not. There there hundreds of thousands of hectares of reedbed along the Okavango River. People harvest the reeds for thatching and other uses, camping out whilst cutting and gathering an area. Apparently, it is not uncommon to set the area alight with a camp fire.

But, there are some areas of unburnt riverbank and we catch glimpses of some wildlife. We see a group of African Skimmers - birds with a longer bottom bill to skim the water for food - and our boatman explains that these birds are in decline in the area and are now at risk. Apparently, the main problem is the boats; the Skimmers lay their eggs on sand banks and the wash from passing tourist boats washes the eggs away. Our boatman goes on to say, 'If you saw *our* wash, it went right up onto the sand'. *Maybe you should drive your boats more carefully to conserve the attractions that are giving you your living then,* think I.

At the town of Ghanzi, we realise that we are not going to be at Mabuasehube on the right date that we have paid for, so we try to phone the park office at Maun. After three phone calls and not being able to speak to anybody who understands that we want to change our dates, we give up and go to the tourist office to see if they can help. The nice lady there tells us that there is a parks office in town and it will be easy to find if we can give two fat ladies a lift there. She does not quite phrase it like that, but that is how I translate it when I see our prospective passengers. We have to shift a lot of gear to get them in. The very nice lady at the local parks office needs to make four more phone calls to the Maun HQ before she gets our simple date change agreed.

As we drive towards our bit of Kalahari, a check of our map shows that we need to go to Tshane and then take a trail to Mabuasehube. In Tshane, I ask someone the way and he tells me 'Straight down, straight down the road'. We get to the end of the tar and then it is sand. Deep sand. Into four-wheel-drive, low range, and we are still struggling. There is nearly 60 miles of this to go, and after fifty metres I want to give up. At this speed, it will take far too long and in this gear we will not have enough fuel to get there and back. I call it a day. What a shame that we have had to pay in advance to visit a park that I now consider too difficult to get to. On our way back, the man whom I had asked the way flags us down and asks why we have turned back. 'Sand', I say. 'Too much sand'. 'Ahh, yes', he says. 'There is too much sand that way. You should go to Lokhwabe (another village). There is a better road that way. It is all gravel.' 'Thaaank yoouu, ' I say, through gritted teeth.

This is not the first time we have come across this sort of thing and I know it will not be the last. I just wish he could have told us of the other road in the first place, but such is life.

On our way to Lokhwabe we spot a parks office. We call in and ask if they can tell us where the road to the park is. Four of them have a bit of a conflab, but it would seem that, although they all work for the National Parks, they have very little idea of where the nearest park is or how to get there. They suggest we carry on to Lokhwabe and ask someone there. *Africa!*

After a while, and three attempts, we find the road. It is quite good – not gravel all the way and actually pretty hard going in places, but certainly a lot easier than deep sand all the way.

Upon reaching the park and presenting our booking papers, the man in reception is totally confused. We have been allocated campsite KTENG-03, which he does not understand. All the campsites have a designation of a letter group, but this man has never heard of ours. He phones the booking office in the capital, Gaborone, going over the heads of the people in Maun with whom we have booked. After half an hour with several phone calls to and from HQ, the person at the other end appears to ask our man where he is calling from. I hear him say, 'Gate three'. I then think the person at the other end says something like, 'If you look out of your window, you can see camp KTENG, and site 03 is there'. Not more than 50 metres from his office and he has never heard of it. Now he knows where it is, he is able to direct us to it. We stand in the doorway of his office and he says, 'You see that green roof over there? That is your camp'. Whilst on a roll, we ask where are the best places to see any wildlife. 'Everywhere', he replies. This sounds good. Off we go to pitch our tent.

Botswana is currently experiencing the longest, driest, dry season for many years. I have seen many photos of lions sleeping in the shade of - or even in - people's tents. I have great expectations. But with the pans (waterholes) all dry, I think the lion food has wandered off to wetter places and the lions have gone with them. So we do not stay as long as planned, even after all the hard work getting here. When the man at the gate asks why we are leaving early, I explain my theory about all the animals going off in search of water. He agrees that is probably the case.

The roads here seem to track endlessly through the Kalahari desert. On one of these roads, somewhere in the middle of the desert, the speed limit suddenly drops from 70mph to 30mph. This was unnoticed by me at the time, but, unfortunately, the speed trap noticed me still doing 45mph, resulting in reams of paperwork and a £20 fine.

Later in the day, after we have made camp, Helen pops out to the shops. Somehow she reverses into a tree, denting the driver's door and bending the running step. I am not sure how she managed to reverse into a tree and yet hit the side of the car near the front and damage the driver's door. It must be a woman thing.

I make a start on fixing this damage and remember that the car was making a juddering noise, which seemed to be getting worse throughout the day, so I crawl underneath for a look. Bad news: the rear universal joint on the prop shaft is knackered. I hope tomorrow will be better.

By mid-morning the next day, we have the prop shaft repaired, having been directed to a shed where a man specialises in repairing prop shafts. What luck and what service! So, now we head for Moremi Park in the Okavango Delta – the only river delta in the world that does not empty into the sea. Instead, it empties into the Kalahari Desert. Apparently, here lions abound.

On our first morning, I get up early, sit outside with my tea and book and watch the sun come up. Later, talking to a couple of rangers, they tell me that, whilst I was reading my book, two lions walked along the edge of campsites 5 and 6 and then through camp 7. We are in camp 6. *I was slurping tea and two lions were prancing about behind my back!*

Then next morning, I set my chair the other way around, but still I see nothing. When Helen gets up, we notice lion paw prints in the sand all around the edge of the tent and the car. It would seem that this time when the lions visited, not only were we facing the wrong way, but we were also asleep.

We go on some game drives to increase our chances. We see a lot of elephants, zebra and giraffes. Commonplace but great to see, nonetheless. Then, as we are driving along, a leopard appears from out of the bush. I stop the car, heart pounding, and it walks slowly past, almost within arm's reach of me. It stops by the back of the car and sits down. We crane our necks to see. After a couple of minutes, it just carries on along the track. We turn around to follow it. He (or she) then turns off into the bush again. We continue a bit further and wait at what we think is the other side of the bit of bush that the leopard went into. A group of five antelopes is standing near the area we are staking out. They glance at us and then look about with a startled appearance before suddenly taking flight. We fully expect our cat to be the reason for this alert so we wait a bit more in anticipation, hoping that the leopard will come chasing out of the bush. But nothing happens. In the end, we give up and carry on, still very excited with our encounter and buzzing with misplaced optimism.

A few days later, from a place called Gweta, I have a chance to drive on the Makgadikgadi salt pans. It is about 60 miles across vast wilderness to get to our destination. We have the GPS coordinates locked in and we are off, with a healthy dose of trepidation. This is an area you might have seen in an episode of Top Gear, in which Clarkson stands in front of the camera and says things like: 'If you run out of fuel, you die'; 'If you break down, you die'; and 'If you run out of water, you die'. *If you do not have the vast resources of the BBC planning, backup, rescue services and mobile canteen, you die.*

My map shows what looks like a narrow stretch of salt pan, only about 30 miles wide. We are heading for an area called Kudu Island where, apparently, tourist groups are taken to see the salt pans. After about 30 miles of this hostile and desolate environment, following the GPS seemingly to the edge of the world with not another sole in sight, I think Helen's enthusiasm is starting to wane and worry is starting to set in. Then we come to a vast area of tussocky dead grass. Driving over this shakes the car a huge amount, giving Helen a dose of motion sickness on top of her dose of worry.

We reach one salt pan and I drive about on it, but, in order to reach our goal, we will have to cross some more rough ground. Helen is not very happy about this so, with regret and with due deference to my little navigator, we turn back, leaving this amazing, desolate and hostile wilderness behind. Another long-time dream of mine is thus nipped in the bud.

The next morning, I find that my dream drive, although incomplete, had not only made Helen car sick, but it had also made the car itself sick. We now have a broken torsion bar on the front nearside suspension. In less than a week's time we hope to put the car up for sale, but now we have a mega problem.
We were lucky that when the torsion bar broke, the suspension settled down on the rubber stops. These limit the amount of up and down movement of the car and also stop the car falling into a heap on the ground. Having taken the micky out of the Top Gear presenters, I

now realise how close we could have come to dying. There is nothing, absolutely nothing, out there and the area does not get a lot of visitors. There are no real or defined routes, it is just follow your nose to somewhere over there. Had we broken down completely, even if someone else had passed by, they could have passed half a mile or more on either side of us and not seen us. There are no phone signals out there. It cannot be understated how desolate and hostile the Makgadikgadi is - and certainly how lucky we were - and also, possibly, how foolish we may have been. There are many places in Africa where it is recommended that you travel in convoy. I am not sure whether this is one of those places, but I would certainly recommend it for what it is worth.

Leaving Gweta, we limp along with the front nearside suspension sitting down on the rubber stops. Luckily, we are on tarmac all the way now as we head northwards. We stop early afternoon for the night at a camp called Elephant Sands, a mile or so up a very sandy track. We come across some South Africans stuck in the sand and offer to tow them out. It seems that every time I have broken suspension, I have to tow somebody else out of trouble.

Here, there are elephants galore. Twenty-four hours a day, elephants visit a waterhole just a few metres from the bar and patio area. It is an artificial waterhole, filled two or three times a day by bowsers from nearly 20 miles away. The camp invests in bringing this water in, as it not only creates a big attraction to draw customers, but it also, apparently, stops the elephants digging up the water pipes in the camp.

Across the main road is a conservation area where we had hoped to do a game drive, but, with our broken suspension, that plan has to be scrapped. In the morning, we go for one last look at the jumbos at the watering hole. Whilst there, a pack of Wild Dogs - also known as painted dogs - turns up. This is the cherry on the top for us. We have been to a lot of game parks in six countries hoping to see these animals. They are considered endangered throughout their range in Africa and here we have a pack of eight or nine right in front of us in camp. *Woweee!* Right up to the end, the excitement keeps coming.

Our last stop in Botswana is Kasane. Once we have the tent up and have had a cup of tea, I go and ask in the camp workshop if there is anywhere I can get my suspension fixed. The workshop staff are very helpful. They phone around and, in no time whatsoever, locate a torsion bar. They can get a second hand one flown in tomorrow. My knees give a bit of a wobble on hearing 'flown in', but it is nothing to worry about; the little plane flies back and forth a lot and they often put small parts on for friends at no cost. That cheers me up.

Later on, I have trouble getting the main bolt undone so I pop along to the workshop again to ask if I can borrow a longer spanner than the one I have. Instead of lending me a spanner, they send a strong but incompetent fool to help me. At least the camp has a swimming pool and a bar so Helen can have a swim and a drink by the pool while I lie under the car with my new-found friend, struggling, sweating and swearing.

Unfortunately, the specialist bolt breaks. I do not blame my new friend for this. The bolt was very seized – that was the main reason I was having problems undoing it. But, following this, my unable assistant tries to fit the replacement parts with a big hammer, despite my attempts to stop him.

I dispense with his help in a hurry. Then I have to dismantle more of the car to get out the bits that he has hammered together in the wrong position. Once I have it all apart, I reassemble it all in the correct position – without the aid of a hammer. Now I just need to wait for the new nut and bolt to turn up. In all the things I have read about the pros and cons of coil or leaf spring suspensions, nothing is said about torsion bar suspension. Lying under my car, I wonder why.

For a bit of relaxation and to calm down whilst waiting for the parts to turn up, we take an afternoon boat trip on the Chobe River. With Botswana on one side and Namibia on the other, we see lots of wildlife on the river banks and a fantastic sunset. Back to the tent for dinner and a glass of red. *Ahhh, wonderful.* Forgetting about the suspension for a moment, life could not get much better.

The bolt arrives the following morning, just in the nick of time, so it is back under the car for me to finish the job. Our carnet de passage expires today so I get a hustle on and repair the car so we can leave the country legally.

Job done. We are up and bouncing again. We need to go to the ATM to get some money to pay for our car parts and then it is off to Zambia where we hope we can sell the car and go home.

Kazangula is our exit point. There is no town but there is a raft-like ferry that crosses the Zambezi. Having cleared Immigration and Customs with our carnet stamped - unbeknown to us, however, it was not stamped properly and will later give us months and months of problems back in the UK - we head down to the ferry to cross back into Zambia.

Botswana is fantastic and we desperately hope that we can come back one day, having discovered so much more than last time we visited.

Botswana – real 4x4 country

Salt pan driving

Another African carwash

Elephant Sands Camp – Helen makes a new friend

ZAMBIA (AGAIN)
31 October

We cross the Zambezi on a basic, raft-like ferry and, on entering Zambia, we have to pay for a month's visa and, now that our carnet de passage has expired, we also have to pay for a month's temporary import permit for the car, as well as a month's insurance, carbon tax and Interpol registration. If we are lucky and sell the car quickly, we will only be in Zambia for a few days. We will not be getting value for money on these things, but that's life.

The drive from the ferry to the town of Livingstone is less than 40 miles. Our plan is to put 'For Sale' signs in the car windows, park it somewhere visible around the town, and hope we get a buyer. With this scheme in mind, Helen had researched a couple of potential places to stay and rejected the nice camp on the riverbank of the Zambezi, just above Victoria Falls, and had earmarked a backpackers' lodge in the town centre. Unfortunately, Helen had put her cross on the map in the wrong place, so we are now looking in the wrong area. I get fed up with driving around and not finding it and opt for the first place I see advertising rooms.

We check in and Helen puts a sign on the car where it is parked in the yard. One hour later we get an inquiry from someone who eventually buys the car. There is a lot of faffing about from him as he tries to find out about import duties, Interpol, and re-registration. He also gets a mechanic to come and do an inspection. My maintenance regime, put under scrutiny, holds up well.

We start negotiations and agree a price in US Dollars. It is not as much as we were hoping for, but we decide it is more important to sell the car than get the right price. We have had a fantastic time, so we are happy with any reasonable price and our buyer says he will pay us in hard currency. He turns up with a carrier bag of Zambian Kwachas – not really to our liking, but it is money. Unfortunately, there is nowhere in this town to change it for a more usable currency. We will lose a bit more on the exchange but we are going home, so we are not going to worry.

Our car is gone. We are not sentimental about cars - they have always only been a means of transport - but this one, well, we are a bit sorry to see this one go. For the last year, we have travelled in it, we have slept in it, it has carried us through some difficult terrain, we have rescued it, and it has rescued us. It has taken us on a journey of a lifetime. The Toyota will now carry on playing in Africa and we are going back home to reality.

With the money from the sale of the car we can afford a flight home, so we book a bus to Lusaka, packing only what we can carry and leaving the rest in the car. It is quite a long and uneventful drive to the capital but, just to prove that we are still in Africa, the bus breaks down on the main road as we arrive into the city. We are in the middle lane with smoke pouring out of the back of the bus. We all exit as fast as possible into the traffic steaming along either side of us. Once safely away from the bus, we realise we need to go back to reclaim our luggage. Eventually, we retrieve our bags and leave the bus quietly smouldering behind us as we walk down the road to find a hotel. It is Africa to the end.

In the country's capital, business and banking centre, we try eleven banks and Bureaux de Changes to exchange our Kwachas for some more user-friendly currency. In some we have no joy at all, in one we get £600 and from the rest we get dribs and drabs of UK Pounds, Euros and US Dollars. At one bank, we take their only £25 and at another we take their final 40 Euros. But eventually, at the airport, we get a few US Dollars and we are all done, bar about three quid's worth of Kwachas. *Not bad, but last minute or what?*

We grab virtually the first flight available and, boarding this, end our African adventure on the 5th November 2013, eleven months after leaving home and just a few days before my seventieth birthday when my driving licence expires. I can only say, *What a fantastic experience.* We have driven all the way from Rochford to Cape Town and, although we end our journey in Lusaka - which was not our aim - our true aim has been realised; the bit between the start and the finish; the travelling. So this trip also proves the truth in our motto: 'The journey *is* the destination'.

Possibly the only Toyota 4Runner to make it from Essex, UK, to Cape Town, South Africa

AFTERWORD

The inspiration for this journey came from a previous visit to Africa when I spoke to some Germans that had shipped their British registered cars to Namibia for their holidays. It was then that I saw the 'need' for us to buy a car at home and drive to Cape Town.

I would class the whole trip as an outstanding success. That said, we did make a number of mistakes - possibly even blunders - in the lack of planning, and in equipment choice. We had our previous trip to draw upon and I think the only thing wrong that time was the suitability of the car. This time, however, we were planning to travel for a longer period and into wilder places. Africa is still a big unknown and, accordingly, the planning was a lot of guesswork. Sometimes during the preparatory stages I was buzzing with anticipation, and sometimes I was wondering if it was going to be a journey too far. But, in the event, the whole thing was easy, much easier than I would have expected. I spent a lot of time wondering, *Why have I not done this before?* and, *Why aren't a lot more people doing it?*

We crossed twenty-five countries and drove some 28,000 miles – more than half the Earth's circumference! Some of those miles were a long, endless drag, necessary just to get to Africa. But most of the driving was great, and so different to what we are used to at home. And all of it so much more exciting. When I was a lad of about twenty or so - and probably for some years more than that - I loved driving and would fight to be the driver among my group of friends when going out. As I got older, the magic and romance waned and, more recently, I find motorways and long-distance driving tedious and Helen has to do her fair share at the wheel to help me out. In Africa, the years rolled back and I was a kid again. I let Helen drive only when I got fed up on long, good tar roads – and, of course, the time in the carpark when she reversed into a tree and bent the car. Even after the disastrous, or near disastrous, trip to the Makgadikgadi salt pan, I still felt excited about the driving and was not looking forward to getting home and driving on English roads again. Having greatly enjoyed re-visiting the driving enthusiasm of my youth, I will inevitably revert to the grumpy old man on the tedious British roads.

We anticipated that there would be a lot of wildlife parks on this trip. We had even wondered if there would be too many, would we get fed up with them? There were a number of animals on our wish-list to see, such as the Mountain Gorillas, the Shoebill bird, leopards and cheetahs. We were also pleasantly surprised to see various other species that we were not aware we would cross tracks with. I had desperately wanted to fulfil my long-term dream to see the Mountain Gorillas and when that did not work out, I expected to be really disappointed. The excitement of the whole trip allowed even big failures like that to pale into insignificance. On the other hand, we saw thousands of elephants, which we have encountered before, but we never got tired of watching these huge beasts.

I enjoy some bird watching. I am not particularly good at it, as I have a bit if a memory problem, and there have been times when I have seen a new and exciting bird only to find that when I look in the book to identify it, I have already seen it. I did put some effort into seeing the Shoebill and was pleased that I did. There were a number of other birds I had hoped to see, and some I did, others I did not. But many of the birds are amazing and it adds another dimension to the reason for being out in that magnificent wildness. Even Helen, who has no real interest in bird spotting, was thrilled at some of the large or colourful birds that we saw.

The landscapes that we drove through were unbelievable and a very humbling experience, making us feel very small in the grand scheme of life; the vastness of the sand deserts, the bleakness of the miles of the volcanic lava fields, the brightness of the salt flats. We stood at the bottom of - and at the top of - some spectacular waterfalls, and the memory of standing on the rim of an active volcano looking down into the boiling cauldron will stay with me for a long time. The weather played a huge part in our experience; we drove around one side of Mount Kenya but did not see any of it due to low cloud, and we got within sight of Mount Kilimanjaro – or it would have been within sight if that were not also in low cloud. But the majesty and huge scale of Africa was ever present.

On our journey we met a lot of people a lot better equipped than us and a lot more organised than us. We also met people less well-equipped and more adventurous than us. But there are so many options of what to do and how to do it. In my opinion, Africa is in a world of its own, and the options are limitless.

The car was always intended to go on a one way journey. I did not want to spend too much on it in case it blew up, or got to a state of being irreparably broken, or was stolen. I also knew that cars cost a lot more in southern Africa than they do in Europe, so I could probably make a healthy profit on selling it there. But I had not seriously thought this through. The reason cars are more expensive there is the import duty. Our car, when sold, would attract an import duty of one hundred to one hundred and fifty percent the value of the car. That is the value the tax man in the given country puts on the car, not what the actual purchase price is. We, on the other hand, having finished our journey, only wanted to get rid of the car. Prior to starting our journey, we thought that we would wait for a good price when ready to sell, but that attitude changed as the journey progressed. When it is all over, the price almost becomes irrelevant; we only wanted to get rid of the car and go home.

The car did us proud. We had to get a lot of things repaired, but then so did everybody else we spoke to. It was a roughty-toughty machine by English standards, but in wild Africa, the suspension was barely up to the job. All in all, we were very pleased with it, whatever its shortcomings, and we still have no idea what is the best vehicle to take - it depends a lot on what kind of trip you want to do. We met one couple in a Citroen 2CV, and two Englishmen on 1937 Velosette motorcycles, and a number of Germans in huge great four-wheel-drive lorries. Each to their own – you have your own dream, you make your own journey.

One minor problem we had was the size of our fuel tank. I did my calculations of fuel capacity on probable distances between petrol stations, plus a safety margin. With the exception of the Turkana route, it all worked out fine. That said, I did not give the tank size any thought when we bought the car; it was only later that I considered it and had no idea what to do about it, so we just went with what we had. Our 58 litre tank seems a bit pathetic, now I know that other cars have 150 litre, or twin 90 litre, tanks. There were a number of places that I would have liked to have gone to that would have exceeded our safety margin. My only consolation is I think we managed a successful trip, even with our limited fuel capacity.

The tent was another decision: big tent, small tent or roof-top tent; all have pros and cons. I think it mainly depends on what you want to do. On our previous trip, we had a small, two-person-sized tent and we spent eighty-seven consecutive nights in it on one stretch of the journey and were very happy with it. This time we took a big tent – big enough to stand up in – and, again, we were happy with it. A big advantage of the larger tent was that it gave us shade from the sun and shelter from the rain. Also the porch gave us a relatively contained area to sit in the evenings, burning antimozzie coils if necessary to make it more comfortable. However, due to the larger size, it was an awkward thing to erect and was like playing with a large parachute if there was any wind. We fairly often had to tie one end to the car. If you have space in the vehicle though, the benefits of a larger tent probably outweigh the negatives. We spoke to people using roof-top tents and they were also mostly happy, although some people mentioned that the convenience of being quick to put up and down, and being out of the way on the roof, should be weighed up against having nowhere to sit in adverse weather. Swings and roundabouts – you pays your money, you takes your pick.

I picked out a few tools to take; my theory was that if a job needed a big tool kit, it was too big a job for me. The tools I took were sufficient to tighten nuts that came loose, grease the points underneath regularly and change the oil and filter, and repair the odd puncture. It worked well for us. We met a number of other people who seemed to carry enough tools for fleet maintenance, but who is to know what is right?

I think we should have invested in a sat nav. I did look at them, but I am not a technophile, and in my quick look I could not find maps for Africa, so I abandoned the search pretty quickly. This was a big mistake. Our maps were (mostly) fine for the open road but our biggest problem was in the cities. It would have even been handy in Europe to navigate the main cities. More than a year after we set off, and now back in the UK, we have a smartphone with GPS sat nav and all the maps we could ever want. I am sure this phone would have been a lot easier to get the sim cards working, but this is all much too late now. I feel a certain sense of pride, though, that we managed it the old fashioned way and our achievement is all the greater for it.

One big failure for us was our camera. We often travel light, so we have a smallish camera, a semi-compact thing, which produces mediocre images. This time, however, we did not need to worry about carrying it about, as we were in the car most of the time, and I wish we had upgraded for a full thirty-five mil. jobbie with a long lens. So the records of our trip of a lifetime are a collection of substandard photos, but we have to be a bit philosophical about it all – we have done it, that is the main thing. We have the T-shirt and our memories.

In virtually every country we went to, we saw the whole spectrum of lifestyles and living standards. There are people living in nice houses with cars, phones, TV and all the trappings of most people in the western world today. There are masses of people living in a feudal state, with no running water, no electricity and poor sanitation - apart from having a mobile phone, they are living in conditions that the western world saw the back of some one to two hundred years ago. And there are people still living a traditional life; herding goats, living in mud or grass huts, and dressed in a loin cloth or a bit of goat skin just big enough for the job - a way of living that went out in the western world maybe a thousand or more years ago. Sometimes different classes co-exist side by side, and sometimes they are only a few miles apart, but there is a huge difference between rich and poor and the difference is much greater than anywhere I have witnessed in the western world.

Africa is also very tribal; many tribes traditionally do not get along, so there is always inter-tribal conflict somewhere. Tribal boundaries rarely coincide with national boundaries and, in most areas, physical boundaries do not exist - it is an imaginary line across the desert or through a bit of jungle - so I suppose it makes little difference to the local tribes. I don't think these areas feature too much on the police radar. I know very little about it apart from what information I have picked up and from what tales I have heard, which often comes in the form of advice: 'Do not go to that region as there are many bandits there'. A lot of the conflicts are in remote areas, and it seems to me that they are just left to get on with it – the police are content to let these tribes shoot each other, while staying out of their way. However, looking at some small area on the map, and finding out that it is possibly as big as the UK with no proper towns, no proper roads and no proper communications, I realise there must be a difficulty in policing such places. I would also imagine trans-frontier conflicts are not easy to patrol, with the police blaming cross-border miscreants. I was also told by police officers in two different countries that laws are difficult to implement as people just ignore them. I imagine few people would be willing to argue a point of law with a man with a gun, especially if he has no compunction about using it, and is from a different tribe.

I have had a small glimpse of life in African countries and have spoken to both white and black Africans. In my opinion, Africa will be 'Africa' for many generations to come. It is still wild and lawless, with a cacophony of cultures and attitudes that defy the western mind. We have been told that in local communities people do not like it when someone else shows signs of 'progress', getting on a bit with their life; many people do not want to lose their friends, so they maintain the status quo. It is these cultures and these attitudes, plus the general African psyche, that will hold Africa back for many more years to come. But it is a fantastic continent to visit - a world apart - and we love it.

We are not professional travellers; I am a retired plumber and Helen was an office worker. We have cobbled together our journeys, taking opportunities as they come, and they have always had to be on a tight budget. We made our luck and we made our moments. I am now seventy, Helen is not so old. We have travelled a fair bit and have always got on well together. On this trip we have spent twenty-four hours a day, seven days a week together for a year and, not only are we still talking, we are still the very best of friends. I could not wish for a better travelling companion. I hope she feels the same. Well, she did ask me to marry her when we got home, so I suppose that's a good sign.

I firmly believe that if we can do it, anyone can.

Hopefully my maintenance regime means our Toyota is still playing in Africa

ABOUT THE AUTHOR

Michael Banks, known as Mick to family and friends, was a plumber from Essex with a thirst for travel. His wife, Helen, described him as a 'multitool of a man', which came in handy when he had to fix the car on the roadside or in the desert.

This was not his first adventure, but it was his greatest and, sadly, his last. Mick died in July 2015 and this book is published in his memory.